THE NEW COMPLETE

Airedale Terrier

by GLADYS BROWN EDWARDS

ILLUSTRATED

Drawings by the Author

THIRD EDITION . . . Second Printing

1979
HOWELL BOOK HOUSE INC.
230 Park Avenue
New York, N.Y. 10017

Library of Congress Cataloging in Publication Data

Edwards, Gladys Brown.
  The new complete airedale terrier.

  Published in 1966 under title: The complete airedale
terrier.
  Bibliography: p.
  1. Airedale terriers. I. Title.
SF429.A6E3 1978   636.7'55   78-7051
ISBN 0-87605-005-4

In memory of

Lou "Lionheart" Holliday, dean of West Coast Airedalers, whose life-long experience and interest in the breed contributed more to Airedales and Airedale breeders than can ever be realized.

Lou Holliday and Rip of Lionheart

Clonmel Monarque
(Ch. Warland Whatnot ex Ch. Kathleen McCaura)

Contents

Ch. Eleanore's Royalty of Lionheart (Ch. Rockley Roasting Hot ex Ch. Ridgemoor Sweetberry).

Ch. Lionheart Copper (Ch. Eleanore's Royalty of Lionheart ex Lionheart Comet III).

Airedale gun dogs, Hilltops' High Noon and Arne of Oregon, follow the path of a flushed pheasant in anticipation of its being brought down for a retrieve. Dogs such as these are typical of how versatile the breed can be and why Airedales are so highly favored by so many dog lovers.

Acknowledgements

Wᴇ GRATEFULLY acknowledge the assistance given in compiling data for this book—from the many breeders in this country who furnished pictures and information on their dogs, from the breeders in other lands who contributed in varying ways. Most especially do we thank Marjorie Schonher for her statistics on pedigrees and champions, without which we could not have traced the background of the dogs mentioned herein; Barbara Strebeigh for statistics, clippings, and other material collected in her many years of association with the breed; Caroline Strong for her collection of valued old club bulletins, various old stud cards and similar Airedalia; Art Mayo for photographs and helpful ideas; the late Bert Heath for the loan of a decade of old *Kennel Reviews* which originally featured Airedales and which filled in several otherwise blank spaces in the history of the breed; the late Lou Holliday for pictures, hunting stories, and history of the breed and individuals on the West Coast, as well as advice through the years on everything pertaining to Airedales; and Jane Messeck, who furnished data on German Airedales as well as "human interest" stories of Airedales in this country.

We wish we could have made the story on each strain of Airedales as comprehensive as, for instance, the Lionhearts, on which we had the most complete data on all facets—hunting, obedience, show, and history—but when such was not available we had to build up the story from cold statistics or whatever else we had collected on our own.

Our sincere thanks are also given especially to Mr. Haruki T. Endoh, who wrote the story on Japanese Airedale activities; Carl-Olof Jungfeldt for material on Swedish Airedales; Captain Soya-Jensen for that on the breed in Denmark; and Mrs. C. M. Halford, Miss E. M. Jones, Miss A. M. Jenkinson, Pat McCaughey and Fred Cross for very complete information on English Airedales.

The foregoing are but a few of those who aided in this work, as will be seen by reference to others in the course of the book.

—Gʟᴀᴅʏs Bʀᴏᴡɴ Eᴅᴡᴀʀᴅs

Three on a match!

The "Gingerbred" bowl.

GLADYS BROWN EDWARDS has enjoyed a love affair with the Airedale for most of her life.

When Mrs. Edwards was nine years old a gift to her family of an Airedale puppy was her introduction to the breed. It was a happy introduction too, because it started the future fancier on a course that would eventually benefit all Airedales and their people everywhere.

While in grade school Gladys Edwards saved her money to buy her own first Airedale. This puppy, Lionheart Imp, came from Lou Holliday's Lionheart Kennels, then located in Montana. The Airedale's versatility was second nature to young Imp. Among her many talents was that of draft dog. In her harness and cart she always caused a small sensation among passersby as she traveled to and from the local dairy for supplies. Apart from her workaday chores, Imp enjoyed some successes in the show ring. On one occasion she won second in the *Sporting* Group at a local dog show held in conjunction with a county fair.

Mrs. Edwards' next Airedale started her on the road to showing and breeding in earnest. This one was also from the Lionheart establishment and her owner named her Crosswind. She was a daughter of Ch. Lionheart Cold Steel and founded one branch of the Ch. Lionheart Comet family. Crosswind's son, Ch. Studio Top Brass, was an influential sire whose name is in the background of leading, current American-bred winners.

Through her excellent monthly column in *Popular Dogs* magazine, Gladys Brown Edwards became familiar to thousands. She wrote this column for many years, imparting news and much-sought-after information to all her readers. She also wrote numerous feature articles in the same publication, thereby widening her following beyond the Airedale fancy. She has also held the office of secretary for the Southern California Airedale Association and the United States Lakeland Terrier Club.

Following the death of her memorable Ch. Studio Liontamer, Gladys Brown Edwards involved herself in the Arabian horse fancy as both writer and artist. Her interest in horses, as with Airedales, also began in childhood and today she is one of the most highly-respected figures in the purebred horse world.

Mrs. Edwards is the author of two books on horses *The Arabian—From War Horse to Show Horse* and *Know the Arabian.* She is also a staff writer for *Arabian Horse World.*

As an artist Mrs. Edwards has earned particular renown in both the horse and dog fancies. Her talent for sketching surfaced in early childhood, and by the time she was in high school she was regularly haunting libraries and book stores for veterinary and anatomical texts to help her more accurately depict her subjects.

Following graduation from high school, Gladys Brown Edwards won a four-year scholarship to the Chouinard Institute of Art in Los Angeles. Interestingly, she won this scholarship for her portrait of Charles A. Lindbergh, the famous pioneer aviator.

At Chouinard she worked in all media and studied numerous art theories. One of her instructors was Millard Sheets, later to become a world-famous figure in the art world.

Mrs. Edwards executed many breed models used for trophies, and other sculptures she has created show the ideals in .horses, dogs and cattle. Her pastels and oil paintings are particularly recognized for their remarkable fidelity to life. She has been commissioned by many owners to paint portraits of their animals because of her universally-recognized ability.

Her diagrams in Chapters 12 and 14 of this book provide a glimpse of Mrs. Edwards' deep understanding of her subject. These diagrams were designed and executed to teach!

A person of many and varied enthusiasms, Mrs. Edwards' interests also embrace aviation, archaeology, American Indians, armor and history. Gladys Brown Edwards has reached for and achieved knowledge and proficiency in many disciplines. How fortunate for the Airedale fancy that the "King of Terriers" is one of her long-term interests!

Foreword

THE LORDLY *AIREDALE,* "King of Terriers," is one of the world's favorite dog breeds. His combination of good looks, trainability and sound temperament has won him numerous friends all around the globe. A loyal companion to working men and presidents since the era of gaslight, the Airedale has truly earned the fame and tributes coming his way ever since he first emerged on the Yorkshire fells in the mid 19th Century.

The colorful story of how the Airedale developed and rose to fame is a fascinating part of the breed's greatest written tribute, *The Complete Airedale Terrier* by Gladys Brown Edwards. Since 1962 this classic has guided new puppy owners, first-time exhibitors, breeders, judges and those seeking to further their knowledge of the breed.

The Complete Airedale Terrier comes by its great reputation honestly. Its authority is the result of Mrs. Edwards' many years of close association with the breed, her first-hand knowledge of the great dogs and memorable fanciers and her own personal successes as a breeder, exhibitor, commentator and artist. A total joy, it is a book to enjoy and learn from, written for Airedale lovers by an Airedale lover.

The world of dogs, like many other endeavors, changes constantly. The dogs and fanciers at the top one day are replaced by new names and faces the next. The last edition of *The Complete Airedale Terrier* was published in 1966, and much change has taken place in the breed and the entire sport since then. Happily, *The NEW Complete Airedale Terrier,* Mrs. Edwards' own update of her enduring masterpiece, makes the story of the Airedale current. It records the events that have occurred since the last edition was published, what dogs put their stamp on the breed, what fanciers achieved prominence and how the Airedale has made important forward strides since that time.

A bright, new chapter in *The NEW Complete Airedale Terrier* traces the leading producing families and sire-lines into the present.

GLADYS
BROWN
EDWARDS

English and American Champion Warland Ditto

At left is a drawing taken from the well-known picture of Ditto as he appeared in 1921. It shows him in the trim used at the time plenty of hair on the neck, but very little leg or facial furnishings—the latter probably due to a very hard coat. At the right is a sketch made from a tracing of the drawing of the 1921 version, but with the padding of hair removed from the neck and more furnishings added to legs and muzzle, as well as chest. These drawings show that many an old-timer would look less "old-fashioned" if he were given a modern trim and had the more luxuriant, if less practical, furnishings of today.

14

This chapter also reports in detail the impact of Ch. Bengal Sabu and the effect of many other imports arriving in America since publication of the second edition.

Chapters on British activity and on the Airedale in other foreign lands are expanded and updated. These spotlight more recent developments in England, Germany, Sweden and Japan. "The Airedale Boom in Australia" is an all-new chapter that will come as an exciting revelation for all fanciers—a whole new world of Airedale activity and the joy of discovery it will bring you. This edition also presents new material on the breed in obedience and a brand-new, invaluable chapter on showing the Airedale by June Dutcher, who is famous throughout the Airedale fancy for her "Coppercrests" Airedales that have distinguished themselves in the strongest competition.

With many new pictures of Airedales from around the world and Mrs. Edwards' famous sire-line charts updated, *The NEW Complete Airedale Terrier* offers the reader more than ever before. Every Airedale fancier, enthusiastic beginner and seasoned veteran, will want this newest edition for the information it contains and as a continuation of the Airedale's story from previous editions. *The NEW Complete Airedale Terrier* is a splendid tribute to the breed from one of its best friends, and like previous editions, it belongs in the hands of all who share their lives with the "King."

—THE PUBLISHER

Otter Hounds in the River Aire at Gargrave, near Skipton.

1

Early History of the Airedale

THE PICTURESQUE Valley of the Aire in West
Riding, Yorkshire, was the birthplace of the Airedale—"The King of
Terriers"—largest of his sporting clan. Although the exact date is unknown, historical data indicates that it was about the middle of the
nineteenth century that the Airedale was evolved to fit the sporting
needs of the residents of the Aire Valley.

The Cradle of the Breed

Located less than a hundred miles south of the Scottish border, the
Aire Valley, although heavily industrialized, afforded endless opportunity for sport involving dogs. Its varied terrain—ranging from bleak
grouse moors to wooded glens, from rocky fells to river lowlands—
harbored myriad species of game: upland birds, rabbits, hare, marten,
badger, and otter. In town, during those mid-nineteenth century years,
were the inevitable rats, fair game for any Terrier.

The many mills and factories lining the Aire River made the stream
untenable for the otter and the fish that are his prey, so otter hunting
was necessarily confined to the Wharfe and other nearby streams.
Properly done, it required a pack of Otterhounds plus a Terrier or two.
Needless to say, this was beyond the means of the average factory
worker, although an occasional sportsman kept a couple of Hounds
and, with a few Terriers, could expect to have fair luck along the
streams. Water-rat matches, with teams of Terriers contesting for

A panoramic view of Wharfedale from the fells above Grassington, Yorkshire.

The River Aire at Bingley with the parish church overlooking the weir.

points, were another popular sport. Less creditable, but a diversion that in its way contributed to the working abilities of the Airedale, was the intriguing (if illicit) pastime of outwitting the gamekeepers on estates that were "off limits" to the average citizen. And because some shootable fur or feather occasionally "happened along," many of the Terriers of the Aire Valley were broken to the gun and trained to retrieve.

Terriers in Early Writings

As far back as the sixteenth century, Terriers were depicted in engravings and paintings, as well as mentioned in writings as a specific type. Although later writings gave the Terrier a rather indefinite description, Daniel in *Field Sports* (1760), wrote: "There are two sorts of terriers, the one rough, short-legged, long-backed, very strong, and most commonly of a black or yellowish color, mixed with white; the other is smooth-haired and beautifully formed, having a shorter body and more sprightly appearance, and is generally of a reddish-brown color, or black with tanned legs. Both these sorts are the determined foe of all vermin kind and in their encounters with the badger very frequently meet with severe treatment which they sustain with great courage, and a well-bred, well-trained terrier often proves more than a match for his opponent."

Sydenham Edwards gives a most enlightening description of the Terrier and his work in the *Cynographia Britannica* published in 1800: "... The Terrier is high spirited and alert when brought into action; if he has not the unsubdued perseverance like the Bulldog, he has rapidity of attack, managed with art and sustained with spirit; it is not what he will bear, it is what he will inflict. His action protects himself, and his bite carries death to his opponents; he dashes into the hole of the fox, drives him from the recesses or tears him to pieces in his stronghold; he forces the reluctant, stubborn badger into light. As his courage is great, so is his genius extensive; he will trace with the foxhounds, hunt with the beagle, find with the greyhound, or beat with the spaniel. Of wildcats, martens, polecats, weasels and rats, he is the vigilant and determined enemy; he drives the otter from the rocky clefts on the banks of the rivers, nor declines combat of a new element."

Terriers of the period were described by *The Sporting Dictionary* (1803): "... of even the best are now bred in all colors—red; black with tan faces, flanks, feet and legs; brindles; sandy; some few brown-pied; and pure white; as well as one sort of each color rough and wire-haired, the other soft and smooth; and what is rather more extraordinary, the latter not much deficient in courage to the former, but the rough breed must be acknowledged the more severe and invincible biter of the two."

Edwards gave a somewhat similar description but mentioned that the ears varied—some short, some erect, some pendulous, and were usually cropped. He also said that the white color had been in demand in recent years. The white Terriers were more popular because darker ones were often mistaken for the fox by myopic members of the field and the Hounds were halloed off the line, or what was more serious, the Terriers were mistaken for the fox and killed by the Hounds—which could readily happen after the Terrier had been in a fox-earth and smelled more fox than dog. Experience showed the white Terriers were relatively safe—hence the predominately white color of the Fox Terrier.

Rawdon Lee, in the "Terriers" volume of his *Modern Dogs* (1903), graphically describes Terrier ways and Terrier days: "Few sporting country districts are, or were without their own special strain of terriers, in which appearance was of little object as long as gameness predominated. By 'gameness' I do not mean partiality for fighting or cat-killing, and standing being cut up piecemeal without flinching or whimpering, but killing vermin and going to ground after fox, badger or otter—wild animals, and not tame, domesticated or semi-tame creatures. I have seen a dog of great excellence and gameness in a street fight which would yelp and run away when a big buck rat seized him by the nose. The north of England was usually prolific in producing terriers; the working artisans in the manufacturing centers owned them; the masters of hounds who hunted the foxes in the hills and mountains, where horses could not follow, required a terrier that would bolt a fox or worry him in the hole if he refused to face the open. Some had a dash of Bull Terrier in them, others had not."

Working Terriers

Various hunts—among them the Belvoir, the Quorn, and the Grove—were noted for their working Terriers and had their own special breeds. Although in the 1860s the Smooth Fox Terrier quickly became the darling of the show gods, the other Terriers went their usual ways, diligently working for their living, unadorned by Dame Fashion, and, we must admit, somewhat scorned by her. Even the Wire, country cousin of the Smooth Fox Terrier, was shrugged off as a "working Terrier."

In its restricted sense, the term "working" Terrier means one small enough to go to ground after animals and bold enough to force them to retreat. With the exception of the Lakeland, whose job it was to kill the fox, working Terriers were expected to bolt the quarry, hard as it might argue back, or to "mark" its location by barking so it could be dug out. Such Terriers, to go to earth, necessarily had to be small, so were often outweighed, though not outgamed, by their antagonists.

Although the "Waterside Terriers," later known as Airedales, were too big to go to ground, they were good for everything else required of a sporting Terrier. Their especial forte was, however, the pursuit of the water-rat in matches arranged for the purpose. These highly competitive matches were regular events along a three- to six-mile radius of the Aire River, and on Saturday afternoons when two well-known dogs were pitted against each other, the whole countryside turned out to follow the match, watching the proceedings with the keenest interest. Stakes of from one to twenty-five pounds were posted, and a referee was appointed to score the Terriers. Added zest was given by side bets, a whole week's pay literally "going down a rat-hole" when a spectator backed the wrong dog.

The Terriers worked both sides of the stream as indicated by their owners, swimming from one side to the other when so directed. When one dog located a "live" hole, it counted two points as a "mark," and both dogs were made to stay back while a ferret was put into the hole to bolt the rat. The rat usually bolted directly into the river, with both dogs going after him like Dollar Day shoppers after a bargain. In his first dive the rat would swim from thirty to forty yards under water, the Terriers meanwhile anxiously swimming about, necks stretched high, expectantly waiting for the rat to surface. If a dog's owner sighted the rat first, he would whistle or wave to his dog; then both Terriers would take off, each deadly determined to get to the quarry first. The dash was usually to no avail, for the rat would again submerge and torpedo away in another direction, only to cause the same furor when he came up for air. Gradually his dives would get shorter, and the nearest Terrier would send his score up one point by making the kill. Often the dog would, in a well-timed dive, catch the tiring rat under water and bob triumphantly to the surface with the crunched animal in his mouth. Many times a dog that lagged in making kills would catch up on his score by being first to locate the rats, the score for the "mark" being double that for the "kill."

The Airedale's Antecedents

Before the evolution of the Airedale can be adequately appreciated, it is necessary to have some idea of the character of the canine ores comprising the alloy that is the breed. The "earth" ancestor of the amphibious dog of Aire was that region's version of the old rough-coated working Terrier, variously known as the "Broken-coated Working Terrier," "Old English Black-and-Tan Terrier," "Rough-coated Black-and-Tan Terrier," and so on; but actually he was not always "rough" nor was he always "black-and tan." His coat was occasionally almost smooth, sometimes almost wooly, but mostly it was hard and wiry. Color varied from red, through various grizzles and bluish-grays, to black-and-tan. Even the latter was not the familiar pattern of today with the black saddle and rich tan, but rather more like that of a

Manchester—black, with tan points on muzzle, eyebrows, inside of legs, and on feet; and he often had a blaze of white on his chest. Before the many outcrosses were made, he was about the size of a large Fox Terrier—a good twenty pounds in weight. It was not until the interest in the waterside matches grew to large proportions that a lively interest was taken in improving the Terrier's swimming ability, scenting power, and in developing an undercoat impervious to water. The Otterhound, or at least what passed for an Otterhound in those days, had all these wanted attributes, and there is no doubt that the Otterhound, or "Hound for otter," was used for the nick. Holland Buckley even names the man who first made the cross, a Wilfred Holmes, near Bradford, and sets the date as 1853. According to Mr. Buckley, "this produced a dog that was as game and hard as the Terrier and better able, by increased size and weight to hold his own with the larger vermin that abounded in the country of 'Broad Acres.' Frequent crosses between the Hound and Terrier were made, and the puppies found a ready sale amongst local sportsmen. These were again bred amongst themselves until, in about a dozen years, a variety of these crossed-Terriers became established in the localities around Otley, Shipley and Bradford; and the dogs had an excellent reputation all over the County for work and fighting pluck. The question of general uniformity and type was not worried over. These Terriers could nearly live in water, and even in the coldest weather would rather be in than out of water, and in the neighbourhood of Bingley were first called 'Waterside Terriers.'"

From all accounts, there was a regular cat's cradle of crosses in the ancestral mesh of the Airedale; the proximity of the vast flocks of sheep on the moors arouses suspicion that the inherent tendency shown by some Airedales toward herding might trace to a sheepish incident involving a Border Collie or other sheepdog.

The Bull Terrier is another that fights his way into the discussion, refusing to be completely downed in his claim to a boost to Airedale spirits. Some state that the Bull Terrier cross did not occur, while others stoutly maintain that it did. But if it did, it surely must have been an admixture to the "original" rough-coated working Terrier, not the later edition, the Waterside Terrier. Support of that theory is given by Gersbach-Jager's *The Police Dog*, written in 1910: "The Airedale Terrier was developed in the part of Yorkshire lying between the Aire and the Wharfe rivers—a great factory and quarry district. Some fifty years ago the workingmen of that section bred a terrier of about 15-20 lbs. in weight and reddish in color. These dogs, a variety of the old hard-coated terrier, were great fighters, and were used for that purpose. Later the Bull Terrier, also a great fighting dog, was crossed with these terriers to give greater size. The result, dogs up to 30 and 35 lbs. and used for rat-pit matches and against each other. The final step in producing the Airedale Terrier was the crossing of these Bull-and-Terriers with Otterhounds of Wharfe Valley."

This version is quite different from some others, but does place the Bull Terrier cross before the Otterhound invasion, although the dates do not quite jibe with Buckley's. Bull Terriers are also referred to in the article on the Airedale in *The American Book of the Dog,* by Shields (1891), in which a Yorkshireman is quoted: "I owned three (Airedales)—Smuggler, Crack and Ben—and they were as good dogs as I ever saw. Ben was the largest and he would probably weigh some 40 to 45 pounds. They breed them much larger now than they did then. When I had them it was over thirty years ago. Crack was first owned by a Leeds gentleman and weighed not more than 35 pounds when in fair condition. He was matched and fought in the pit, in Leeds, with a Bull Terrier, weight 33½ pounds. Crack was to come any weight; the Bull Terrier was to be 32 pounds only, but they let him in at the above weight. I saw the fight and bought Crack as soon as it was over. Crack outfought him, and killed him dead in 48 minutes, and fought fully as quiet as the Bull Terrier. He had better grit, for if the Bull Terrier could, he would have jumped the pit, I think, but Crack pinned him and held him until he finished him. Either of the other two, Ben or Smuggler, would fight just as keen. The Airedale fights much faster than the Bull Terrier and their thick hair seems to sicken the dog they fight with."

Further mention of the early Airedale was made by this same Yorkshireman, regarding the bitch "Floss," who fought a Bull and Terrier bitch for three-quarters of an hour. The Bull had the upper hand for thirty minutes but then "Floss set to and killed her. My men told me that she wagged her tail all the time and never made a sound, though receiving terrible punishment. The Bull and Terrier weighed half again as much as she did." Several bitches named Floss were mentioned in early pedigrees, but it is doubtful that this particular Floss is a close relative, in view of the time—the fights having taken place in the late 1850s or early 1860s.

"Stonehenge" (J. H. Walsh), in his *Dogs of the British Isles* (1884), looked down his aristocratic nose at the interloper from the North, scorning his work and his breeders "whose pockets were not deep," and claiming the dog completely lacked gameness because a few well-chosen correspondents (unnamed) had picked up some Airedales at random and matched them against trained pit-fighting Bull Terriers. The Airedales, supposedly having been made into quick cold hash by the fighting machines against which they were pitted, did not impress Mr. Walsh, so for several years in his writings as editor of *The Field,* he continued to ridicule the breed from this standpoint alone. In spite

23

of Mr. Walsh, it is obvious that some Airedales in particular could fight, and what is more, they fought silently, like the Bull Terrier, thus giving further weight to the theory that such a cross was used.

With Bull Terriers allegedly used in the manufacture of the Airedale, a short tour into their history is timely. Bull- and bear-baiting had been very popular up to the 1830s when they, along with dog-fighting, were declared illegal. While the first two bloody pastimes were discontinued, prohibiting pit-fighting merely added to its zest and it was continued behind closed doors. Because the Bulldog was too slow, Terrier blood was introduced to that of the Bulldog to evolve the breed known as Bull-and-Terrier. The resulting cross was stated to be "even better adapted for mischievous sport" than either the Bulldog or Terrier. Although the Bull-and-Terrier was game, he was an undeniable mongrel in looks, being short-legged, broad-fronted, thick-set, and with a broad, blunt muzzle with considerable lay-back. But as more Terrier crosses were made and the Bull was buried further back in the family tree, the Bull-and-Terrier gradually took on the appearance of the Staffordshire, though his colors were those of the Bulldog—fawn, brindle, pied, and occasionally white. It was about the time the breed progressed from Bull-and-Terrier to Bull Terrier that the first crosses were reportedly made into the Airedale foundation stock.

The Bull Terrier did not take on his sleek appearance as the "White Cavalier" until after 1862, when a breeder named James Hinks crossed the Bull Terrier with the elegant, but now extinct, Old English White Terrier. The resulting all-white, long-headed dogs rapidly won the public's favor away from the broad-headed, old-fashioned type, and for several decades Colored Bull Terriers were not bred—in fact, it was not until after World War I that the Colored Bull Terrier, as we know it today, was re-introduced. If the cross with the Airedale had been made after the Bull Terrier had become dominantly white in color, it would have to have been after the 1860s. Certainly more white would have cropped out in the Airedale in subsequent crosses (as it does in all similar white-crossed dogs) than the blaze on chest and occasional white toes that show up even today. Since minor white markings are also seen in the oldest Terrier paintings, and on Bloodhounds, it would seem that they could have been inherited from some factor other than the Bull Terrier. If this argument holds any water, it might give weight to the theory that any Bull Terrier cross was used before that breed was all-white—i.e. before the late 1860s, at least.

Although some researchers credit the rough-coated Welsh Fox-hound or Harrier rather than the Otterhound with assistance in founding the Airedale, the majority agree that the Otterhound cross was more likely. Whether they were purebred Otterhounds, Welsh Hounds, or mixed, will never be known at this date, but, whatever their breeding, they had all the qualities necessary for the work.

The Otterhound is thought to be a direct descendant of the old Southern Hound, ancestor of many English scent Hounds, with a cross to the shaggy Griffon Vendeen, another of the same variety, both slow but sure trailers. A few writers indicate there might be a distant Water Spaniel admixture, some mention the Bloodhound, while an occasional modern writer will put the cart way in front of the horse and claim that the Otterhound descended from the Airedale!

Two other breeds which modern writers try to credit with founding the Airedale are the Welsh and Irish Terriers. However, as breeds, both the Welsh and the Irish were in embryonic stages themselves when the Airedale was being developed, so could not possibly have taken a hand in the evolution of the Airedale, although all were founded on the same basic stock—the old rough-coated Terrier. The first Airedales to be exhibited under the breed name were shown in 1883, the first "Welsh" in 1886, and the first class for "Irish" Terriers was established in 1873. But with all colors, sizes, and shapes being shown in the latter, it was merely a class for any Terrier bred in Ireland.

The first Welsh were admitted to the Kennel Club studbook in 1885 under "Welsh (or Old English, wire-haired black and tan) Terriers." For a while there were classes for old English and also for Welsh Terriers, and one dog, "Dick Turpin," gained a unique fame by winning in both classes. Later the Old English faded from the scene and the Welsh became the sole representative of the old working Terrier on the show bench until the advent of the Lakeland in 1920. The early Welsh were short-headed, large-eyed, and often bowed of front, so some exhibitors found a quick way of winning by crossing Airedales with Wires, and entered these smart-looking, long-headed, black-and-tan Terriers in classes for either (or both) Welsh or Old English. They won for a while, but the admirers of the Welsh soon prevented their winning the club specials and the old type Welsh again took over until a later date when it too was "smartened up" by the useful Fox Terrier. While misadventures of the Welsh have no real bearing on the founding of the Airedale, the mere fact that Airedale-Fox Terrier crosses won in the first Welsh classes should preclude any claim that the Welsh Terrier, as now known, played any part in the evolution of the Airedale. That the two had a common ancestor, there is no doubt.

As the Airedale progressed, size became a touchy problem and the following dictum was written into the Standard in 1902: "It is the unanimous opinion of the club that the size of the Airedale Terrier as given in the above Standard (40-45 lbs.) is one of, if not the most important, characteristics of the breed; all judges who shall henceforth adjudicate on the merits of the Airedale Terrier shall consider under-sized specimens of the breed severely handicapped when competing with dogs of standard weight; and any of the club judges who, in the opinion of the committee, shall give prizes or otherwise push to the front, dogs of the small type, shall at once be struck from the list of specialist judges." The strong wording had its effect, few judges wishing to face such a penalty. In later years this emphasis on "large" dogs was taken—for a while—to mean the bigger the better. Fortunately this trend, too, was stopped, although not before some specimens reached 24 inches, yet remained within the former weight limit, hence were generally lathy and lacking in substance.

The Irish Terrier, as well as the Welsh, has been credited with playing a part in the evolution of the Airedale, but this seems doubtful; by the time the Irish Terrier itself had developed to the point that it would breed true, the Airedale was well on his way to fame. Use of the Irish in later years, to sharpen expression and improve placement, size, and carriage of ears, may possibly have occurred in a few isolated cases, but seems rather doubtful.

The similarity of all of the sons of the old rough-coated "black-and-tan" Terrier is very marked in pictures of early champions. Even the Wire was of the same outline, and except for the cropped ears of the Irish and his fleeter build, it would be difficult to distinguish the breeds from the pictures if it were not for the coat markings. All the breeds had the same faults—they were long-cast, short-necked, and (again excepting the Irish) cloddy, with a snipey appearance as a result of lacking facial furnishings. While the smaller breeds could tap other sources to improve the breed quickly if so desired—like the Smooth refining the Wire, the Wire aiding the Welsh, etc.—the Airedale had no other large breed of similar type sufficiently advanced in fashion on which to rely. The breeders had to refine the rough ore themselves, heading toward a known ideal, striving always for Terrier quality on a dog of un-Terrier size. And while trying to breed the Hound *out* of the Airedale externally, they wanted to keep valuable Hound attributes internally.

While the average 40-45 pounds of early Airedales seems small in these days of 60-pound dogs, the news in 1879 of a 45-pound "Terrier" caused disbelief and ridicule among the cognoscenti who contended that a dog which was too big to go to ground was unworthy of the name "Terrier." It is true that the Airedale's size would preclude his going to ground and hence prevent his doing the work which gave the tribe its name of "Terrier" (from "terra," earth). But the Airedale, as he continued to improve, became all Terrier in type and character so that finally even his first antagonists admitted that he belonged to this distinguished clan.

A Tribute to the Airedale
by Albert Payson Terhune

Albert Payson Terhune sums up the Airedale concisely in an article

26

in *Nature Magazine:* "Among the mine-pits of the Aire, the various groups of miners each sought to develop a dog which could outfight and outhunt and OUTTHINK the other mine's dogs. Tests of the first-named virtues were made in inter-mine dog fights. Bit by bit, thus, an active, strong, heroic, compactly graceful and clever dog was evolved —the earliest true form of the Airedale. Then the outer world's dog fancy got hold of him and shaped and improved into the show-type Airedale of today. The process was not long, for the newly evolved dogs were quick to adapt themselves to their creators' wishes. Out of the experiments emerged the modern Airedale. He is swift, formidable, graceful, big of brain, an ideal chum and guard. There is almost nothing he cannot be taught if his trainer has the slightest gift for teaching. To his master he is an adoring pal. To marauders he is a destructive lightning bolt. In the Southwest and elsewhere these traits have been made use of by numerous sportsmen. Airedales do the work of pointers and setters and other hunting dogs. For nose and steadiness and snappy retrieving and for finding fallen birds, these field-trained Airedales have given surprisingly good accounts of themselves. There is nothing thrown away in an Airedale's makeup. Every inch of him is in use. Compact, wiry, he is 'all there.' No flabby by-products. A PERFECT MACHINE—a machine with a BRAIN, PLUS. He shows phenomenal powers of brain and instinct found in few other dogs. Fashion can never rule the Airedale out of existence. Too many people have learned to value him above any other breed. He is here to stay. He has won his right to PERMANENCE."

A litter of seven males by Ch. Eleanore's Royalty of Lionheart ex Ch. Lionheart Comet III. The second puppy from the left became Ch. Lionheart Copper.

Airedale Jerry (Rattler ex Bess), whelped in England in 1888 is credited as the foundation sire of the breed.

Ch. Cholmondeley Briar (Airedale Jerry ex Cholmondeley Luce).

28

2

Development of the Breed

UNTIL 1957 it was thought that the first dog show was held at Newcastle-on-Tyne in 1859. However, recent research has shown that Newcastle was antedated at least a decade by Cleveland, which catered to Terriers, Toys, and Spaniels. Other shows had been held in the 1840's for the same breeds, with some of the exhibitors having a go in the rat-pit with their Terriers after the shows.

The First Dog Shows

The Newcastle event was for Pointers and Setters only, and "The Druid," in "Saddle and Sirloin," gave what is probably the first critique on a dog show and reported that the show took place in a tent, with the public excluded. Macdonald Daly's column in *Our Dogs* gives further data on this: "A 'peeping Tom' found a hole in the tent and gave his pals a running commentary on what was going on. He reported that the judge, Capt. Percy Williams, was 'king at nowt else but slape (smooth) coats and white 'uns.' To Captain Williams thus fell the honour of being the first of many thousand judges, throughout the world, to have their efforts disparaged by ringside critics!" The dogs in question were Fox Terriers, the entry consisting of sixteen Smooths and sixteen "hairy 'uns."

The same year Newcastle held its much publicized first show, Cleveland also staged a show for gun dogs and Terriers. Birmingham, however, had the first championship show, which was held in

29

December 1859 with classes for gun dogs. The following year Terriers were added.

The dog-show sport was quickly taken up by all classes, for anyone owning a dog that even vaguely resembled some identifiable variety was free to join in, and shows were held at frequent intervals and in every part of England. However, for fourteen years the game was entirely unsupervised. Anything could happen, and usually did, and the scandals resulting from shady practices of certain over-eager exhibitors almost caused reputable owners to discontinue showing. In due course the need for a governing body with powers to enforce its decrees became obvious, and in 1873 the Kennel Club was established. A *Stud Book* was initiated, the first volume of 600 pages having a listing of 4,027 dogs, but of course there was then no breed named *Airedale*, so any embryonic Airedales were merely listed as one of the rough-coated Terriers in the "non-sporting" classification. The only other classification was for "sporting" dogs (i.e., gun dogs and Hounds), but in the next volume a separate classification of "Terriers" was given these most sporting of all dogs.

In 1864, Keighly Agricultural Show, the first dog show in the Aire Valley, was held. Included was a class for "Broken-haired Terriers," and at Craven, Otley, and Bingley similar classifications followed during the next ten years. Not only were Waterside Terriers entered in these classes, but also competing were Dandie Dinmonts, rough Fox Terriers, Bedlingtons, "Scottish" Terriers, and even the antecedents of the tiny Yorkshire.

It was not until 1879 that the *Waterside* or *Bingley* Terriers were mentioned by name. In that year the noted dog authority and author Hugh Dalziel, after judging at Bingley, wrote in his report: "The class for Broken-haired Terriers, the Bingley Terrier par excellence—was an exceedingly good one." In his book published that year he describes the Bingley Terrier as having the appearance of a giant Bedlington or Dandie Dinmont, and "appearing to have a lot of hound blood." In the 1870's the Bedlington and the Dandie were quite similar, differing mainly in size and in length of leg; the Bedlington was far from the Whippet-like dog of today with his crew-cut and shaved jaw, and had only a slight arch of loin. Although more on the leg than the Dandie, the Bedlington was more long-cast than "square," so the comparison between the early Airedale and Bedlington is not so grotesque as might seem.

The publication of Dalziel's comments brought immediate "outside" interest in the breed but also brewed a storm of protest among its fanciers for pinpointing Bingley as the home of the breed. It was thought that the name *Airedale* was first suggested by Dr. Gordon Stables, who judged these Terriers at Bingley the year before Dalziel, for previous to the latter's comments, the name *Airedale* had not been given the breed in any other connection. At any rate, some fanciers held a meeting in Bingley and decided that in the future the breed should be known as the "Airedale Terrier," and when Mr. Dalziel judged again in 1880 he mentioned the "Broken-haired Airedale Terrier" in his report. There was still confusion about the name, however, and at the Birmingham show in 1883 the show committee arranged a class for "Waterside Terriers." And for many shows that followed, two or all three names were used—possibly to ensure being right on one of them. During this period Airedales were classified in the studbook under "Broken-haired Scotch or Yorkshire" Terriers, and not until 1886 did the Kennel Club bow to the Airedale name.

Refining the Airedale

Having passed the first "Hound-Terrier" stage, the Airedale had begun to lose some of his coarseness and to give a glimmer of his potential as a show Terrier. John Q. Dogowner was beginning to appreciate this rough-and-ready Northerner, but it was the out-and-out fancier who had visions of "knocking 'em dead" in Terrier competition with this dramatic dog that could dominate the ring through sheer size and magnificence—once he was given the necessary polish.

While the Yorkshire breeders always remembered temperament and working ability along with an awakened appreciation of conformation and showmanship, the Southern fanciers were interested primarily in show points. With this singleness of purpose the latter breeders were able to improve conformation and quality much faster than had been the case hitherto. Fortunately, in the ensuing years character and versatility were not ignored, and, in fact, were brought more and more to the attention of the public as the Airedale was used for purposes never dreamed of in his native Yorkshire.

The problem of evolving a smart, though large, Terrier from the amalgamated tribes of sporting dogdom was no easy one, with Hound ears, light eyes, soft backs, and "off" coats being among the eyesores that cropped up in even the best of litters.

The descriptions of parents of the best early winners indicated that the sires were often the large, somewhat Houndy dogs, but the dams were neat, rather small, very hard-coated, and sometimes even smooth bitches, fiery and Terrier-like through and through. It was doubtless because of such variation in parents that litters were far from uniform, as Holland Buckley mentioned in his book, *The Airedale Terrier*: "...it would have been possible, if one were so minded, to have benched specimens from any one litter in Airedale, Old English Rough-Coated Terrier, Otterhound and Welsh Terrier classes, with a fair chance of winning honours." However, by selecting the best from such litters; and breeding "Airedale" type to similar type, it was finally possible to breed fairly true—although some would always have such faults as a large ear, soft coat, oversize or undersize, as can plague us even today.

Early Winners and Producers

Wharfedale Rush, a good winner in the first shows, was the large, Houndy type, but Venus III was the neat, Terrier type. Newbould Test was the leading winner for about five years, his colors finally being lowered by Colne Crack at Otley in 1890. Crack, of real Terrier type, was considered the best seen up to that time. Airedales had improved to such an extent by 1891 that a team consisting of Cholmondeley Briar, Cholmondeley Bridesmaid, and Briar Test won over eleven other teams, many of which represented the then most popular breeds—Fox Terriers, Dandie Dinmonts, and the "Scotch" Terriers. This win caused much comment and gave the breed a great boost in the fancy.

There is no need to name all the winners of the breed's early days, for many of them did not breed on. There is one line that did, however, and to which every leading sire of today traces in direct tail male down through Int. Ch. Warland Ditto, then for twelve generations back to old Airedale Jerry. The "Adam" of this family tree is actually, so far as is traceable, a dog named Rattler, but since it is his son who made more of a name for himself, it is he, Airedale Jerry, to which credit is usually given for founding this phenomenal line.   F. M. Jowett, in The *Complete Story of the Airedale Terrier* (1913), says: "Airedale Jerry, whom I remember well, was a dog who did a lot of winning in the north of England, but was never quite up to Championship form. He was a big, strong-boned dog with a long, typical head and a real hard, wiry coat, but overdone in ears. His sire was a dog named Rattler, who won many prizes, and his dam, Bess, was by Champion Brush, who was by Champion Bruce, so his pedigree goes back to the very first dogs that were exhibited." Just as Jerry was more noted than Rattler, so was Jerry's son, in turn, of even greater fame. This was Ch. Cholmondeley Briar, the sole surviving pup of his dam's first litter. Briar's dam was Cholmondeley Luce, said to be a good-headed one, very Terrier-like in character, with small ears and good coat, but a trifle undersized.

Briar won about 170 first prizes, starting his career at six months. He was the winner of the first challenge certificate offered for the breed (1893), winning a total of nine up to the year 1897, and started the fad for bristly names, most of which just had the "briar" with a prefix. Mr. Jowett gives a good description of Briar: "Ch. Cholmondeley Briar was bred at Queensbury near Bradford, and he was first exhibited at some small local show under the name of Red Robin . . . He had a beautiful long, clean, typical head, with great power in front of the

32

Ch. Midland Royal (Ch. Master Royal ex Madame Briar).

Ch. Master Briar (Briar Test ex Betty).

eyes, nice small ears, lovely neck, and clean, well-placed shoulders, with good, short, firm back and well-set, gaily carried tail. His bone and legs and feet were extraordinary, and as round and firm as an English Fox-hound's, and being well covered with hair, gave him an appearance of immense strength. In color he was dense black on his back with rich golden tan on his legs and quarters, and his coat was both straight and hard. He had any amount of substance, yet he was all Terrier, with nothing houndy or coarse about him. He was well up to standard weight, and when mature I would say he was a little over . . . Ch. Cholmondeley Briar will always be remembered by Airedale Terrier breeders, as his name appears in nearly every first-class pedigree of the present day (1913), if it is only traced far enough back, and he stamped his own grand type and character upon his breed in a remarkable manner."

The next in this line is Cholmondeley Briar's son, Briar Test (whose dam was by Ch. Newbould Test), a winner in good company, very similar to his sire, but lacking quality of head. His main claim to fame is as a sire, for Ch. Master Briar (1897-1906) was his son, and here the dynasty developed another branch. Master Briar (out of a small bitch named Betty and bred by A. P. Bruce) was all Terrier in type and quality, and was said to be one of the best-headed Airedales bred up to that time (yet his sire did not become a champion because of a "plain" head). Master Briar's qualities as a "laster" were passed on to many of his get. As a puppy he was described as having a well-shaped head but faulty ears, and as a youngster he did not win well. Even with maturity he was usually beaten by Ch. Rock Salt. However, he kept improving with age—his ears came up and his clean skull not only did not coarsen but also filled up before the eyes, and he became noted for great strength of muzzle.

There are two main lines of descent from Master Briar, that of Ch. Clonmel Monarch and that of Crompton Marvel. Monarch was the favorite of Holland Buckley, who bought him for the Clonmel firm at six months of age. This is Mr. Buckley's description of Monarch, written about 1910: "Probably the nearest approach to the Standard was Champion Clonmel Monarch, who, if he did not absolutely fill the bill, was certainly the nearest approach to the ideal I have ever seen; and this dog has had a great say in the type and character of the modern Airedale: A beautifully balanced terrier, with a long, clean, grandly shaped head, eyes that were ablaze with terrier fire, dark and well-set, muzzle very powerful and with that rare barrel-like formation under the eye which is the hall-mark of only the truly great; his front was irreproachable, with great bone, hard and flat. Legs and feet like bars of iron. He was short in back yet with plenty of liberty. Tail set on gaily at a defiant angle. The smallest possible ears, well-set, and always well carried. The only jarring note in the tout-ensemble of this extraordinary dog was his coat; which although hard and wiry, was—as is not seldom with Champions of this breed—decidedly wavy; a failing he inherited from his sire Master Briar."

Of Crompton Marvel, Mr. Jowett said: "He was a beautiful terrier I always thought unlucky never to become a full champion, as he was full of quality, with beautiful coat and color. He will be remembered chiefly by breeders as the sire of the great show and stud dog Ch. Crompton Oorang, who is the sire and grandsire of more champions and first-class show dogs than any Airedale Terrier living at the present day (1913)."

With the bloodlines of all great modern sires funneling back through English and American Ch. Warland Ditto, we will bring the "Master Briar" line directly up to Ditto, then mention some of the other dogs and bitches which contributed to Ditto's background. All of these are repeated time and time again in extended pedigrees of today's winners, as nearly all of today's winning Airedales are strongly line-bred to Ditto.

Clonmel Chilperic, although not a champion, was the next dog to pass on the line of Monarch, his sire. Chilperic's greatest son was Ch. Master Royal, a high-class dog that was sold to Joseph Laurin's Colne Kennels in Canada, where he stood at a $75.00 fee, a large sum for those days.

In England, Master Royal had sired Ch. Midland Royal, who is the next sire to carry this line along. W. J. Phillips, in *The Modern Airedale* (1921), mentions Midland Royal along with the growing interest in the Airedale in the early 1900s: "He is still in my mind as a model of perfection and what I should require in a young puppy with championship aspirations, to this day. His beautiful quality and all-around richness at this age, made him other worshipers besides myself. North Country men predicted a great future, their prophesies proving quite correct, although having the great Crompton Oorang as his chief opponent. Royal for many years was a force to be reckoned with. So enamored was the writer with these two great strains, the Cromptons and the Midlands, as embodying all that is great in the Airedale, that he at once decided that here was the foundation for a new kennel, which was afterwards known as 'Tintern.' The stock left by Royal has done much to bring into popularity our favorite, for not only was he a dog of great character, but he also had the size that so many of our winning dogs about this time lacked."

Although Midland Royal sired many good winners, he is now more noted as a "sire of sires." Among the main lines were those of Primrose Royalist, Elruge Monarch, and Midland Rollo, who handed the baton on through succeeding generations to Ditto. Midland Rollo's son Requisition is the next transmitter of the line, then his son Wadsworth Royalist, who in turn sired Cragsman King. King was the sire of Cragsman Dictator, a war-baby of 1917 who eventually gained great fame as a sire, with Ditto being his most famous son. Dictator, Ditto, and Ditto's dam, Ch. Warland Strategy, all were imported to America, with Ditto and Strategy gaining further great honors in the show ring, and all of them making their influence felt in subsequent generations. Strategy was better known over here as "Doreda" Warland Strategy, Doreda being the prefix of her new owner, Mr. Joseph Dain, in Illinois. Imported in 1919, she went Best in Show in St. Louis on her first outing in this country in 1920, was shown with great success during 1920 and 1921, then was retired. Although it deals a blow to our "sire line" story, it is to Strategy rather than Dictator that many breeders credit the excellence of Ditto as a sire, for line breeding to Ditto brought vastly better results than did line breeding to Dictator.

Ditto was imported by the Anoakia Kennels in 1922 and on the dispersal of those kennels in the same year, he and several other top Airedales were purchased by Chris Shuttleworth, who had originally brought Ditto over for Mrs. Baldwin. Ditto was advertised by Mr. Shuttleworth as the "World's Greatest Airedale Stud," and he was well patronized by the Western fancy, although the Eastern Airedalers did not care to ship such a great distance and so lost out on his use. Lou Holliday said that when he saw Ditto in 1926, Mr. Shuttleworth told him Ditto's score was then eighteen champions. Just how many were Canadian, Continental, and South African, as well as American, cannot be determined at this late date, but Ditto's English champions (eleven) are a matter of record.

A study of Strategy's bloodlines seems in order, for she contributed much to Ditto's prepotency. And when her full sister, Warland Wingate, was bred to Ditto, his most prepotent son, Ch. Warland Whatnot, was produced. Strategy's sire was Ch. Rhosddu Royalist, a dog that went quickly through to his title in England and was imported to America when well along in years. He made a name for himself as a sire in both countries, with his daughters, especially, bringing him fame through their produce as well as wins. Royalist, whelped in 1913, was out of Maesgwene Trixie, a consistent winner and granddaughter of Ch. Rockley Oorang (a dog eventually owned by the Colne Kennels in Canada and one of the greatest winners of his day).

Rhosddu Royalist is another line of the Master Royal clan, representing the "Primrose" breeding of W. T. Chantler, who started his kennel in 1887. Primrose Rebound was the sire of Ch. Rhosddu Royalist, and Rebound's sire was Primrose Royalist, by Ch. Midland Royal. Thus both the sire and dam of Ditto trace through the same tail male line—through Midland Royal to the Ch. Clonmel Monarch branch of

Airedale aristocracy. There are several other crosses to the Master Royal line in Ditto's pedigree, as well as many to the Crompton Marvel branch of the Briar family tree, mainly through Ch. Prince of York (known in England as Dany Graig Commander), and through the previously mentioned Ch. Rockley Oorang.

Strategy's dam was Warland Enchantress, whelped during World War I and founder of the modern "Warlands," although J. P. Hall, owner of these highly successful kennels, was "in" Airedales from 1895. Enchantress' sire was Cheltenham Cadet (by Ch. Clonmel Cadet) and her dam was Camperdown Flyer (by Brown Jug Perfection, another son of Midland Rollo). Clonmel Cadet was by Petronius, who was by Ch. Master Royal.

Although we have traced the direct male line of Cragsman Dictator (Ditto's sire) from the days of old Jerry, it is worthwhile to have a look "inside" his pedigree, for the "ladies" and the bloodlines they brought in also contributed to the excellence of this line. Dictator's dam was Cragsman Lady Girl, who was by Wadsworth Elite, a son of Tintern Desire (who was in turn a son of Ch. Crompton Oorang). The dam of Cragsman King (Dictator's sire) was Cragsman High Lady, who brought in the line of Ch. Soudan Swiveller, who was sired by a dog considered one of the greatest sires of his time, Elruge Monarch. High Lady's dam, Gray Flossie, was by Leighton (also Leyton) Mainspring, by Ch. Crompton Oorang, and Flossie's dam was Leighton Peggy, by Ch. Midland Royal.

Dropping down again to the dam of Dictator (Lady Girl) we find that her sire (Elite) was out of Laval Queen, a daughter of Requisition and full sister to Wadsworth Royalist, and thus a granddaughter of Midland Rollo. Lady Girl's dam was Bramshall Queen, whose dam, Harrington Kitty, was by Tintern Desire, and Queen's sire was Culminton Tyrant, by Springbank Radium. Even a casual glance through this breeding will show that the blood of Ch. Clonmel Monarch and Crompton Marvel is compounded again and again, and would probably show more such concentration of bloodlines if some of the "deadends" that are not traceable at this distant date could be taken back to their source.

Ch. Clonmel Marvel, easily confused with Crompton Marvel of the same approximate era, was used often as a cross with bitches of the Master Briar line and was very helpful in correcting the soft or linty coats sometimes encountered in that family. It was the Clonmel Marvel-Master Briar cross that produced Ch. Clonmel Monarch; his sire was Ch. Master Briar and his dam Richmond Peggy by Ch. Clonmel Marvel (by Clipper ex Cholmondeley Mona). W. L. Barclay described Marvel in the 1919 Airedale Club Bulletin: "Clonmel Marvel probably weighed 47 pounds. He had the hardest coat, bar none, I have ever had my hands on. He was black on body in his early days in England, but went red on the body, so that when he finally went down to defeat under his grandson, Clonmel Monarch, he was as red all over as an Irish Terrier. His eyes might have been darker, but he was deep-chested, well ribbed up, grand at the quarters, and stood on strong, straight, heavy-boned legs. He probably had a clean head as a puppy, but when I first saw him his head had gone coarse and we would today call him plain-headed. His ears were better than other dogs of that time but that is all that could be said of them. He had a very heavy muzzle and long punishing jaw almost devoid of whisker. The hair on his face was rough, but I cannot imagine that great old terrier with a long white linty mess of soft whisker about four inches long hanging all over his muzzle."

The other "Marvel" was Crompton Marvel, who, like Monarch, was by old Master Briar, his dam being Woodland Judy, by Ch. Rock Salt, a grandson of Briar Test. Unlike Clonmel Marvel, whose influence was mainly through bitches bred to the Briar-line sires, Crompton Marvel set up his own dynasty, which rivaled that of Monarch in quality and numbers. W. J. Phillips said that "Crompton Marvel is probably one of the best of the uncrowned Airedales that ever lived. That he did not obtain the coveted title of champion was more by bad luck than anything else. Built on ideal lines and bred from the best possible strains, he quickly made a name for himself at stud at a very early age. One of the great dogs to claim him as a sire was Ch. Crompton Oorang. After one defeat as a puppy, at Birmingham National, this Lancashire product never looked back—he won the coveted title of champion, and as a sire proved even better worth by his wonderful consistency in breeding. A few of the best of his progeny are: Ch. Dany Graig Commander (now Prince of York), Ch. Crompton Performer, Ch. Rockley Oorang, Tintern Desire, Ch. Clonmel Imperious, Ch. Rebound Oorang, etc."

Mr. Barclay further described this line in the 1923 Club Bulletin: "In reviewing the get of Crompton Oorang it is hard to know where to begin. They came to America in shoals... Ch. Rockley Oorang was the most consistent winner of any of Oorang's sons and probably had the greatest number of wins to his credit. After a most successful career on the English bench Rockley Oorang was sold to the late Joseph Laurin of Montreal. The dog spent some time in the Colne Kennels before being shown in the United States. As I remember him he was a short-backed dog, standing on straight legs and feet, weighing about 48 pounds, rather greyish in color, tan markings not too distinct, and having large ears. He had a good muzzle, good length of head, and dark eyes. One of the best known of Ch. Rockley Oorang's get was Ch. King Oorang, who was a good one. He had strong positive good points rather than a lack of faults. He was black in body color with a rich tan. He had a very long head with about the right amount of whisker and had strong straight legs and good body. He was a very big specimen but gave the impression of great activity as well as substance and strength. His ears were well carried and his quarters were especially good. Although larger than most of the Airedales shown at that time, he was all terrier and won a large number of prizes in England before he arrived in America...

"Although probably Crompton Oorang's best son, Prince of York was not his greatest son. Tintern Desire, whose name lives in the pedigrees of succeeding generations, will be remembered long after Prince of York is forgotten. Tintern Desire, by Crompton Oorang ex a Midland Royal bitch, was one of the first bred by Mr. Phillips, now so well known as a writer, breeder and judge of Airedales. Desire is described as a large, strong-boned dog on racy lines, a nice length of neck, a front of the best, a long clean head and real terrier character, with very dark, well-placed eyes. He weighed about 52 pounds. As a sire of Airedales he can stand in line with the best half-dozen that the breed has produced."

In Summary

While these old-timers may seem of little consequence with the passing of time, they nevertheless have had their influence on modern Airedales—some set the type, others the character, they all had good points and bad points, but help the breed along they all did. Their names are repeated time after time in all Airedale pedigrees. And in modern strains of show quality, in all lands, the name of Ditto is "dittoed" right down the column of names, further intensifying these bloodlines.

So ingrained is the hunting instinct in the Airedale that big-game hunter and Best in Show winner have the same ancestors, and some are even litter mates. All the hunting strains and multi-purpose Airedales which combine show quality with hunting and other working potentials, trace to Ditto, and consequently to the noted dogs mentioned in his background, while such strictly utility strains as the modern "Oorangs" trace over and over again to Ch. Rockley Oorang, Elruge Monarch, and Tintern Desire.

The best known of the combined show and utility lines is that of Lionheart, representatives of which have won many Groups, Specialties, and even Bests in Show, yet have made an enviable record on big game as well as on upland game and waterfowl. This line has the further distinction of producing many obedience workers, some of which are also champions, holding all degrees including that of U.D.T. This one strain in itself symbolizes the versatility of the "show" Airedale.

English and American Ch. Cast Iron Monarch (Walnut King Nobbler ex Lady Conjuror).

3

Early Days in America

THE FIRST Airedale known to come to America was Bruce, a hard-boiled customer brought over by C. H. Mason, well-known dog expert from Bradford, Yorkshire. Although he left no purebred descendant in this country—there being no Airedale bitches here at the time—Bruce is nevertheless in the pedigree of everyone's Airedale, for he was the sire of Ch. Brush, who sired Bess, the dam of none other than Airedale Jerry, root of the family tree. Bruce was the old-fashioned "fighting kind," and the last heard of him was that he was sold for $21.00 at a dog auction at the American Horse Exchange. But Bruce was good enough as an individual to win first in the class for Rough-Haired Terriers in New York in 1881.

The next Airedales to be exhibited were two listed as "blue-and-fawn" in color, belonging to Mr. Lacy. Mr. Mason's book *Our Prize Dogs* (1888), which contained critiques of many of the dogs exhibited in the East at that time, mentions a lone Airedale named Tatters, whelped in 1885 and owned by Dr. Al Watts, that was winner of the Miscellaneous Class at Boston in an entry of nine very miscellaneous dogs. As with all the dogs in the book, Mr. Mason pulls Tatters apart piece by piece, with occasional praise of visible virtues, winding up with the comment: "A useful-looking second-class dog." Obviously no booster for the Airedale, Mr. Mason went on to say: "Here is a breed almost unknown in America. It is more than probable that a good specimen of the breed has not been exhibited here, and prospect of improvement is not bright." Other writers of the period reflected

Mr. Mason's opinion that the breed would probably not become popular, mainly because of the shaggy appearance of these then-untrimmed specimens.

Early American-breds and Breeders

From breeding operations started at Charlotte, Virginia, in 1897 came the Brushwood Airedales by Broadlands Brushwood (Best of Breed at the New York show in 1898), and very distinct from the fashionably bred "Monarchs" and "Marvels" of a few years later.

Other early sources of American-bred Airedales were two kennels in New York—that of J. Lorillard Arden, and about a year later that of DeWitt Cochrane. Both showed with fair success, but it was not until Mr. Arden bought Ch. Clonmel Marvel and Ch. Clonmel Sensation from Holland Buckley that the star of the Airedale in America began to rise.

Then the well-known horseman Foxhall Keene brought over Ch. Clonmel Bed Rock and Ch. Clonmel Coronation. And Theodore Offerman had many a successful season with his York Kennels, housing the imports Ch. York (previously Dumbarton) Sceptre; Ch. York (previously Tone) Masterpiece and Prince of York (known in England as Dany Graig Commander); Ch. Bolton Woods Briar; and Ch. York the Conqueror. Among the homebreds of the York Kennels were Ch. York the Hayseed, by Masterpiece, and Ch. York the Haymaker, by The Hayseed. William S. Barclay, noted for his articles in magazines and club bulletins, bred many of the Wyndhills founded on Monarch blood that appear in the pedigrees of today's winners. Among them were Ch. Wyndhill Tackle, Ch. The Gamecock, and Wyndhill Vandal (who sired three champions although he never gained the title himself). Mr. Barclay's daughter, Caroline Strong, still breeds Wyndhill Airedales today.

Russell Johnson bred the good bitch Red Hackle, and also Ch. Red Sunlight. The latter, bred to her grandsire (Monarch), produced Ch. Red Raven, the dog considered to be the best American-bred son of Monarch.

Lynford Biddle purchased the imported bitch Dumbarton Vixen, who produced Ch. Babs to Ch. The Gamecock, and Babs bred to Ch. The Chorister produced another great American-bred, Ch. The Norseman. Another product of this strain was Ch. The Riding Master (though he was sired by the imported Ch. Endcliffe Crack).

Boston was the other main area in the East in the thick of the early Airedale wars. Arthur Merritt, originally from Northern England, imported several good Airedales, the most famed of which was Ch. The New King, in whose honor the New King Bowl was named. The early Boston area Airedales resembled Rock Salt in type, just as those in

Philadelphia favored that area's leading sire, Clonmel Monarch. And The New King, a son of Ch. Rock Salt, was no exception. The New King nicked well with Clonmel Monarch bitches, thus pulling the two Briar Test lines together, as Rock Salt was by Rock Ferry Test, who was by Briar Test. This line has not survived as a sire line, but is in the blood of certain families through the dams.

A Boston breeder who started early in the Twentieth century and long maintained an interest in the breed was George West, whose best-known Airedale was probably Ch. Vickery Soubrette, sold to the Vickery Kennels and campaigned by them. This bitch, Best in Show at the Eastern Dog Club Show in 1914, was winner of the New King Bowl six times.

In Canada the Colne Kennels of Joseph Laurin made history with their imports and sales of innumerable puppies. Mr. Laurin, then vice-president of the Canadian Kennel Club, introduced the breed to Canada in 1899, and he never balked at paying a high price for a good Airedale, paying $7000 for four Terriers imported in 1901. He spared no expense to further the interests of the breed, bringing over the best of both sexes, not only great winners but also proven sires and dams. Among the imports were Willow Nut, winner of over 130 first placements and sire of more than 75 winners; the famous Ch. Dumbarton Lass, winner of fifteen championships (this was before challenge certificates were issued) and dam of many noted winners; Ch. Colne Lucky Baldwin (brother of Crompton Marvel and Ch. Rock King); Ch. Master Royal, who gained his fame in England rather than after importation; Ch. Mistress Royal; Ch. Freeman Terror; and many others. But the one best known in the later days of the kennel was Ch. Rockley Oorang, who also gained his renown as a sire mainly from his English-bred stock.

Ch. Rockley Oorang was bred in Yorkshire, England, in 1905 by Sid Perkins, who sold him to Mr. Roper. After campaigning the dog to the heights of Airedale glory, Mr. Roper sold him to Colne Kennels. Later, Mr. Perkins established his Rockley Kennels in Toronto, Canada, and the first Airedale he imported was Llangollen Nellie in 1911, this bitch having a litter by Ch. Crompton Oorang shortly after her arrival in Canada. Nellie formed the foundation of the Rockley strain in Canada, a strain that had a strong influence on American as well as Canadian Airedales from Coast to Coast. The fame of the Rockleys reached its peak during the 1930s, and among the later importations (1936) were Tri. Int. Ch. Cotteridge Brigand, subsequently sold to Holland; Ch. Warland Wondrous; and Ch. Warland Warboy, one of the last imported (1941). The influence of the Rockley Airedales on American bloodlines is inestimable, with Ch. Rockley Roasting Hot accounting for twenty American champions. The

Ch. Maralec First Mate (by Maralec Bingo Boy ex Maralec Surprise) won well during the early 1940s. He is shown in a Best in Show win under Hubert Doll, Tom Gately handling.

Ch. Warland Warboy (Ch. Warland Wattotstuff ex Blue Flash) shown taking a Best in Show win, handled by Phil Prentice.

44

bitches were equally good as producers and winners—the sensational Ch. Rockley Riot Act producing three champions, and her sister, Ch. Rockley Hidden Treasure, six. Both, by the way, were sisters of Rockley Roasting Hot. Their dam, Rockley Glitter, founded a many-faceted family of American Airedales, all among the big-time winners. Ch. Greenburn Infractious, a good winner in the 1940s, was straight Rockley-bred, his pedigree in the third generation listing Brigand, Warboy, and Wondrous. He was, however, bred by the Greenburn Kennels, not by Mr. Perkins, and the blood of the foregoing Airedales was doubled, since his parents were full brother and sister.

The Eleanores of Mrs. Loree, the Gingerbreds of Mr. and Mrs. Perry, the modern Lionhearts of Lou Holliday, many of the Trucotes of Mrs. Smit (later Urmston), some of the Airelines of Charles Ryan, the "First Mate" branch of the Maralec Airedales, many of the Tedhursts and some of the Freedoms are strong in Rockley bloodlines. Many more trace to Rockley-imported dogs and bitches, if not to Rockley-bred stock, as in the case of Eng. and Am. Ch. Warbreck Eclipse. But this is the "air age," so back to the early 1900s.

We can only touch lightly on the early days and refer readers to the many books on the breed written from 1910 to 1921 for detailed information on breeders and winning dogs. So far as possible, we will try to name those—both people and dogs—influential in the breed at the time, but whose strains have had an effect on today's Airedales, rather than just those who won the most prizes.

W. E. Baker, author of *The Airedale Terrier* (1921), took up the breed about 1905, and his Tanglewood prefix became well known. Ch. Tanglewood Una and the excellent brood matron Brosna Bacchante, whose produce was among the winning Airedales as far away as California, were among the best of his early stock. Andrew Albright, Jr., made his contribution to Airedale history with his imported Ch. King Oorang and Ch. Tintern Royalist and owned several good bitches. George Batson, who for a while owned some of the York dogs in partnership with Mr. Offerman, later imported Ch. Soudan Swiveller and Ch. Soudan Stamboul, both widely represented by their get in the Far West as well as in the East. These two dogs were later owned by William Wolcott's Kenmare Kennels, which also obtained or bred such top ones as Soudan Sapphire (known in England as Ch. Springbank Diamond), Ch. Kenmare Sorceress, Ch. Primrose Royston Tess, and Bothwell Sorceress (daughter of Kenmare Sorceress).

Earle Woodward was one of the earliest and one of the most successful breeders in the Chicago area. His Ch. Earlwood Warlock is still remembered not only for his wins in breed competition, but also for taking Best in Show at the great International event in Chicago. Although he was well patronized at stud, Warlock's line does not survive in direct tail male today. Francis Porter's Abbey Kennels housed some of the best Airedales of the time, including Ch. Freeman Terror, Ch. Clonmel Isonomy, Ch. Abbey King Nobbler (a great winner and sire but another whose influence is found in female rather than sire lines), Ch. Springbank Sceptre, Ch. Clonmel Command, and Ch. Clonmel Imperious. Fighting it out with the Abbeys were the Vickerys, who bought Ch. Prince of York, Ch. Tintern Royalist, and many others, plus the superior bitch Ch. Vickery Soubrette.

In the Far West, one of the earliest breeders was R. M. Palmer, whose book *All About Airedales* is a classic on the working Airedale. Mr. Palmer, who owned Ch. Matlock Bob (by Ch. Midland Royal) and Ch. Lake Dell Damsel (a daughter of Bob), stressed working ability along with show points. The Lake Dell Kennels were in Washington.

Other Western breeders who took up the Airedale before 1915, were George Downer and James Keefe in Montana. The former was the breeder of Ch. Kootenai Radiance and Int. Ch. Kootenai Chinook, who was eventually owned by the Vibert Kennels in New Jersey and advertised as "The most widely known Airedale Terrier in the world." Mr. Downer bought the magnificent sire Elruge Monarch to head his stud, and although this lost the dog to Eastern use, he was of immense value in leavening the quality of Western Airedales. Mr. Keefe's prefix was Mountain View, and he bred many good ones whose names can be found in extended pedigrees of modern Airedales. Crack Oorang, a son of Crompton Oorang out of a Midland Royal bitch, was advertised at stud by the Chief Kennels in Montana. Among his kennel mates were Chief Chinchinoo (by Elruge Monarch) and Chief Kootenai (by Ch. Prince of York). An imported dog, Marshall Tinner, headed the Flathead Kennels in Montana, which like others in that State emphasized hunting ability while giving plenty of publicity to prize-winning ancestry. Also located in the big-game area of Montana, though a few years later, were Lou Holliday's Lionheart Kennels. This strain proved to be a foundation strain of the West Coast Airedales and is still an important line today, so it will be traced in detail later.

Airedales were well represented in Oregon, also, and Ch. Red Raven (mentioned earlier) headed the kennels of Dr. H. V. Adix in Estacada, bringing Monarch blood to the West Coast. Other lines in the kennels were those of Crompton Oorang and Master Royal.

Among other Westerners who brought the "varmint dog" to the attention of the big-game hunters was S. C. Dietz of Colorado, whose stock was of Elruge Monarch, Clonmel Monarch, Tintern Desire, Crompton Oorang, Midland Royal, and other leading lines. C. P. Hubbard, although having his main kennels in Iowa, had another in Wyoming. He was one of the very earliest pioneers to introduce the Airedale

Ch. Matador Mandarin (1929).

Ch. Tiger of Deswood (1938).

Ch. Aireline Bombsight (1943).

to the public as a big-game and general sporting dog. Ch. The Gamecock was purchased by Mr. Hubbard and was of material aid in building up a good working strain.

C. W. Buttles, first publisher of *The Kennel Review,* was an early breeder in Missouri, and his Elmhurst Kennels produced many a fine show dog, importing several also. In Ohio, the town of LaRue was made famous by the Oorang Kennels founded by Walter Lingo mainly on the Crompton Oorang line—the "Oorang" being taken from that dog's name. This strain will also be detailed in due course, in the proper section.

Airedales were far from rare in Texas and the "Deep South" in the first decade of this century and became progressively more numerous as the years went on, with many big kennels located there and some of the best imports and strains represented.

Frederick C. Hood's Boxwood Kennel fits in between the "early" and the "intermediate" days of the first decade or so of the new century, and one of its early champions was Young King Nobbler. But the climax of this establishment's career was the homebred Ch. Boxwood Barkentine's Best in Show win at Westminster in 1922.

Bulletins of the Airedale Terrier Club of America in the 1920's gave the impression that Airedale activity was largely confined to the Eastern seaboard and a few States east of the Mississippi, as the shows reported were those wherein club challenge trophies were offered, and, of course, Westminster. The foregoing has shown, however, that Airedales were well distributed all over the country. All over the North American continent might be more exact, for the Airedale flourished from Alaska to and including Mexico, and entries were heavy in shows from Washington to Texas and from California to all points East.

The breed was well on its way upward and onward by its second decade in this country and nearly every big Eastern show saw the latest "greatest Airedale ever bred" making its American debut, usually from a boat conveniently docking a day or so before the show. The wins of these dogs were far from discouraging to other exhibitors, but only gave them the idea to bring over another super Airedale and see if it could knock the spots off the latest sensation. This spirit persists to this day and Airedale exhibitors still find it refreshing to bring over a current winner from England, a more recent example being Harold Florsheim's Eng. Ch. Westhay Fiona. This bitch, coming over just in time to win the Group at her first show, then went on to win the Terrier Group at Westminster in 1957.

Although Fox Terriers, both coats, hold the records of Westminster wins, Airedales have fared well among the larger breeds. Ch. Kenmare Sorceress started the parade in 1912, with Ch. Briergate Bright Beauty

A group of working Airedales in Montana, circa 1916. The second dog from left was by the import, Marshall Tinner and was broken to pack and harness.

Ch. Fallcrest Harry (Tri. Int. Ch. Cotteridge Brigand ex Fallcrest Charm), shown with his handler Tom Gately.

49

following in 1919, Ch. Boxwood Barkentine in 1922, and Ch. Warland Protector of Shelterock in 1933. The last win is probably responsible for pulling the breed from the lowest ebb of its depression back to sound footing. At any rate, 1931 had shown the lowest registrations of Airedales since 1907, but they mounted steadily after Protector's win until they are now back in the multiple-thousands.

Establishment of the Great Kennels

The early "teens" saw great kennels founded from Coast to Coast. The most famous of the California kennels started during this period was Anita Baldwin's Anoakia Kennels, which at one and the same time housed Ch. Tintern Tip Top, Whitebirk Tyrant, Cyprus Cadet, Int. Ch. King Oorang, and a couple of Anoakia-bred dogs. Later, Chris Shuttleworth took over the Anoakia Kennels, and with Ditto heading his stud, showed under the name Chrisworth.

The Criterion Airedales of George Binney furnished foundation stock that "lives on" in modern strains, and established about this same time were H. M. Robertson's kennels. Mrs. Greggains' Flashlight Kennels won well up and down the Coast, especially in the 1920s with Warland breeding. Later Mrs. Greggains had several spectacular wins with her Ch. Flashlight Protector, a son of Ch. Warland Protector of Shelterock. The Flashlights furnished much foundation stock on the Coast, especially in the San Francisco area, and among other good points were noted for beautiful coats and rich coloring.

Dr. Frank Porter Miller bought the Canadian-bred Ch. Colne Master Oorang, winning many of the top spots with him as well as with Fancy of Anoakia. In 1921 George Binney's Criterion Kennels featured Ch. Warland By Product, a son of Ch. Neville's Double of Primrose ex Warland Enchantress, who was the dam of the immortal Int. Ch. Warland Strategy and Warland Wingate (dam of Ch. Warland Whatnot). George Harker's Bighorn Kennels in San Fernando made canine headlines both in hunting exploits and in the show ring, his "head man" being the versatile Lionheart Politician. Irving C. Ackerman made room among his Wires long enough to take in the big-time winner Ch. Criterion Warland's Double and stop his sale to the East. Double, later sold to the Estancia Kennels, had the honor of going Best in Show at Long Beach as well as several lesser events.

The Portola Kennels imported Warland Whizbang and his dam, Ch. Warland Waterlily. Lily was by Ch. Warland Whatnot, while her son was by Int. Ch. Flornell Mixer, both of which were highly successful sires in England and in this country. Lily and Whizbang were later sold to Texas.

Ruel Riley, on the advice of Lou Holliday, purchased Ch. Dendale

Tantalizer, a son of Ch. Cragsman Dictator. Tantalizer was very influential on the Coast and was a good winner. Several of the dogs bred by Dr. Warta's Pappio Kennels in Omaha were owned in California and did very well—as they also did in the East—Pappio T.N.T. taking Best in Show at Santa Clara.

In 1926 Lou Holliday moved his Lionheart Kennels to Southern California and before long the "Lionhearts" dominated the West Coast scene with their many wins. These kennels featured the bloodlines of Elruge Monarch through Dakota Bri and others, such as Killarney Sport. Dave Hicks did well with his Pepper Tree Kennels, and his Pepper Tree Don, a son of Ditto, contributed to the foundation of the modern Lionhearts by siring Ch. Lou's J. M.

In Central California Dr. A. P. Deacon was well known for his hunting Airedales. His printed testimonials on bear dogs, 'coon dogs, cougar dogs, and various types of "gun dogs"—all Airedales—apparently paid off, for he mentions selling 237 Airedales in 1922, all over America, Alaska, China, Canada, and the Hawaiian Islands. About this time Chris Shuttleworth was doing a bit of exporting, too, selling one dog to a British army officer stationed in India, and a brace of Airedales (including two by Ditto) was shipped to President Obregon's kennels in Mexico.

Skyline was one of the best-known kennels in the Portland area. Washington had its share of breeders also, Ray Sheldon being heard from most often, but Paul Lancaster in the "Inland Empire" started his Quarryhill Kennels in the 1920s and maintains his interest today.

George Ainsworth's Morning View Kennels of Havelock, Nebraska, bred top Airedales with regularity. Heading his stud was Dakota Bri, whose get became widely known throughout the West.

Denver had many Airedale enthusiasts, with Edward Allen leading in the 1920s with Ch. Rose Bri, a Group winner who consistently placed high in Airedale classes from the Coast to Texas. Rose was by the Canadian-bred Ch. Ruler's Double, first shown on the Coast, then purchased by Ted Dealy of Dallas, Texas. Traced back several generations, Airedales from Mr. Allen's kennels will be listed in the pedigrees of many of today's winners, especially those on the West Coast.

The Marathon Kennels in Wisconsin owned Ch. Clonmel Cadet, a dog especially noted for his classic head with powerful foreface. Cadet is in the ancestral branches of Warland Strategy's family tree, and his sire, Petronius (by Ch. Midland Royal), was a full brother of Leighton Peggy, great-granddam in the direct tail female line of Cragsman Dictator.

The Midwest was the site of several powerful kennels in the 1920s. The Briergate Kennels in Illinois owned Ch. Rex Persaltum, a much-used sire of the period who later went to Virginia. The Caswell Ken-

51

nels in Ohio showed many a top Airedale, and their stud dogs were headed by the great Ch. Tintern Tip Top, purchased from Anoakia. The Davishill Kennels in Kentucky took the measure of import and homebred alike in the Eastern shows, taking several Bests in Show. Among the homebreds of Davishill that made Airedale history were Ch. War Boy of Davishill, Ch. Man o' War of Davishill, Ch. War Bond of Davishill, and the greatest of all, Ch. Warbride of Davishill, Group winner at Westminster and runner-up for Best in Show at that event. Ch. On Guard was another Ohio dog that was used extensively throughout the country. The Briar Croft Kennels in Ohio had really great dogs at stud, such as the famed Ch. Rhosddu Royalist, Ch. Boy, Ch. Briar Croft Authority Nut Brown, Ch. Briarcroft Perfection, Ch. Briar Croft Elms Knight, and Briar Croft Flornell Imperator. Nut Brown won at Westminster and the parent club specialty in 1923; Perfection (by Wawasee Whinbush Maxim) won the summer Specialty in 1924, with feminine honors taken by a kennel mate, Ch. Briar Croft Sweet Memory (by Ditto); and Perfection also won the parent Specialties in 1925 and 1926.

The Doreda Kennels in Illinois owned the great sires Eng. Ch. Doreda Craigmillar Prince, Eng. Ch. Doreda Cragsman Kingsway, and Cragsman Dictator, who, although untitled, out-sired both the other two. A. L. Zeckendorf, well known for his "Freedom" Airedales, first took up the breed when in Michigan, but later moved to Connecticut and his dogs were well to the forefront from then on.

Dr. Thatcher's Cliffdale Kennels in Texas stood various imported dogs at stud, including Stockfield Desire (a son of Ditto), who came to the United States by way of Canada. The Thornbrook Kennels in San Antonio owned the imported dog Narrowdale Nimrod, litter brother of the great Int. Ch. Polan Maxim.

Tennessee was also well up in Airedale news as a result of the excellence of the Chickasaw Kennels. Their stud dogs included Int. Ch. Craigmillar Prince and Ch. Elmhurst Emperor, but their Airedale that will go down in history is Ch. Doreda Kathleen McCaura, purchased, as was Prince, from the Doreda Kennels. Kathleen's most famous son was Clonmel Monarque (by Ch. Warland Whatnot), and she was also the dam of Ch. Chickasaw Sunny Kathleen. G. L. L. Davis' Daystar Kennels in Missouri bred many a good one, and confused the "Davis" mixup further by buying one or two of the "Davishill" prefix.

Sheldon Stewart's Shelterock Kennels started on the road to Airedale immortality about 1925, the year in which their Ch. Geelong Defiance was Winners at the Specialty. Through importation of the very best dogs and bitches, and a well-planned breeding program, the "Shelterocks" were on the top for nearly two decades, making spectacular wins. As their Ch. Warland Protector of Shelterock has a place in modern sire lines, he and his most sensational son, Eng. and Am. Ch. Shelterock Merry Sovereign, will be mentioned later. C. Rasmussen's Hekla Kennels were begun in the early 1920s, and Hekla brood matrons have earned the kennel a place in the sun by their produce that "bred on."

Harold Florsheim started his Harham Kennels about this same period, importing many good dogs—possibly more than any other exhibitor—and also breeding dogs that have contributed to the excellence of the modern American Airedale as well as making history in the show ring. Barbara Strebeigh's Birchrun Kennels were also founded at this approximate time. Although at first her kennel did not attain the heights noted by the major exhibitors of the period mentioned, Barbara herself, as officer of the Club and especially as editor of the Newsletter, did more for the breed in America than has any other one person. Her lively comments and work on the Newsletter brought together all Airedale breeders, who up to that time were starved for news, not just show results, but interesting items about breeders and dogs. And not show dogs alone, but hunters and pets also. As if this were not enough, it was the importation by Barbara (and Mrs. Tuck Dell) of Bengal Sabu that not only took the Birchrun Kennels to the aforementioned heights in show wins, but resulted in a major change of top-winning bloodlines in this country, almost eclipsing the long-established American lines. Of this, more later.

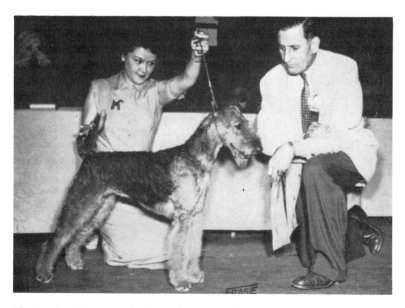

Ch. Benaire Crown Jewel (Ch. Harham's Expert Explorer ex Ch. Aireline Storm Queen).

Ch. Rockley Riot Act (Tri. Int. Ch. Cotteridge Brigand ex Rockley Glitter).

4

American Bloodlines to 1960

THE CUSTOM now is to give the name of the countries involved when using the champion prefix from one or more countries other than the United States, but in this chapter we will use the term "Int." for "International Champion" on the older dogs originally designated by that prefix. While most are English and American champions, some were Canadian, South African, Indian, Continental, etc., and as we are not certain of the countries concerned on some of these widely traveled dogs, we have left the old terminology. Modern winners will be given specific titles, when known. Also, in respect to the older sires and dams, information as to champions produced was often taken from advertisements, stud cards, or write-ups, and where the totals do not tally with the number of known American champions, it can be assumed that some of these were of Canadian or European origin.

The Moorhead Marquis Line

In reference to the lasting qualities of English-bred sire lines and the incomprehensible fading away of the American-bred lines, it is interesting to note the following comment from a 1926 *American Kennel Gazette*: "Another new one was the English champion *Flornell Mixer*, which, rumor says, was one of the highest-priced Airedales ever imported. Airedales are one of the breeds in which America can hold her own with England, so a fancier should watch his step and not throw away a big sum in importing Airedales. We generally win with home-breds. Flornell Mixer won the limit class and went Reserve Winners. He is the property of Mrs. Stanley Halle ... The open and winners class was won by Ch. Briarcroft Perfection, which looked better than last year. He also took the medal for Best Airedale. In his present form he is good enough to compete with the best terriers of all breeds. It is not often one sees a better terrier."

Apparently the writer did not know that Perfection's sire, Wawasee Whinbush Maxim, was one of those imports on which "money was thrown away." Nevertheless this line did not breed on at all, in the sire line, while that of the "high-priced" Mixer is the one which carries on the Moorhead Marquis branch from Ditto. Shortly after the foregoing show, Mixer won the title of Best Airedale at the Sesqui-Centennial show in Philadelphia in an entry of sixty-seven judged by Russell Johnson.

The next dog of this line to be imported was *Int. Ch. Walnut Challenger*, brought over by Fred Hoe. Challenger was Best of Breed at Westminster and won the Specialty in 1931 and 1932. He sired *Ch. Eleanore's Knight*, a successful sire of champions but whose un-crowned son *Maralec Bingo Boy* was destined to become outstanding in this respect. Bingo Boy founded his own line, to which the majority of this dynasty's champions trace. His son, *Ch. Maralec First Mate*, was equally sensational as a sire but also was an outstanding show dog. Among other outstanding wins, he was Best of Breed at Westminster in 1947. Bingo Boy's dam was Miss Hot Trix by Ch. Rockley Roasting Hot, while First Mate's dam was Maralec Surprise, also by Roasting Hot. The Challenger line is doubled here in the background of Surprise—Eleanore's Princess (dam of Surprise) being out of a daugh-ter of Challenger. Also in this breeding is the American-bred line of Ch. Willinez Warrior Bold, a really good one.

Ch. Warland Whatnot Line—Ch. Warland Waterman Branch

Another grandson of Ditto imported at the same time as Flornell Mixer was *Ch. Warland Waterman*, a son of the main transmitter of the Ditto line, Ch. Warland Whatnot. Waterman, brought over by Louis Bader of Dover, Massachusetts, was Winners at the 1927 Specialty and Best of Breed at Westminster, and also won the New King Bowl at the Eastern Dog Club show. A son of Waterman, *Ch. Wrose Cargo*, was imported in 1928 by the Penny Ponds Kennels of Long Island, and his claim to Airedale immortality is through his siring *Ch. Wrose Anchor*, the latter the sire of the tremendously successful Int. Ch. Warland Protector of Shelterock. The line breeding to Ditto is interesting in the case of Anchor: Cargo's dam, Wrose Marchioness, was a daughter of Ditto, while Miss Gabrielle, Anchor's dam, was by Flornell Mixer ex Singram (by Marquis, a son of Ditto). Since Whatnot's dam, Warland Wingate, was a full sister to the dam of Ditto, there is a still greater concentration of the bloodlines delineated in the history of Ditto.

Now we come to the immortal *Int. Ch. Warland Protector of Shelterock*, whose dam was Warland Sprite, who was by Clee Brigand ex Seacot Soubrette (a daughter of Whatnot). Soubrette's dam, Seacot Sylph, was out of Warland Watchful, a litter sister of Whatnot, and Sylph's sire was Cragsman King's Own, by Cragsman King. Clee Brigand was a litter brother of the more famous Int. Ch. Clee Courtier, and a grandson of Whatnot via Clonmel Monarque. Brigand's dam, Clee Charming, is out of Warland Stella, by Ditto.

Protector was bred in England by J. P. Hall of "Warland" fame and was purchased as a puppy by S. M. Stewart's Shelterock Kennels. Together with Covert Dazzle, his scintillating kennel mate, Protector was campaigned in England under the guidance of Bob Barlow for about a year, during which time they, as a pair and separately, won eighteen "championships" in Great Britain, twice Best Brace, Best of all breeds in show, and Protector was runner-up for BIS at Crufts.

Mr. Stewart's dream of "breeding a real 'flyer,'" literally came true when he mated Protector and Dazzle, producing *Int. Ch. Shelterock Merry Sovereign*. Whelped December 27, 1934, he won his American title in 1936 at consecutive shows in a period of twenty-six days. He was the leading American-bred Terrier, all breeds, for that year, and placed in twelve Groups. This record convinced Mr. Stewart that the English should have a chance to see a first-class American-bred Airedale (though of English breeding), so he did the then unprecedented thing of sending him to England to "have a go," fully cognizant of the set-back the quarantine period might have on the dog. Merry Sovereign came out fighting fit, in magnificent condition, and scattered famous dogs to the right and left on his way to the title of "Best Exhibit in Show" at the huge Kennel Club Show at Olympia in London. He again won his championship in successive shows and was runner-up for Best in Show at Birmingham, England's oldest championship show, which averaged an entry of about 3,000 dogs at that time. Although the tail-male line of Merry Sovereign is eclipsed by other lines in America, he was a very successful sire of brood matrons—his blood being in the background of many of the best Airedales of England and America through the dams. There are two main lines from Warland Protector in this country, but considering the twenty-five champions sired by this dog, the line, so far as tail male is concerned, is lagging. Only reference to pedigrees of brood matrons brings out the great influence Protector has had on the breed.

Ch. Warland Whatnot Line—Clonmel Monarque Branch

Clonmel Monarque was a great stud force but, like his grandson Walnut King Nobbler, never became a champion—in fact, he was rarely shown. That he was widely used as a sire was a tribute to the excellence of his get, six of his sons and daughters gaining the title, with others carrying on the line as sires or producers with remarkable success. Clonmel Monarque, who was whelped in 1921, was one of Whatnot's first sons, the latter having been whelped in 1920.

Monarque's greatest claim to fame at this date is through his son *Ch. Clee Courtier*, sire of thirteen champions as well as two untitled dogs that did more in the way of continuing the line than did some of the more famous winners. The uncrowned Clee Brigand, older brother of Courtier, founded a line in England but did the greatest amount of good to the breed through his daughters. Courtier was a magnificent show dog, and as J. Ethel Aspinall said in *The Airedale Terrier*, he seemed to exercise a dwarfing effect on certificate winners of other breeds, as witness his many Best in Show awards. He won a total of fourteen c.c.s at England's largest shows, including Crufts.

Walnut King Nobbler Line

The most fabulously successful of the Courtier lines is that of *Walnut King Nobbler*. This dog was whelped in 1930 and was bred by Major J. H. Wright, whose Ch. Murose Replica brought him more fame fifteen years later and whose Ch. Holmbury Bandit was a great sire of the 1940s. Nobbler was originally named Holmbury Good Lad but renamed under the "Walnut" prefix of his new owner, Sam Bamford. Nobbler was the sire of seventeen English and nine American champions as well as some that acquired their titles in other countries, and several were in the "international" category. Nobbler's dam was Holmbury Brunette, who was by Neadwood Captain ex Taff Queen (whose sire was Ch. Mespot Tinker). The latter was A. J. "Towyn" Edwards' most famous dog and his stud card gives him credit for siring sixteen champions, of which eight were English.

Walnut King Nobbler Line—Tri. Int. Ch. Cotteridge Brigand Branch

Much of the success of the Nobbler line is through his son *Tri. Int. Ch. Cotteridge Brigand*, founder of a branch responsible for more American champions in the last decade than all other lines combined. Brigand was imported to Canada by Sid Perkins, and the few litters he sired there before being sold to Holland gave even more fame to the "Rockleys." While the Cotteridge Brigand line was much less influential in England, its dominance in American bloodlines cannot be denied. Brigand's full brother, Ch. Aislaby Aethling, however, contributed heavily to English lines. Brigand's reputation as a sire could have been made by the one litter which produced Ch. Rockley Riot Act, Ch. Rockley Roasting Hot, and Ch. Rockley Hidden Treasure, for Roasting Hot founded the line that produced 97 of the 130 champions of the Brigand dynasty, and the two bitches also founded strong families of their own.

   Ch. Rockley Roasting Hot was purchased by Mrs. Eleanore Loree of Summit, New Jersey, and although he had a good show record, it was not as outstanding as that of Riot Act. Whelped April 19, 1937, Roasting Hot gained his title while still under a year of age. What enduring fame he may have lacked in the show ring he made up for as a sire of twenty-one champions.

   Roasting Hot's leading son is *Ch. Eleanore's Royalty of Lionheart*, this branch producing fifty-four champions in the last decade, with Ch. Roy el Hot Rock and Ch. Eleanore's Brigand being the other main contributors. Royalty was bred by Mrs. Loree and purchased as a young prospect by Lou Holliday. It is as a sire that he will best be remembered, but he made a fine record in the show ring, being one of the Airedale elite to have an all-breed Best in Show win to his credit, many Group placements, and a Specialty Best in Show. The Specialty Best in Show win took place in 1947, the first year the Ch. Lionheart Comet Bowl was on offer for winners of the Southern California Specialty. And it is a tribute to Royalty's success as a sire, and as a sire of sires, that in the decade since it was first offered, only two winners of the bowl have not been his direct male-line descendants.

   Of Royalty's sixteen champions, *Ch. Lionheart Copper* had the most notable show record and also established a strong clan of his own in this remarkable patriarchy. He was best of breed on 29 occasions, three times first in the Group and had twenty other placings. Copper's dam was Ch. Lionheart Comet III by Int. Ch. Cast Iron Monarch, and of course of the famed "Comet" family, which will be mentioned later.

   The line from Copper which has become the most influential is that of *Ch. Studio Top Brass*, whose dam was Crosswind of "gun dog" fame. Crosswind was by Ch. Lionheart Cold Steel, and in keeping with the metallic naming system, I had applied for "Battle Axe" as first choice for a name, this seeming beautifully applicable, as she was tough and—as a pup—willful, so, when that was not allowed by the AKC, the second choice, "Crosswind" was. This name was chosen because I was taking flying lessons at the time and could think of nothing harder to handle than crosswinds. That should explain this rather un-Airedalish name. Brassy too was an independent individual who loved to hunt, but he was destined for the show ring. He had style to the nth degree and passed this attribute on to most of his get. He won the first Pacific Northwest specialty in 1950 and the next year was BOS to Ch.

Ch. Rockley Roasting Hot.

Ch. Roy El Hot Rock (1945).

Ch. Roy el Tiger Lily (1946).

Lionheart Enchantress (1948).

Ch. Sierradale Chica, U.D.T. (1939).

Raylerock Mica. Two generations later the combination of these lines resulted in the production of Ch. Hilltop's Happy Josh and Ch. Hilltop's Kintla Challenge, as will be noted under their sire's name.

Ch. Studio Liontamer brought Brassy the most fame of his nine champions. Liontamer's first Specialty win was the Pacific Northwest event in 1952, followed the same year by his taking the Southern California 25th Anniversary Specialty, in an entry of 87 Airedales— the largest in America in thirty years. Next he won the California Airedale Terrier club's Specialty at San Mateo, then, three years after his first win, he again took the Southern California affair. He was never campaigned on circuits, and was never away from the West Coast. Shown 21 times after he was out of the puppy stage, *Liontamer* (Simba) won 15 Bests of Breed, and placed in the Group 14 times. Six of these were Group firsts, including Golden Gate, Beverly-Riviera and Harbor Cities (Long Beach). The latter Group win was especially impressive, for finishing in back of him were several famous Best in Show winners. The 1952 SCAA Specialty was judged by Percy Roberts, who had also officiated at the Westminster show that year.

Liontamer is a full brother of five other champions. Those of a later litter almost didn't make it into this world at all, for their dam, Lionheart Enchantress, nearly died as a result of blood poisoning. This was because of her rushing in "where Greyhounds (if not angels) feared to tread," and killing a huge, gone-wild tomcat in the woods. The Greyhounds had caught the cat but had let go when he got too tough. Ellie (Enchantress) had never seen a cat close-up before, but it was damaging her gawky friends so she did something about it, silently finishing him off, but he got his revenge "posthumously" when the wounds from his claws brought on the infection. This was an astounding affair for Ellie, since she was a mild-mannered bitch who liked nothing better than to carry a toy football around all the time... without even puncturing it.

The line from *Liontamer* was originally carried on mainly through the first of his five champions, *Ch. Hilltop's Rocky Top Notch*, but another branch, which has proven to be even more productive started from an untitled dog, *Coppercrest Brandy*. Since this was a later development taking two generations more to break into the limelight, it is detailed in the next chapter. Rocky's exploits as a gun dog are worthy of note in themselves, but it is his career as a show dog, and as a sire that gave him a place in Airedale history. He too won the Pacific Northwest Specialty and at the same show won the Group. He won several other such firsts and like his sire, once he was mature he placed in the Group every time he was Best of Breed, except one. His dam was Lionheart Impact, who was by Ch. Lionheart Banner ex Ch. Lionheart Comet III. Two of Rocky's sons have carried on for him, one by show

61

Ch. Studio Top Brass (1948).

Ch. Studio Liontamer (Ch. Studio Top Brass ex Lionheart Enchantress), owned by the author, was BB at the Golden Gate KC show under T. H. Carruthers, III. He went on to win the Terrier Group this day and was handled by John Edwards.

Bennett

successes, including the Southern California Specialty, but no branch line descends from him. This was Ch. Hilltop's Happy Josh. The other was Ch. Hilltop's Kintla Challenge, the first Airedale bred on the West Coast to win Best of Breed at Westminster, which he did twice. This feat was repeated around two decades later by another dog of the Top Notch dynasty, and all but one of whose ancestors in tail male lineage had won the PNW specialty. This one exception was not a champion (he may have been used only for hunting, but memory fails me on this) but it is through him, *Hilltop's Blitzkrieg*, that the line has descended—a similar situation to that from *Coppercrest Brandy*. But then when you think of it, all the descendants of Walnut King Nobbler trace back to an uncrowned king, Nobbler himself.

The dam of Challenge and Josh is Cowboy's Cowgirl of Foxglove, a bitch of Replica and intense First Mate breeding, and they were bred by Mr. and Mrs. Frank Slama of Corvallis, Oregon.

The second main branch from Top Brass is that of *Can. and Am. Ch. Lionheart Skyway,* full brother of Liontamer and sire of Ch. Saltash Royal Guardian (Winners Dog at the 1957 Southern California Specialty) and Ch. Sundown Forty-five (Reserve to Guardian at that show). Skyway himself was best of winners at the 1955 Specialty, which was won by his older brother, Liontamer. Skyway's litter sister, Ch. Lionheart Starlight, was winners bitch—making a "family" clean sweep of the top spots. Skyway subsequently became owned by Mary Curran in Canada.

Going back to Copper, we come to the second of his leading sons, *Ch. The Sheik of Ran-Aire.* The Sheik was another outstanding show dog, although he was never campaigned nor widely advertised by his owners and breeders, Mr. and Mrs. George Rankin of North Hollywood. Winner of the Southern California Specialty in 1951, Sheik won several Groups, climaxed by a Best in Show at San Mateo. Ch. Boulder Gulch Son of the Sheik, bred and owned by Florence Fisk Fried, was the Sheik's most successful son, and was a Group winner as well as placing in Groups several times. His litter sisters, Ch. Boulder Gulch Little Sheba and Ch. Boulder Gulch Show Girl, won the California specialty in consecutive years. "Sonny's" dam brings in a variety of bloodlines. She is Patshee Patricia, tracing to Walnut King Nobbler in tail male, and her dam was Trucote Dazzle, by Ch. Tiger of Deswood (a son of Merry Sovereign). Son of the Sheik sired Ch. Gooch's Prince Charming, was Winners Dog at the 1956 Southern California Specialty.

Ch. Hot Shot of Ran-Aire, founder of the secondary branch of the Royalty dynasty, was out of a full sister of the Sheik. Hot Shot was Winners at the 1949 Southern California Specialty and Best Opposite to Ch. Roy el Tiger Lily in 1951. He sired the Champions Sundown

Ch. Hilltop's Rocky Top Notch (Ch. Studio Liontamer ex Lionheart Impact).

Annie Oakley and Sundown Trigger, the latter winner of the 1954 Southern California Specialty and known as "the Giant Killer" for his success in bowling over the currently successful winners from time to time. "The "Sundowns" are bred and owned by Mr. and Mrs. Adrian Eichorn of Malibu, and Trigger and Annie's dam was Marbeth Surprise (by Copper out of a bitch by Ch. Lionheart Cold Steel); hence, their breeding is very similar to that of the "Liontamers." A son of Trigger was Winners Dog at the 1954 Specialty but unfortunately was lost soon afterwards.

Going back to Roasting Hot we find the two other main branches of this line. Of these, the line of *Ch. Eleanore's Brigand* is still going strong while that of Ch. Roy el Hot Rock seems to be dying out. Brigand was a full brother of Royalty, and although his name has a piratical ring, he proved his royal lineage by being second only to his brother in the number of champions sired by sons of Roasting Hot. In the "spice litter" sired by Brigand, there were three champions: Eleanore's Allspice, Eleanore's Marjoram, and Eleanore's Ginger. But it was Ch. Aireline Bombsight that gave Eleanore's Brigand his high score. Bombsight's dam was Ch. Fiesolana, who was by Ch. Towyn Speculation ex Stockfield Melody. Speculation was by Warland Michael ex Warland Maple (a full sister of Warland Protector of Shelterock). Michael also was out of Warland Sprite, dam of Protector and Maple. Bombsight was bred by Charles Ryan and sold to the Milroy Kennels in Canada, where he had a successful career. Repurchased by Mr. Ryan, Bombsight was first shown in this country at the 1947 Specialty, when just under four years of age, and so impressed Percy Roberts that he bought a half interest in him. At this show Bombsight went on from the classes to Best of Breed, downing seven champions en route. He was Best of Winners at Westminster but had to bow to the four-and-a-half-year-old Ch. Maralec First Mate for Best of Breed. Two of Bombsight's best-known sons are Ch. Tedhurst Pilot and Ch. Breezewood Ballyhoo.

Ch. Tedhurst Pilot was bred by Ted Becker, and his dam was Ch. Tedhurst Aviatrix, who was by Roasting Hot ex Tedhurst Bruna of the Rampart, a daughter of Ch. Warland Warboy. Ch. Tedhurst Cadet is a son of Pilot ex Tedhurst Belle, the phenomenal producer of champions.

Ch. Breezewood Ballyhoo, owned, trained, and exhibited by Jane Ruth, is out of Breezewood Bonfire, who was by a son of Ch. Squire of Siccawei ex Bourbon-Ayr Manhattan (by First Mate). Whelped in 1952, Ballyhoo has won three specialties and one Group, and has already sired two champions.

The third of the main Roasting Hot lines, that of *Ch. Roy el Hot Rock,* was very much in the forefront for a while; but due to the main representatives of later years being bitches, the tail-male inheritance has stopped abruptly. Hot Rock was bred and owned by Roy Latham and whelped in 1945. His dam was Ch. Eleanore's Glittering Girl, who was by Ch. Eleanore's Knight ex Roasting Hot's sister, Ch. Eleanore's Hidden Treasure. Hot Rock, known as "Jeep," was shown nineteen times, going Best of Breed fourteen times, placing in the Group eleven times, and was Best Terrier six times.

Ch. Roy el Red was Jeep's most prominent son, winning the *Dog World* Award by acquiring his title in three straight shows. The story of this line concerns its daughters more than its sons, for two of the former made Airedale history on the West Coast. The first was Ric Chashoudian's Ch. Roy el Tiger Lily, twice winner of the Southern California Specialty (1948 and 1950) and Best of Opposite Sex to Copper in 1949. Lil was by Hot Rock out of Hot Rock's own dam, Glittering Girl, and though this breeding may be considered close, it was nowhere near so close as that of Ch. Hazelin's Red Hot Mamacita. 'Cita was sired by Ch. Hazelin's Red Hot, who was by Roy el Red out of Red's dam and granddam, Glittering Girl. 'Cita's dam was Ch. Annjiehills Bloomer Girl, by Hot Rock, which also brought in the name of Glittering Girl, and gave her a large percentage of the pedigree. Like Ric Chashoudian, Mamacita's owner, Daisy Edwards Austad got started as a professional handler with a good Airedale. 'Cita won the Texas Specialty, was Best of Opposite Sex to Liontamer in the Silver Anniversary Specialty—an honor she had had the previous year to the Sheik and which she repeated at the age of seven and half years to Liontamer's grandson Josh at the 1957 Southern California Specialty. She won several Groups and placed in many others.

Ch. Highmoor Rival is another son of Roasting Hot who started a line that produced champions. This traces down from Rival through Dalehaven Chief Rival, and his son Dalehaven Debonair, who sired Ch. Comrade Speed King. The latter is a Group winner and also a sire of champions. Chief Rival is the maternal grandsire of Only Girl of Ran-Aire, dam of the Sheik.

Going back now to Cotteridge Brigand, the most successful branch after that of Roasting Hot is the branch of Eng. Ch. Monarch of Tullochard, a great-grandsire of *Ch. Squire of Siccawei,* to whom this line owes its fame in America. The line traces down from Monarch to Rural Defiance, then His Lordship of Tullochard to Esquire of Tullochard, sire of the imported Squire. Squire traces to Walnut King Nobbler in many lines, with nearly all the rest of Matador Supreme of Mandarin blood. Many of the names that appear unfamiliar are full brothers or sisters of those we know very well in America. For instance, Fierentina, granddam of Esquire, is a full sister of Ch. Fiesolana, and their dam, Stockfield Melody, is a sister of Ch. Aislaby Joceline of Shelterock. This breeding has already been mentioned

66

under that of Bombsight. Melody's sire, Ch. Aislaby Aethling, a full brother of Cotteridge Brigand, won thirteen c.c.s by the time he was two years of age, seven of them in succession. Aethling was Best in Show at the National Airedale show for two years in a row, BB at the Midland Airedale show, and Best Terrier at Cruft's in 1934. Squire's dam, Siccawei Pica was by Leader Writer, a son of Newsboy Call and a full brother of Ch. Ridgemoor Sweetberry. The latter was a bitch who founded a strong family in this country, as will be noted later. Many of Squire's antecedents were "war babies" and were in their prime during the period when no championship shows were held in England. Squire, with his dozen champion sons and daughters, is high on the sire list, with Ch. Tedhurst Equity at the moment supplying the main sub-branch. Owned at one time by Charles Ryan and Percy Roberts, Squire later became the property of the Whitehouse Kennels of Harry Reinhart. A son of Ch. Tedhurst Equity who has done exceptionally well is Can. and Am. Ch. Tedhurst Major, a Best in Show winner in Canada and winner of a couple of Groups, as well as several placements, in this country.

The Canadian-bred *Ch. Fallcrest Harry* was another son of Cotteridge Brigand to found a line in this country. Harry's line is carried on down through Ch. Croftlyn's My Own Mickey, a good winner. Mickey's son Airelore Perfection, in turn, has sons siring champions, thus carrying on this branch. The other line from Harry is through Ch. Croftlyn's Sir Galahad, also a sire of champions.

Ch. Rockley Robin Hood, a Canadian dog as his prefix indicates, founded a line in this country that might not be noted for many branches but it did feature a few big winners. Ch. Greenburn Infractious is the dog that started this line on its way to fame, and was by a son of Robin Hood—Greenburn Sir Michael. Mike's dam was Rockley Bess, who was by Ch. Warland Warboy. Robin Hood's dam was Ch. Warland Wondrous, a daughter of Walnut King Nobbler. Infractious was out of Greenburn Gingersnapper, a full sister of Sir Michael, Infractious' sire. She was also full sister to Greenburn Inquisition, dam of Ch. Acres Sal of Harham. When Infractious was owned by the Ker-Wel-Aire Kennels, he was described on the stud card as having a "long, clean, perfectly balanced" head, but Infractious had offspring on the "pony-headed" order, rather round-skulled and broad, during the years he was owned by the Copperdale Kennels in San Francisco. However, this complemented the cobby conformation of the Copperdale dogs. And with the clean-skulled Replica stock of the same kennels, the result was very good and the combination produced several champions. Infractious was more widely advertised than any dog of his time and was well patronized at stud. Although he did not himself sire many champions, his grandson, Ch. Orlaine's

Ch. Greenburn Infractious (Greenburn Sir Michael ex Greenburn Gingersnapper), shown with his handler George Ward.

English Ch. Son of Merrijak (Holmbury Murraysgate Merrijak ex Nelson Lassie).   *Tauskey*

Roustabout, had the record number of Group wins by an Airedale—twenty-seven—until the advent of Eng. Ch. Westhay Fiona who was imported by the Florsheims.

Walnut King Nobbler Line—Ch. Walnut Clipper of Freedom Branch
The second longest Walnut King Nobbler line in this country is that of *Ch. Walnut Clipper of Freedom,* owned by A. L. Zeckendorf's Freedom Kennels. Clipper's dam was Walnut Happy Maid, by Ch. Tavern Leatherface, who was by Ch. Stockfield Aristocrat. So far as extending the line is concerned, Clipper's most noted son is Ch. Freedom Free Lance. Clipper was also a good brood matron sire, one of his daughters, Ch. Walnut Amethyst of Freedom, being dam of three champions, while another, Freedom Forget Me Not, topped this number by one. Forget Me Not's son, Ch. Freedom Full Force (by Free Lance), is the leading sire of the Free Lance line. Ch. Freedom Fireworks, another son of Clipper ex Amethyst, was ten times Best of Breed and also won a Group. Ch. Lance of O'Samequin, Best of Winners at the 1943 Specialty, is another son of Free Lance. Lady Filigree, a full sister of Full Force, was dam of Ch. Aireline Supreme (by Bombsight). Supreme had an enviable record of Group placements and wins, as well as a Best in Show, but died in his prime. He had acquired his title without a defeat.

Walnut King Nobbler Line—Int. Ch. Cast Iron Monarch Branch
Although the sire line founded by Int. Ch. Cast Iron Monarch is not a long one, he has been influential through the success of some of his daughters as brood matrons. One of these was Ch. Lionheart Comet III and another was the Best in Show winner Ch. Tesque Muldavin—though the latter was more noted for her show wins than as a producer. Some puppies of this line (as is also the case with the line from Infractious and several others) have a blaze on the chest, and occasionally white toes, this latter marking disappearing when the puppy gets its new coat. Color Bracer of Merzhill, a son of Monarch, has also sired champions.

Ch. Clee Courtier Line (from Whatnot)—Ch. Matador Mandarin Branch
Going back now to the Clee Courtier main line, we come to a branch with more offshoots and taproots than a banyan tree. This is the branch from *Ch. Matador Mandarin,* which has a record second only to that of the Walnut King Nobbler line in this country, with eighty-one American champions tracing to Mandarin in tail male in the last decade. Mandarin sired only one male champion, Ch. Stockfield Aristocrat, but this dog was a sire of sires, as the whole line seems to be. Mandarin won five c.c.s in succession, going from novice to Best in

Show at Birmingham and also winning this high honor at the National Terrier show and at Bath.

Ch. Stockfield Aristocrat was the winner of nineteen c.c.s in four years, and sired nine champions. He was sold to Japan along with several other good Airedales, but during his career in England he won many Bests in Show as well as other high honors. Aristocrat's dam was Gleeful Wendy, by Ch. Ileene Brigand, who was by Ch. Mespot Tinker.

Carrying on this line was *Ch. Waycon Aristocrat,* sire of only two champions, but they "made" him, for they were the great sire *Ch. Wolstanton Bostock* and the good winner and producer Ch. Warland Wedding Gift. Waycon Aristocrat's dam was Ch. Sweet Damsel's Legacy by Warland Protector, and this was one of the many instances where Protector aided in giving producing ability to a line. Bostock sired five English and one Continental champion. Among his best sons was Ch. Broadcaster of Harham, while his daughter Ch. Ridgemoor Sweetberry founded a very strong family of her own. Chathall News was a prominent progenitor in the English branches of this line. Berrycroft Atoppa, unable to compete in championship shows due to World War II, was another son of Bostock who founded an enduring line, as did Waycon Designer, an uncrowned son of Waycon Aristocrat.

Carrying on the *Broadcaster* dynasty, *Ch. Harham's Expert Explorer* had the most sensational show career and sired the most champions, but his line at present is shorter than that of *Ch. Harham's Rocket.* Broadcaster's dam, Lady Conjuror, was also the dam of Cast Iron Monarch, who was by Stockfield Aristocrat. Expert Explorer, bred and owned by Harold Florsheim's Harham Kennels, was Best of Breed thirty-five times from 1949 to 1953, including twice at Westminster (1950 and 1953), and won the Terrier Group eight times.

Ch. Harham's Rocket won thirteen Bests of Breed and one Best in Show. His dam, Adoration of Aldon, was by Cotteridge Brigand, who was by Warland Protector ex Eng. Ch. Warland Wishbone. Ch. Ardendale Repeat Performance was an especially well-named dog so far as siring champions was concerned, dittoing down the line with seven title holders. Of these, Ch. Ardendale Mr. Trouble sired three more, and his line is carried on by Ch. Gingerbred Number One Boy, a California-bred dog that had the distinction of winning his title in the East, taking Best of Winners at Morris and Essex, Best of Breed at Plainfield, Middlesex, and the New England Specialty. On his Eastern tour he was accompanied by his litter sister, Ch. Annjiehill's Show Off II, making the trip unique in that she took all her points at these shows, including the New England Specialty. A full brother of Mr. Trouble, Ch. Ardendale Trouble's Double, is also the sire of champions.

The third of the Broadcaster lines is that of *Ch. Oakhaven's Flam-*

Ch. Stockfield Aristocrat (Ch. Matador Mandarin ex Gleeful Wendy).

Ch. Harham's Rocket (Ch. Broadcaster of Harham ex Adoration of Alden).

71

ing Rocket and includes Ch. Buckthorn Blackjack, grandsire of Pixie of Alii, Hawaii's first champion bitch. Blackjack was sired by Cinnibar Rags ex Ch. Buckthorn Sal, a Best in Show winner sired by Flaming Rocket. Sal was out of Vasona's Liberty Bell, who was Lionheart-bred throughout and sired by Ch. Lionheart Cold Steel.

Returning now to *Bostock,* we find the excellent sire line of Berrycroft Atoppa. Unable to compete in championship shows himself, due to wartime cancellation of such events, Atoppa sired a number of champions and sires of champions. Among them was *Ch. Holmbury Bandit,* the breed's first postwar champion in England, and sire of seven champions, of which three were in one litter: Weycroft Wondrous, Weycroft Wishful, and Weycroft Wyldboy. Both Wondrous and Wyldboy were imported to America. In England, Wyldboy had a remarkable show career, but gained his American title after a rather slow start. He proved to a laster, however, and at the age of eight years polished off the younger dogs for a Best Opposite placement to Fiona at the 1957 Morris and Essex Show. His death a few months after his Morris and Essex showing was a great blow to his owner, Mrs. Claire Dixon, and his handler, Sheila Lyster.

Eng. and Am. Ch. Murose Replica was undoubtedly the most famous of the *Bandit* sons and was older than Wyldboy. He won seventeen c.c.s in fourteen months, and in this country, though well along in years, he won the Specialty, was Best of Breed at Westminster and Morris and Essex, and won six Groups as well as a Best in Show.

Although Replica sired four champion sons, three non-champions have done more in carrying on the line in this country, with another untitled son carrying the load in England. Replica was whelped April 15, 1948, and was five years of age when imported.

As to the bloodlines behind Replica, Atoppa's sire and dam were both by Ch. Waycon Aristocrat; Bandit's dam brings in Briggus Bonnie Boy (by Junemore Bonnie Boy ex a daughter of Mandarin) and again Bostock as the maternal grandsire. Replica's dam, Murose Lassie, has Shelterock Merry Sovereign as her paternal grandsire, and this dog was also the grandsire of her dam. Here the influence of Merry Sovereign on the distaff side begins to show up. Replica was widely advertised in America. Wyldboy was not—nor was he shown often. After the dispersal of the Buttsark Kennels, which had imported him, Replica was sold to Mrs. Griffin's Copperdale Kennels in California. There he was bred to bitches of all bloodlines and shapes, with the resultant variance of type in the first generation. Greenburn Infractious was also owned by these kennels at this time, and second- and third-generation crosses of the two lines have produced some fine Airedales.

As has already been seen, many a strong line is founded by a dog that never became a champion, and that is the case of *Waycon Design-*

Ch. Weycroft Wyldboy of Clairedale (Ch. Holmbury Bandit ex Judy of Peelshall.

Ch. Sierradale War Drum, U.D. (Ch. Rusty Dusty, U.D.T. ex Ch. Sierradale War Bonnet).

73

Ch. Harham's Expert Explorer (1948).

Ch. Bengal Bahadur of Harham (1950).

Ch. Aireline Star Monarch (1951).

74

er, son of Ch. Waycon Aristocrat. Designer's dam was Ch. Flower of Fashion, by Ch. Aislaby Aethling. Designer not only sent the Merrijak line on its way to glory but he also figures prominently "through the middle of the pedigree" in the background of many winners and producers. Designer's son *Can. Ch. Murraysgate Monty* carried on the line, siring Holmbury Murraysgate Merrijack. Monty was sold to Canada after winning eight Bests in Show at open and member shows, Dan Hargreaves of British Columbia importing him. Monty's career was mainly during the championless war period, but he did win his classes at the first London postwar show shortly before exportation. The "Merri" of this line comes from Murraysgate Merry Mascot, a daughter of Merry Sovereign. She belongs to a well-known producing family, as will be shown later. Mascot, bred to Ch. Warland Warboy, produced Murraysgate Merriment, dam of Monty. Monty's son, Merrijack, unfortunately died young after the start of a promising career, with one c.c. to his credit, but he had sired Ch. Son of Merrijack and thereby won his place in Airedale history. Son of Merrijack's dam was Nelson Lassie, by Cashton Herald. Son of Merrijak was hard to condition—a trait that some of his get inherited—and this caused him to be retired without gaining his title in this country although he lacked only a few points. He turned out to be a sensational sire and outstripped Replica as a sire even though he was never advertised.

In England, Son of Merrijak had sired Ch. Bengal Bengali, winner at Crufts, and *Bengal Bahadour,* who, after his importation by Mr. Florsheim, was known as Bengal Bahadur (without the "o") of Harham. These dogs were litter brothers but Bahadur started more slowly than Bengali and it took him some time to get under way in this country, but once in condition he was almost impossible to stop. Among his thirty Bests of Breed were those of Westminster in 1954 and 1955, and in addition to winning a Best in Show and two Groups, he had several Group placements. He also won the "New King Bowl" four times and Illinois Specialty once.

King of the Merrijak line is *Can. and Am. Ch. Aireline Star Monarch,* owned by Charles Marck of El Cajon, California. As his prefix indicates, he was bred by Charles Ryan, then in partnership with Percy Roberts. This great campaigner has eighty-two Best of Breed wins to his credit, and sixty-six Group placements, topped off by five Best in Show wins. Star Monarch's dam, Aireline Classic, is by First Mate out of Aireline Queen. The latter is by Ch. Eleanore's Brigand. The fact that Star Monarch sired three champions in one litter, the dam being Ch. River Aire Rock-C, U.D.T., would indicate that he nicks well with the Roasting Hot lines of Lionheart bitches, Rock-C being of that breeding.

Another line from Merrijak is that of *Ch. Ardendale Revenger,* whose dam is Ardendale Top Me. His son Ch. Westbank Etaoin Shrdlu proved himself by winning the Northern Ohio Specialty on his first venture into the show ring, then going on to a Group third. He has placed in several other Groups. This dog's young son, Ch. Westbank Main Event, also owned and bred by Jane Merrill, finished his championship at ten months of age, in seven consecutive shows, winding up with points to spare in four- and five-point entries.

Ch. Clee Courtier Line—Matador Supreme Branch

Matador Supreme was a full brother of the sensational Mandarin. His son *Ravenslea Red Pepper* was purchased by J. P. Hall especially to mate with Warland bitches. One of these, Ch. Warland Watto of Oxenhill, by Briggus Bonny Boy (who was by Ch. Junemore Bonnie Boy), produced Ch. Warland Wattotstuff, sire of the famous *Ch. Warland Warboy.* (Wattotstuff is usually misspelled—leaving out the second "t.") Watto was herself exported to America, where she won the points at both the Specialty and Westminster in 1938. Blue Flash, dam of Warboy, was a granddaughter of Red Pepper and purchased especially as a brood bitch for the Warland Kennel.

Ch. Warland Warboy was imported to Canada by Sid Perkins of Rockley fame and was shortly thereafter sold to Mrs. Joseph Urmston. Warboy was Best of Breed at the 1945 Westminster show but no Specialty was held that year, nor was the "Airedale Bowl" offered during the war years. However, Warboy won the "New King Bowl" three times, was Best in Show on several occasions, with numerous Group placements and wins. Although he is credited with only nine champions in this country, he is named in the background of many of today's winners. The line of Can. Ch. Shining Rip Rap, founded by Rockley Man o'War, is the longest Warboy line at present although many of the Pepperidge Airedales are strongly linebred to him.

Ch. Clee Courtier Line—Ch. Warbreck Eclipse Branch

The fourth of the Courtier branches is that of *Ch. Warbreck Eclipse,* a dog that had been practically unshown in England, so had none of the usual fanfare when he was imported by James Manning. He was entered at Westminister, but Col. Guggenheim's Wolstanton Superb was Best of Breed, placing over Flornell Tavern Maid, who was also owned by James Manning. Eclipse, by Ch. Clee Courtier out of Flornell Brentwood Lady, was whelped September 3, 1928, and his only appearance in English shows had been at Leeds, where he was awarded four first prizes. All the contenders for top honors at the 1930 Specialty—Tavern Maid, Eclipse, Superb, and Eng. Ch. Belfort Supreme of Shelterock—were by Clee Courtier, which is in itself a tribute to Courtier's success as a sire.

Digressing from the Eclipse line for a moment, it is of interest to note the influence two of the other foregoing imports had on the breed. Belfort Supreme, a big winner and an English champion, died after he had been here about a year. But he sired three champions, including Shelterock Madame Supreme, the dam of Shelterock My Superex, who was the maternal grandsire of Rockley Roasting Hot. Madame Supreme is the founder of the amazing family of Tedhurst brood matrons which includes Tedhurst Belle, leading Airedale matron as to number of American champions produced. This blood is doubled in Belle's pedigree, for she is by Eleanore's Brigand, by Rockley Roasting Hot, and also brings in lines from Roasting Hot's sister, Hidden Treasure.

Warbreck Eclipse founded a tail male line that is being carried on by the well-known Sierradale line of obedience-trained champions, of which *Ch. Rusty Dusty, U.D.T.,* is probably the most noted, for he holds the bench title and all obedience degrees, as well as being the sire of several champions. May Pridham, owner of the Sierradales, is an obedience teacher, which explains her interest in having Airedales accomplished in this art. Her most famous Airedale, however, Ch. Sierradale Squaw, did not have time for obedience work but acquired seventy-five Bests of Breed, a Specialty win, and numerous Group placings in her career as a showgirl. The Eclipse line comes down through his son *Ch. Rascal of Bri* to Bighorn Duke, full brother of Lou Holliday's Ch. Lionheart Comet, founder of the "Comet" line of famed brood matrons. Rascal's dam was by Int. Ch. Flornell Mixer out of Rose Bri, who was a Group winner by Ch. Ruler's Double. Foundation bitch of this strain was Ch. Sierradale Chica, U.D.T., by Ch. Shelterock Monmouth Squire, a full brother of Merry Sovereign and winner of the Airedale Bowl at the 1936 Eastern Dog Club show. Chica's dam was Lionheart Jill, a daughter of Comet and sired by Eng. Ch. Walnut Gamecock of Brandwood, who was by Walnut King Nobbler. The branch from Rusty Dusty that is longest at present is from *Sierradale Sitting Bull,* whose dam was Chica. His most noted son is *Ch. Sierradale Sitting Bull II,* out of Ch. Sierradale Firefly, C.D., who was a full sister to the senior "Bull." Sitting Bull II was the sire of the famous Squaw. A full brother to Sitting Bull was Sierradale Lone Indian, and two of the three champions sired by this dog were out of Squaw, which makes this very close inbreeding to Rusty Dusty and Chica. Ch. Sierradale War Drum, U.D.T., by Rusty Dusty out of Ch. Sierradale War Bonnet, is among the champions of this line who acquired the U.D.T.

Ch. Clee Courtier Line—Int. Ch. Junemore Bonnie Boy Branch

The last of the Courtier tail-male lines in this country is that of *Int.*

Ch. Junemore Bonnie Boy. He sired two English champions, and one line in this country is brought down through *Authority's Replica,* whose son *Ch. Elmer's First Mate* is the sire of two champions, one of which, Pool Forge Flapper, is the dam of three champions. Another line comes down through Croftlyn's Sir Galahad. Bonnie Boy is more noted for his daughters than his sons, and consequently his line does not show his actual influence. One of his daughters was Cumbrian Chrysoberyl, dam of Ch. Newsgirl Charming, whose family will be delineated later; another is Crosslye Brunette, dam of Tri. Int. Ch. Cotteridge Brigand, star of the Walnut King Nobbler line. Both the sire and dam of Ch. Junemore Bonnie Boy were international champions, and his dam, Int. Ch. Clonmel Cuddle up, was by another international champion—Warland Ditto. Cuddle Up was purchased from Holland Buckley by Mrs. Marriott and spent seven years in India, where she produced three champions. Apparently she was about ten years of age when she produced the litter of which Bonnie Boy was a member, for he was whelped after her return from India.

Foundation Tail-Female Families

The foregoing has been entirely from the tail-male point of view, touching on the feminine side of the ledger only to give the names of dams of outstanding sires. The following line of descent is through the dams—those matrons which seem to pass on their producing qualities to their daughters for generation after generation. These families, as a rule, form the foundations of strains, rather than do sires. Through most of these are found the old "American" lines, tracing back in extended pedigrees to early importations.

There are seven major families—those founded by Ch. Fiesolana, Hekla Cleopatra, Ch. Lionheart Comet, Ch. Ridgemoor Sweetberry, Rockley Glitter, Ch. Walnut Review of Shelterock, and Warland Sprite. Of these only Cleopatra and Comet were American-bred, but their later lines bring in some older American strains. The lines which follow are dealt with alphabetically.

The Ch. Fiesolana Family

Ch. Fiesolana won the challenge certificate at Cruft's in 1938 and was owned in America by the Aireline Kennels of Charles Ryan. Her breeding has already been given under that of her sister, Fierentina, in the pedigree of Ch. Squire of Siccawei. Fiesolana's daughter *Ch. Warland Warbride,* bred in England, was the dam of four champions, but it is to the untitled *Aireline Queen* that most of this family now trace. Queen, by Ch. Eleanore's Brigand, founded six families, of which that of *Aireline Classic* is possibly the most notable. Classic, by Ch. Maralec First Mate, was herself dam of four champions: Aireline Star Monarch, Aireline Merryboy, Aireline Storm Queen (all by Eng.

Ch. Son of Merrijack), and Wyndhill Lillabet, by Ch. Bengal Bahadur of Harham. *Storm Queen* was the dam of the Best in Show bitch *Ch. Benaire Crown Jewel*, Ch. Benaire Miss Chiff, and Benaire Tennessee Storm, all producers of winners. Another daughter of Classic is *Aireline Symbol*, by Squire. Symbol produced six champions, but her daughter *Aireline Peerless Pearl* brought added distinction to the family by producing the magnificent Ch. Axel's Columbus, a dog that won the summer Specialty in 1956, the New England Specialty in 1957, Best of Breed at Morris and Essex in 1956, and Best Opposite to Eng. and Am. Ch. Westhay Fiona at the 1957 summer Specialty. Columbus was sired by the German-bred Ch. Axel v.d. Limpurger Residenz, who also sired Ch. Axel's Duplicate. The sire of Peerless Pearl is Star Monarch.

Another line from Queen is that of *Aireline Atalanta*, whose daughter Ch. Wyndhill Wasp was the dam of Ch. Birchrun Scorpio and Ch. Buckeye Sweet Talk. The third line from Queen is that of *Craigston Happy Birthday*, by First Mate; this line is carried on by the Champions Craigston Hot Rocks (by Lightning Coslea) and Craigston Monopoly (by Bahadur). The fourth line from Queen is that of *Ch. Aireline Passing Review*, a sister of Happy Birthday and producer of two champions, of which one is Rancho Valle Baronessa, by Ch. Lionheart Barrister. Baronessa produced two champions, including the daughter Lawrence's N.K. Only One, who in turn produced Ch. Lawrence's M.C. Shirley's Kim. The fifth line from Queen is that of *Wee Jezebel*, by Roasting Hot; Wee Jezebel has already been mentioned as the dam of Ch. Jezebel's Infractious Son, but here is of more note as to family because she produced the champion bitch Lady Elgin. Queen's sixth producing daughter is *Ch. Aireline Lovely Lady* (sister of Wee Jezebel), whose line comes down through Cotswold Dowager Duchess (dam of one champion) through Blackheath Coca to Ch. Blackheath Geisha Girl, by Son of Merrijak.

The Hekla Cleopatra Family

The Hekla Cleopatra family traces down mostly through *Eleanore's Princess*, dam of four champions. Cleopatra was by the American-bred Ch. Willinez Defiance. Her daughter Hekla's Queen of the East was by Ch. Warbreck Eclipse. Queen was also the dam of Eleanore's Princess, who was sired by Ch. Aislaby Jocelyn of Shelterock, who was in turn by Ch. Aislaby Aethling. Princess' daughter *Ch. Maralec Super Sis*, by Maralec Bingo Boy, was the dam of Bourbon-Ayr Manhattan, by First Mate. Manhattan's daughter *Breezewood Bonfire*, by Aireline Monarch, produced two champions, one of which, Breezewood Ballyhoo, has already been mentioned (Bombsight sire line). Another line to Princess is that of *Maralec Surprise*, by Roasting

Ch. Lionheart Comet I (1933).

Ch. Lionheart Comet II (1940).

Ch. Lionheart Comet III (1942).

Hot, and one of the champion offspring of Surprise is Super Sis of Renidrag. Ch. Maralec Jocelinette, another daughter of Princess, was sired by Roasting Hot. *Maralec First Lady,* a sister of Maralec Super Sis, is the dam of Ch. Quarryhill Princess, sired by Lionheart Local Boy. Quarryhill Princess is the dam of Quarryhill Home Ruler, sire of Ch. Raylerock Mica, a good producing bitch of the Rockley Glitter family.

The Ch. Lionheart Comet Family

The Lionheart Comet family is really the family of her dam, *Lou's Cross,* as this brings in two other producing lines of identical breeding to that of Comet. Cross was by Ch. Lou's J. M. and her dam was Criterion Cute Girl, whose sire had two close crosses to Ch. Soudan Swiveller and whose dam was by the imported Warland By Product. It is through J. M. that the Lionheart line is brought down to Cross, who is by Pepper Tree Don, a son of Ditto and out of Lou's Electress; the latter's dam, Lou's Suffragette, was also by Ditto. Suffragette's dam was Lionheart Cross (by Lionheart Politician ex Lionheart Queen), the foundation bitch of the Lionheart strain.

Comet was the dam of four champions (by three different dogs), and her sisters Carry On and Away were dams of one each and founded families producing several others. These bitches were by Ch. Rascal of Bri, a son of Ch. Warbreck Eclipse. The line second to Comet's is that of Carry On, which produced, among others, *Ch. Buckthorn Sal*—a Best in Show winner and dam of three champions.

Sal was a great-granddaughter of Carry On, and was by Ch. Lionheart Cold Steel ex Vasona's Liberty Bell. Bell also founded another branch through Cinnibar Imp. It is the Comets, however, who brought fame to Lou's Cross. Although five daughters carry on from Comet, three carry most of the fame. *Ch. Lionheart Comet II,* by Rockley Roasting Hot, won two Groups and was second in the Group five times. She was the dam of six champions, the main producer again being a Comet—*Ch. Lionheart Comet III.* The latter was dam of three champions and founded quite a champion-filled and many-branched family of her own. She was the dam of *Lionheart Enchantress,* who was retired to the matron ranks with twelve points toward her title, but who made up for the lack of the final points by producing six champions, including one with a Canadian title as well. Of these, the daughters are Ch. Lionheart Starlight and Ch. Lionheart Clee, the rest being dogs.

Studio Miniature, full sister to the foregoing champions, is also the dam of a champion. Another daughter of Comet III is *Lionheart Irene, U.D.,* by Ch. Lionheart Banner. She is the dam of two champion daughters—*River-Aire Rock-C, U.D.T.*, and *River-Aire Revel, U.D.*, both by Royalty. Rock-C is the dam of two champions by Star Monarch, River-Aire Bonniroxie and River-Aire Brisance. *Muncie of Lionheart* is a litter sister of Revel and Rock-C and is the dam of two champions by Ch. Studio Liontamer, one of which is a bitch—Lionheart Abigail.

Going back to Comet III, Irene's litter sister *Lionheart Impact* is the dam of Ch. Hilltop's Rocky Top Notch, a dog by Liontamer which is very influential in the Pacific Northwest. *Lionheart Comet IV* is, of course, out of Comet III and sired by Royalty.

Backtracking to *Comet II,* we come to another of her daughters, *Ch. Lionheart Baroness* (by Royalty), who produced three champion bitches. A full sister to Comet III (by Int. Ch. Cast Iron Monarch) was the Best in Show winner Ch. Tesuque Muldavin. And a daughter of Comet II by Royalty was Ch. Lionheart Betsey, producer of a line for the Phelaire Kennels in Texas. Again going back—this time to the original Comet—we come to the untitled *Lionheart Jill,* who was by Ch. Walnut Gamecock of Brandwood ex Comet. Jill's daughter *Crosswind* was more noted as a hunting dog than as a producer, and the bitch line stops with her, for she carries on only through a sire line, that of Ch. Studio Top Brass, whose career has already been outlined. Jill's daughter *Ch. Sierradale Chica, U.D.T.*, was more obliging in the family-continuing line, however, producing *Ch. Sierradale Firefly, C.D.*, dam of three champions, and *Ch. Sierradale Osalita, C.D.,* both by Ch. Rusty Dusty, U.D.T. Osalita is the dam of Sierradale Sundance, who is the dam of Ch. Thunderbird Indian Feather.

Again going back to *Comet I,* we come to the final family to be outlined—that of *Lionheart Star,* sister of Comet II. She was the dam of Miss Victory (by Eleanore's Knight), dam of Happy Polly (who was by Cold Steel). Polly was the dam of *Marbeth Surprise,* who was by Copper, and Surprise was the dam of three champions, her daughters being Ch. Sundown Serenade (by Harham's Beaming Boy) and Ch. Sundown Annie Oakley (by Ch. Hot Shot of Ran-Aire).

The Comet line nicked exceptionally well with Ch. Eleanore's Royalty of Lionheart, and the majority of the West Coast winners have at least one cross to Comet, or the blend of the various Comet families with Royalty. At the Twenty-fifth Anniversary Specialty of the Southern California Airedale Association, fifty-three of the eighty-seven Airedales entered traced to Comet in one or more lines, with eleven of the fourteen champions in competition tracing to this bitch, either through the sire or dam, or both. The winner of the Specialty, Liontamer, traced to Comet four times, three of these lines through the sire. Ch. The Sheik of Ran-Aire (winner of the previous Specialty) had one cross to Comet through his sire, Copper (winner of the 1949

Ch. Lionheart Starlight (1953)

Ch. Ridgemoor Sweetberry (Ch. Wolstanton Bostock ex Ch. Newsgirl Charming). *Tauskey*

83

Specialty). Ch. Sundown Trigger, whose pedigree shows three Comet lines, won the 1953 event. And Liontamer and Trigger won the 1953 and 1954 renewals of the California club's Specialty in San Mateo, with the litter sisters Ch. Boulder Gulch Sheba and Ch. Boulder Gulch Show Girl winning in 1955 and 1956 respectively. Little Sheba and Show Girl are by the Sheik.

Although Royalty takes credit for siring the largest number of champions of any Airedale on the West Coast, the majority were from Lionheart bitches, or those tracing in some line to Comet. The leading sires on the Coast are of the Royalty-Comet combination to some degree, diffusing this blood still further throughout the West. Royalty-Comet dogs have won in the country's largest Specialties, on occasion have topped all breeds for Best in Show, and very often have won the Terrier Groups in strongest competition against Eastern and English-bred Terriers. Comet herself was winner of the 1935 Southern California Specialty and was Best Opposite in 1936 to Ch. Shelterock Monmouth Squire, the brother of Int. Ch. Shelterock Merry Sovereign. Comet was defeated only once in her sex, and in memory of this great foundation bitch, Mr. and Mrs. Holliday donated "The Lionheart Comet Bowl," a perpetual trophy won by the Best of Breed Airedale at the Southern California Specialty. Winners of the trophy have already been listed under the "Royalty" section of the foregoing sire lines.

The Ch. Ridgemoor Sweetberry Family

Bred in England, *Ch. Ridgemoor Sweetberry* was by Wolstanton Bostock ex Newsgirl Charming. She was bred by William Burrows and was owned in America by Mrs. Loree. *Newsgirl Charming* founded other families in England, but it is the American-bred lines of the imported Sweetberry with which we are concerned here. Through Eleanore's Margolow and Ch. Warlaine Belle Canto, there are two short lines, with a third and longer line coming down through *Ch. Eleanore's Sweetberry,* dam of three champions including the bitch Ch. Seaward's Hobby. Margolow was sired by Roasting Hot, Belle by Ch. Eleanore's Corporal Jack, and Sweetberry by Ch. Eleanore's Allspice. A sister of Eleanore's Sweetberry, Dillie of Beverwyk, produced Vicky of Beverwyk when bred to Ch. Warland Warboy. Vicky was the dam of *Trucote Dazzle,* who was by Ch. Tiger of Deswood. Dazzle was the dam of Patshee Patricia, by Patshee Captain Courageous, and Patricia was the dam of four champions, all by Ch. The Sheik of Ran-Aire. Two of these, Boulder Gulch Little Sheba and Boulder Gulch Showgirl, have already been mentioned.

Another daughter of Dazzle is Patshee Dutchess, C.D.X., dam of Ch. Elroy's Top Kick, C.D. Dutchess is unusual in that as the result of a severe illness she nearly lost her hearing, and in fact was totally deaf

84

while being trained for the first degree in obedience, learning all her cues by hand signal. She regained enough of her hearing to qualify for the trials, but even so her performance is unique. She and Top Kick are owned and trained by Mr. and Mrs. E. T. McElroy. Dutchess is by Trucote War King, by Warboy, while Top Kick brings in the lines of the Canadian dog, Lamorna Prince Nobbler, a son of Walnut King Nobbler. Top Kick, like Columbus, is not of a sire line that produced enough champions to be included in the foregoing section.

Founder of the longest line and producer of the most champions in the Ridgemoor Sweetberry family was Sweetberry's daughter *Ch. Eleanore's Blackeyed Susan,* also by Allspice. One of her daughters was Milroy's Ariel, by Bombsight, and she produced Ch. Shining Dulcie, sired by Ch. Shining Rip Rap. The strongest Susan line is that of *Milroy's Aireline Susan,* sister of Ariel. Three of her daughters, all by Squire, produced champions, with *Ch. Ardendale Annabell* taking top credit with six, all by Ch. Ardendale Repeat Performance. One of her daughters, Ch. Ardendale Our Best, proved the aptness of her name by going Best in Show on one occasion. However, as often proves the case, it was Ardendale Top Me, one of Annabell's untitled daughters, who has so far been the best producer, with five champions as her score, all by Son of Merrijak.

When the influence of the sires tracing directly to Sweetberry is also considered, such as Ch. Eleanore's Royalty of Lionheart, Ch. Eleanore's Brigand, and the latter's son Bombsight, as well as the remarkable records of others of these lines, it is not hard to realize Sweetberry's contribution to modern Airedales.

The Rockley Glitter Family

Rockley Glitter is another whose heritage is carried on by a son, namely Ch. Rockley Roasting Hot, sire of twenty American champions, including the two "Eleanores" just mentioned. However, her daughters were also outstanding both as winners and as producers. Foremost, of course, was the sensational *Ch. Rockley Riot Act,* litter sister of Roasting Hot and Ch. Rockley Hidden Treasure. Riot Act won thirty-seven Bests of Breed, with three Groups and Bests in Show to her credit, as well as many Group placements. Riot Act was the dam of the "spice" litter, which was sired by her "nephew," Eleanore's Brigand. Of these, the bitches that carried on the line were Ch. Eleanore's Marjoram and Ch. Eleanore's Ginger. Marjoram is the dam of Ch. Trucote Invasion Belle, by Warboy, but it is her sister *Tedhurst Bruna of the Rampart* who proved to be the producer. Her daughter by Roasting Hot, Ch. Tedhurst Aviatrix, is the dam of a pair of champions, but another daughter, by First Mate, was not only an outstanding winner and producer of four champions, but she founded her own branch of this family. This was *Can. and Am. Ch. Tedhurst Pin Up Girl.* Pin Up Girl's daughter *Ch. Raylerock Mica,* by Quarryhill Home Ruler, was most outstanding, winning one Group and placing in several. Mica's daughter *Cowboy's Cowgirl of Foxglove,* by Replica's Cowboy of Buttsark (Ch. Murose Replica ex Ch. Tedhurst Boots), produced three champions by Ch. Hilltop's Rocky Top Notch and described in the "Roasting Hot" dynasty. One of the three was a daughter, Ch. Hilltop's Rockette. The other daughter of Mica is a litter sister of Cowgirl, this being Foxglove Saucy Sal, dam of Ch. Foxglove Studio Joye, by Ch. Studio Top Brass. Joye has already produced daughters which seem destined to carry on as befits the line.

The second of the "spice" litter, *Ginger,* is the dam of *Ch. Annjiehill's Show Off,* by Ch. Roy el Hot Rock. In a single litter by Ch. Ardendale Mr Trouble, Show Off produced Ch. Gingerbred Number One Boy, Ch. Gingerbred Show Off's Own, and Ch. Annjiehill's Show Off II. The "Gingerbreds" are owned by Mr. and Mrs. Chester Perry of Temecula, California, and have the distinction of having an all-champion tail female family for five generations back to Riot Act. Ch. Gingerbred the Boy Friend is the fourteenth champion in tail male. On paper, the line breeding of the Gingerbreds is most interesting.

Going back to Glitter's other daughter, *Hidden Treasure,* we find that although she had three daughters among her six champion produce, the main line comes down through *Ch. Eleanore's Glittering Girl,* by Eleanore's Knight. She was the dam of four champions, her daughter *Ch. Roy el Tiger Lily* (by Hot Rock) was the dam of three, and *Ch. Steelcote Reflection* (Lil's daughter sired by Ch. Lionheart Copper) was the dam of Ch. Steelcote Misty Morn, who was by Ch. Roy el Red of Hazelin. Another daughter of Reflection is Steelcote's Sweetheart, sired by Ch. The Sheik of Ran-Aire, and the dam of Ch. Steelcote's Shooting Star. The intense inbreeding of the "Roy els" and the "Hazelins" has been given under the "Roasting Hot" sire line.

The Int. Ch. Walnut Review of Shelterock Family

The family of *Int. Ch. Walnut Review of Shelterock* is mainly that of Tedhurst Belle. The line traces down from Review through Shelterock Madame Supreme (by Ch. Belfort Supreme); Hekla Protectress (by Ch. Warland Protector); Ch. Wykagyl War Bonnet (by Ch. Shelterock Marvelous Style); directly to the sisters Croftlyn's Princess Royal and Wykagyl Fashionette. Princess Royal's daughter Croftlyn's Toby (by Ch. Freedom Free Lance) was the dam of Tedhurst Lady Joyce, dam of *Tedhurst Belle,* whose sire was Eleanore's Brigand. Belle, with nine champions, is at the top of the "leading brood matron" list. One daughter, by Squire, is the dam of two champions. Her sons Ch. Tedhurst Equity and Ch. Tedhurst Cadet have both sired four champions.

Ch. Tedhurst Cadet (1950).

Ch. Tedhurst Equity (1951).

Ch. Warland Wargift of Harham (Ashleigh War Model ex Warland Merry Wedding).

87

Ch. Westhay Fiona of Harham (Ch. Westhay Jamus ex Ch. Riverina Westhay Flayre), owned by Harham Kennels, was one of the standout winners of all time. At her first show in America she qualified for Westminster by winning the Terrier Group and repeated that performance at Westminster itself. She is shown here winning BB at the Morris & Essex KC under Mrs. J. W. Urmston, handler Tom Gately.

The Warland Sprite Family

The last of the major families is that of *Warland Sprite,* a daughter of Clee Brigand, and previously hailed as the dam of Warland Protector. One Sprite branch was founded by Warland Maple (by Wrose Cargo) sister of Warland Protector. She was the dam of Ch. Warland Wishbone (by Warland Michael) whose daughter Adoration of Aldon produced two champions: Harham's Rocket (mentioned under sire lines) and his sister Adorer. These were by Broadcaster. Adorer produced Harham's Authentic, dam of Harham's Beaming Boy, sire of the Junoesque Ch. Sundown Serenade. The other Sprite branch was Warland Maisie's (by Wrose Anchor); her daughter Warland Gaiety produced *Eng. and Am. Ch. Warland Wedding Gift* (by Waycon Aristocrat). This line then develops two branches, of which the shorter is that of *Warland Merry Wedding.* This bitch, by Merry Sovereign, was the dam of Ch. Warland Wargift of Harham, producer of two champions, including the great Explorer. The other branch is English for a couple more generations, and is from a sister of Merry Wedding, *Murraysgate Merry Mascot.* Her daughter, Chathall Miranda (by Warboy) is the dam of two champions, including the imported Thelwyn Yenolam Merry Mascot, by Thelwyn Command. Another daughter was *Murraysgate Winniedale,* already mentioned under the "Merrijak" sire line, and her sire was Waitland's Warlock, also by Merry Sovereign. A daughter of Winniedale's, imported to Canada by Mr. Hargreaves, is Murraysgate Marlyn, dam of Ch. Gooch's Fraserholm Lass, by Murraysgate Monty.

The Tridwr Milady Family

Although this is still primarily an English family, its leading representative in this country, *Eng. and Am. Ch. Westhay Fiona of Harham,* makes its inclusion necessary in order to give the background of this phenomenal bitch which in one year accumulated more Group and Best in Show wins in America than any other Airedale in the history of the breed. The complete background of the family is given in the chapter on English dogs, so we will only touch on it here.

Sired by Eng. Ch. Westhay Jamus, Fiona is out of *Eng. Ch. Riverina Westhay Flayre,* subsequently owned in Sweden. Fiona made her debut in a show in the fall of 1956, shortly after importation, the object being to secure a blue ribbon which would qualify her for entry at Westminster. Not stopping with merely the "points" or the blue, she went on to Best of Breed and then first in the Group. In 1957 she collected twenty-seven Group firsts, with a scattered few lower placements—but rarely "lower" than second—and seven Bests in Show. Fiona's sire, Jamus, is by Raimon Nobbler of Noremarsh ex

Westhay Souvenir. Nobbler is by Bengal Bash 'em, by Bengal Lancer, while Souvenir brings in a line to Replica through her sire, Westhay Solo King.

Other Families

At first glance it would seem that certain great Airedales of the past left no outstanding descendants, if, in fact, any offspring at all. One of these was Int. Ch. Glenmavis Solitaire of Freedom, a sensational show bitch. However, though not shown in any family mentioned herein, the bloodlines of Solitaire are perpetuated through most of the Freedom strain, with line breeding to her further intensifying this inheritance. Another marvel of the 1930s was Tri. In. Ch. Briggus Princess, and both Princess and Solitaire were by Walnut King Nobbler. Princess is the dam of Ch. La Condesa, and oddly enough, this line is carried on down through a so-called "hunting" strain rather than modern show Airedales.

The Airedales of Hawaii deserve mention, due to an upsurge of interest in the breed to the extent that an Airedale club was formed in 1957. Not too many years ago Airedales were among the "rare" breeds on the Islands, and the formidable quarantine, paralleling England's, discouraged importation of dogs. However, many service men, transferred to the Islands, took along their Airedales, as did other new residents, and the breed flourished in its new home. Entries in shows have been good, averaging higher than in many mainland shows having fair Airedale representation, and the Airedale population has been increasing by virtue of the many new litters being produced. The year 1957 saw two champions crowned, the first Airedales ever to gain the title in Hawaii.

Both the 1957 champions had previously placed in Groups, and the day Thora Sands' Ch. Just Plain Brick gained his title, he also placed second in the Group. Brick, bred in Washington, is by Ch. Studio Top Brass ex Just Plain Dinahmite, by Ch. Studio Liontamer. The bitch champion is Pixie of Alii, bred and owned by Thelma Emanual in Hawaii. Pixie's sire is Surfrider's Poi Boy (by Ch. Buckthorn Black Jack ex Ch. Buckthorn Sal). And her dam is Saltysan's Alii (by Alii O Na Ilio out of Ch. Saltysan's Empress of Royalty) and is predominately "Lionheart" in breeding. Others bring in "Roy el," "Lyon," and "Ouachita."

This chapter has been devoted mainly to bloodlines that have produced the majority of Airedale champions in America prior to 1960. The prospective buyer of a "pet" puppy might wonder why so much emphasis is placed on championships, and Group and Best in Show wins, when all that he himself is interested in is having a typical Airedale of good temperament, not a show specimen. Dog shows are the only place where dogs can be compared with one another as to adherence to the breed Standard, and the more individuals of his breed a dog can defeat in the show ring, the greater is the chance that he is a superior dog himself, especially if those he defeats are of high quality. The title of champion means that the dog is a little better than the average, for he has had to compete with a certain number of dogs of his own breed under several judges. Quality is as important in dogs as in anything else, and "blood will tell," even if the dog is desired only as a family pet and will never see the show ring.

Naturally in this summary we are restricted to the lines producing the majority of modern champions, so there are some of the lesser-known lines not represented. However, nearly every quality-bred Airedale of today traces to one and usually several of these lines, and in this way nearly everyone can trace his Airedale's family tree.

To avoid repetition of the title "Ch.," where individuals already have been mentioned by title, the prefix has occasionally been omitted on subsequent mention of the dogs.

"Hunting" Strains

There are some Airedales in America which, though registered, would not have any relatives whatsoever on any of the foregoing lines since the days of Ch. King Oorang and his contemporaries. These are Airedales of the "Oorang" strain, and since they are almost never exhibited, they naturally would have no show records with the AKC from which to compile statistics. The Oorang strain was founded well before 1920 by Walter Lingo in Ohio, who was interested in the hunting potentialities of the breed. Mr. Lingo decided on the Ch. Oorang line as best suited for his purpose, and so enthusiastic was he about the Oorang line that he used the old dog's name as a trademark. The most noted stud dog of the Oorang Kennels was King Oorang II, who was, as the catalog stated, from "a long line of champions." He was indeed of the most fashionable bloodlines of his time, being by Ch. Rockley Oorang out of a daughter of Ch. Prince of York. Other stud dogs in use during the early 1920s were of intense Crompton Oorang lines with Ch. Abbey King Nobbler or his sire, Ch. Soudan Swiveller, giving added champion-bred background. King Oorang had quite a record as a gun dog, big-game dog, dogfighter and even as a sheepherder!

The Oorang Kennels did things on a big scale in the boom days of the Airedale. They advertised that they could supply any type or size, from thirty-five to one hundred pounds, and the dogs were priced according to show qualities or training. Some of the older stock was sold fully trained as to hunting experience on the type of game specified by the buyer. The brood matrons were kept by local farmers, the litters

91

being brought to the kennels for sale, and apparently the breeding is still handled in this way.

During the boom days, the Oorang Kennels had an extensive publicity campaign, both in the press and by athletic exhibitions. The trainers were Indians, headed by the famous Olympic Star Jim Thorpe of the Sac and Fox Tribe. They had a professional football team, and the Airedales, of course, went along as mascots, putting on acts of their own, especially as "war dogs" in sham battles staged by the teams during the war years. All of this publicity put the Oorang Airedales right on the map. Even after the boom they were advertised in sports magazines, but always as "Oorang AIREDALES," never as "Airedale TERRIERS," which brought about the confusion in the public mind as to an imaginary difference between Oorang AIREDALES and Airedale TERRIERS, a befuddlement that confounds the uninitiated to this day.

Considering the vast numbers bred, it can be seen that all thought of show qualities, except in the very upper tier, was sidetracked. Today the "Oorangs" are still as varied as in the old days with the thirty-five to one hundred pound weight classifications. There is no such thing as an "Oorang type," for they can be tall, short, lathy or cobby, sheep-coated or pin-wire, gray-tan or mahogany, grizzle or black saddled. So can dogs of any other strains which have been bred without consideration of type for several generations. On the other hand, a reasonably typical Airedale of the Oorang strain can produce show-quality Airedales when bred to prepotent, sound and typical individuals of show strains, and several champions have been of such breeding. However, it should be again emphasized that neither Oorang nor any other strain has the corner on the Airedale's hunting potential. The Lionhearts are proof that show-quality Airedales can hunt, train well for obedience, or do anything an Airedale ever could do, and so can other strains. In fact, it is harder to keep an Airedale FROM hunting than it is to find one reluctant to hunt. The foregoing should answer the question so often asked—"What is the difference between Oorangs and Airedales?"

There are several other breeders who also advertise "sporting Airedales" in hunting magazines. Prominent among them are the Lyons, Scarborough, and Ouachita. All are located in rural or mountainous areas where the young stock gets hunting experience, starting out with the puppies following their dams on excursions after small game. Many are then used on larger game, when the opportunity is afforded. These are truly "hunting" strains, in that they get some experience as such. But all of the foregoing are based largely on modern show strains, and some Oorang blood. Familiar names in the Lyons strain are Ch. Warland Warbride (Warboy-Fiesolana) and Ch. Maralec

First Mate. The Scarboroughs show such champions as Warland Protector, Fallcrest Harry, Rockley Roasting Hot, Fiesolana, Ridgemoor Sweetberry, and Aireline Apollo II in their background. Similarly, the Ouachita Airedales have the Champions Broadcaster, Bombsight, Cast Iron Monarch, Fallcrest Harry, and Roasting Hot. It is interesting to note that in this, a "hunting" strain, is found the name of Int. Ch. Briggus Princess. She was the dam of Ch. La Condesa, who was in turn the dam of Ch. Royal Commando. He was the sire of McCoy's Ozark Rambler, close up in the pedigree of the early Ouachitas.

Canadian Ch. Murraysgate Monty

Ch. Riverina Siccawei Phoebus.

93

Ch. Bengal Sabu, owned by Barbara Strebeigh, Tuck Dell and Harold Florsheim and bred by Molly Harms-worth, was one of the most influential sires of modern times. He came to the United States in 1959 as an unshown yearling. By the time he was retired he was a multiple BIS and Specialty winner with a record that included seven Airedale Bowl wins. He fathered dozens of champions and was the founder of an Airedale dynasty that still shines today.

5

American Bloodlines Since 1960

THIS CHAPTER continues the same sire lines and families (plus new families and minus some now unproductive ones) as Chapter 4, but starts around 1960 and takes in part of 1977. Naturally many of the scores for sires and dams of champions will be greater even by publication date than those given here, but these supply an accurate view of these dogs' producing ability.

The Bicentennial Year, 1976, supposedly celebrated this country's divorce from England two hundred years ago. However as far as Airedales are concerned it was the other way around—we are once again dominated by the English—to the point of no return for some famous sire lines, replaced to a phenomenal degree by those of English imports. True, this English-made breed has always been refreshed by imports from the old country, but nevertheless the winning dogs, and a few bitches, at Westminster and the major Specialties often represented several generations of American breeding. This has been drastically changed.

Ch. Bengal Sabu

The importation of *Ch. Bengal Sabu* was of infinitely greater moment than even his importers—Barbara Strebeigh and Tuck Dell—could have possibly foreseen. He was not even purchased as a show dog, but rather for his pedigree (the record and characteristics of ancestors named therein, not just names alone), his conformation, type, movement and temperament, along with careful consideration of the "nick" with their own Airedales' bloodlines and characteristics, including corrective qualities. *Sabu* was casually mentioned in Mrs. Harmsworth's ad in the 1958 *Our Dogs* Annual thus: "The dog puppy Bengal Sabu will be shown shortly and at stud early in 1959" but instead his show career materialized in America where he was imported at only one year of age.

For a dog "not imported to show," Sabu did mighty well when he proved to be a show dog deluxe. Not only did he win "Top Airedale" honors for three years in a row and all the Westminster and New York and Montgomery Specialties in view (for several years in a row) but he founded a dynasty of dogs which continued the pace. This last is mainly through three litters sired in England. So powerful has been the influence of this sire line that, taking alone the New York Specialty wins of the last decade, seven wins have been made by individuals of the *Sabu* line, with only three to those of an American-bred sire line. And even that is not diverse, for these trace back to *Ch. Studio Liontamer,* through two different branches. This same pattern exists for the Montgomery County (summer Parent Club Specialty) show, with *Liontamer* being the only one to break the all-English hold, although there is another English line here, that of *Ch. Lanewood Lysander.* All the other Montgomery wins have been made by Airedales of the *Sabu* line. He himself had won there in 1959, 1960 and 1961.

Ironically, or perhaps "fittingly," the Bicentennial Year Best of Breed at Montgomery County, Ch. Jerilee's Jumping Jericho, carried the American tail-male heritage. And, in the spirit of '76, or at least compromise, his pedigree on the dam side is all-English. That of his sire has at least five generations of all-American breeding.

Most American breeders have used the best English imports from time to time as a top cross on their own breeding programs. This makes for a strong family line since, of course, it always goes back to the taproot bitch with either dogs of the same heritage or of the best outside blood being used as sires of her daughters, granddaughters, greatgranddaughters and so on. With each new sire there can be a change in sire line, though not necessarily, where there are so many of that line, as with *Sabu.* But the tail female line can never change without bringing in an entirely new bitch and starting from there, assuming she is not of that family herself, in which case she merely represents another branch.

The "New English" Lines

Through the current use of the "new English" lines because of their astounding and continued success and resultant popularity, the once-

96

important sire lines of this country, and even some in England of once-numerous lines there, have practically died out "along the top of the pedigree", i.e. the sire line, although still very much alive through the center of some of those documents. There are undoubtedly many Airedales not of these English lines still prevalent in the breed, but these are not represented among the major winners. Many of the bitch families are by dogs of these once-famous sire lines, but even these are becoming scarce since more and more are by the English imports or dogs of those lines.

The New York (Parent Club) Specialty and the outdoor, or summer Specialty at Montgomery County have already been mentioned. Westminster wins in the last decade were much the same, but I have statistics from 1970 through 1977 only. During this period five winners trace to *Sabu* in tail-male, two to *Lysander* and one to *Liontamer*, but the latter winner, Ch. Jerilee's Jumping Jericho, won twice. He was also fourth in the Group, a feat quite rare for an Airedale at Westminster in recent years. It was another dog of this line which won twice in a row at the New York Specialty. This being Ch. Ernie's Jack Flash. However a *Sabu* son, Ch. Talyn's River Rogue, emulated his sire's record by winning three times in a row—1968, 1969 and 1970.

The various Specialties across the country were all but overwhelmed by this new English invasion. Jericho spoiled their "exclusive" attempt again by taking the California Airedale Terrier Club Specialty twice in a row and the Great Lakes Specialty (in addition to his other wins mentioned). Ch. Airewyre's Big Ernie, his son Ch. Ernie's Jack Flash, and his sire won the Pacific Northwest Airedale Club Specialty. Jack Flash also won the California ATC Specialty in 1977. It's almost eerie the way the only line to break the spell traces back to my own Simba, as *Liontamer* was best known. This line is very much in the minority as to numbers, but it packs a major punch in the quality of the wins made by its representatives.

Because of the great shift in sire lines, as reflected in top-level show wins and the most popular and successful sires, the charts presented in the 1966 edition of *The Complete Airedale Terrier* have had to be renumbered and changed, with some deletions. However several lines were still doing well in the previous decade so will be referred to here to connect them with the earlier years, even though they do not now show up on the charts.

A Shift in Emphasis

The 1960s saw the beginnings of the current English tidal wave. The greatest winner in America in the late 1950s and early 1960s was English and American Ch. Westhay Fiona of Harham, this grand bitch won 24 Bests in Show, 60 Group Firsts, and out of the 82 times shown

97

Ch. Querencia's Suerte Brava, owned and bred by Ercila E. LeNy, had a distinguished show career that included first in the Terrier Group at Westminster in 1963.

Shafer

Ch. Bengal Bladud of Harham

Ch. Joklyl Bengal Lionheart

in the United States was Best of Breed 80 times. In England Ch. Riverina Tweedsbairn had gone Best in Show at Crufts, the greatest honor of all, especially for a Terrier in the country that created Terriers. Moreover he was England's Dog of the Year in 1960 and 1961. While America's answer to Crufts, the great Westminster show, did not record an Airedale BIS during this period, Ch. Querencia's Suerte Brava was best Terrier in 1963. In 1964 Eng. and Am. Ch. Jokyl Bengal Lionheart was Top Terrier of the Western states and runner-up for Top Terrier in the United States. *Ch. Bengal Sabu* was the top-winning Airedale from 1959 through 1961, and, until the advent of Ch. Jokyl Superman, was the top sire up to current times, with 40 champions to his credit. He won the Airedale Bowl six times and two other Specialties where the Bowl was not in competition. In his 103 outings, Sabu won seven all-breed Bests in Show, 28 Groups and 49 other placings. It should be noted that except for Suerte Brava, these show-stoppers were all English-bred, and even the latter was by an English import, Ch. Bengal Bladud of Harham, a son of Sabu.

How the Ratings Show it

Several Airedales have recently gone to the top in Group competition, with Ch. Wagtail Woodbine topping the breed for 1976 in *Airedale Quarterly* ratings, which includes Group placements, not breed wins alone, in the point system. And since she, "Bonnie," won several Bests in Show as well as Groups, this was all to her good. She is linebred several times to Ch. Benaire's Queen's Ransome (Ch. Bengal Bahadur of Harham ex Ch. Aireline Storm Queen) and is at least two generations of American breeding except for her sire Ch. Stone Ridge Gingerbred Man, a son of Ch. Jokyl Supermaster. In addition to the Airelines in the pedigree, some notable Ardendale ancestry is seen.

Second in the *AQ* rating for 1976 and "top *dog"* (male) was Ch. Eden's Sal Sorbus, while in the *Terrier Type* system this placing went to Ch. Pequod Blackbeard the Pirate, and further difference in scoring gave *AQ*'s third place to Ch. Jolee Aire Stone Ridge Stomp, with *TT* placing him fifth and listing Ch. Ernie's Jack Flash third. This dog was fourth in the *AQ* index. All of these were top winners, and all in this and the *Terrier Type* system must win at least four Group placements to even get in this type of scoring.

The *Airedale Quarterly* itself is new (started in Fall, 1976) so earlier years' scores cannot be given for it, but some of the *Terrier Type*'s top winners can be named. In 1975 Ch. Jerilee's Jumping Jericho headed the list, with Ch. Pequod Blackbeard the Pirate runner-up. The Knight system, which only counts Best of Breed wins, rated Ch. Argus Stone Ridge Hunky Dory first. In 1974 Ch. Marydale's Pride N' Joy took the *TT* poll and also No. 1 in the Knight list for bitches, but this system gave Jericho first in dogs, and Ch. Pequod Salt Horse was second to him, while Ch. Harbour Hills Klark Kent was second to Pride N' Joy in the *TT* system. In 1973 Klark Kent was No. 1 both systems; Ch. Talyn's Man About Town was No. 2 on *TT* with Jericho in that place on the Knight scoreboard.

In 1972 Ch. Jokyl Prince Regent swept the boards, both systems, with Ch. Harbour Hills Klark Kent assisting, for second honors. The former also took 1971 in stride, both systems again, with Eng. Am. Ch. Jokyl Superman second on *TT*, 5th on Knight, and Ch. Benaire Sock It To Me was second in the latter system.

This gives a fair inkling of the nation-wide placings of the top Airedales, for these last few years. There were many others on both (or all) lists that won well at Specialties, at Westminster and at other prestige shows. Not all dogs can be shown often enough to make a mark via any of these systems, whereas the local boys can (and have) won over some of the top-rated ones. Nevertheless all those mentioned had to earn their way, and (except for the Knight system) had to win over, or at least place among, other Terrier breeds in the Group, and that, folks, "ain't easy." Bests in Show are not given extra points, since what counts is Terrier competition. That's the way it's figured. Bests in Show wins do add something by some kind of analysis, even if only through the prestige achieved.

Recent Status of Earlier Sire Lines

The fate of the various sire-line branches, or even of main lines, can be seen in the accompanying charts. Some which were important in the previous decade or two have disappeared, as far as top-winning (or siring) dogs are concerned, and some lost out through a dog's having had more good daughters than sons, and although well represented, and often extremely influential through the middle of the pedigree. Unfortunately this does not show up in sire-line charts. In the same way a few great brood-bitch families have died out through their having produced outstanding sons, but no daughters (or none which produced at all, or in any quantity of good ones).

Reference to the charts will show the line of descent and the inter-relationship of these main lines. *All*, championship or not, trace back in tail-male to *Int. Ch. Warland Ditto*, and as things seem to be developing, eventually the main show quality lines at least, as represented in highest wins, will show that all funnel back to *Ch. Warland Whatnot* via *Clonmel Monarque*'s son *Ch. Clee Courtier*. However should the *Ch. Warland Waterman* branch from Whatnot (which ended in the previous charts with *Eng. and Am. Ch. Warland Protector of Shelterock* and his descendants) suddenly revive, this could bring that branch again into the picture. Of the five sons of Courtier given in the earlier chart as founding branches, only *Ch. Matador Mandarin, Wal-*

Ch. Ernie's Jack Flash

Ch. Coppercrest Red Marvel (Ch. Town Girl's Challenge ex Ch. Scatterfoot Tim Tam), owned by the author and June Dutcher. *Ludwig*

nut King Nobbler and *Ch. Warbreck Eclipse* remain in force, with the former holding a vast lead, and the former leader, Nobbler, in second place.

The continuity of sire-line references will be continued in the sequence used in Chapter 4, although in the first instance the line has few modern representatives.

The *Moorhead Marquis* line from Ditto has almost died out although Ch. Phelaire Rhoderick Dhu traces to him and is the sire of three champions which could carry on the line for him. One of these is Ch. Phelaire Abner, already the sire of a champion at this writing.

Although the Walnut King Nobbler line is now in second place, it, like Avis car rentals, "tries harder" and accordingly has come up with some outstanding winners and sires, as detailed previously.

The branch from *Ch. Studio Top Brass* is the present leader of this line, via *Ch. Studio Liontamer*. This branch seems especially talented at winning Specialties, for Top Brass won the first Pacific Northwest Specialty, and Liontamer won this and three others, two of which were the Southern California event (one was the largest in 30 years with 87 entries) twice winning the Airedale Bowl; his son *Ch. Hilltop's Rocky Top Notch* also won the PNW Specialty, and Rocky's son Ch. Hilltop's Happy Josh took the 1957 Southern California Specialty. Another son of Rocky was Ch. Hilltop's Kintla Challenge (full brother of Josh), the first West Coast Airedale ever to go Best of Breed at Westminster, and this he did twice, just to prove it was not a fluke. A third Rocky son was the untitled Hilltop's Blitzkrieg, but he sired Walter Hammond's Ch. Town Girl's Challenge, who also won the PNW Specialty, Challenge, in turn, sired two winners of the PNW event, Ch. Thunder's Playboy and Ch. Buckshot III. Playboy kept the game going in great form by not only taking the same Specialty, but also siring Ch. Airewyre's Big Ernie, the 1974 PNW winner who really made it "big" by siring the strong campaigner Ch. Ernie's Jack Flash. Jack Flash carried on the family tradition by winning the PNW Specialty in 1975 and 1976, also annexing the Parent Club (New York) Specialty "in duplicate" too, in 1976 and 1977.

The "Hilltop" Airedales of Mr. and Mrs. Frank Slama of Corvallis, Oregon were often used in hunting all kinds of game. Ch. Buckshot III treed two bears, and according to his owner, Steve Wood, retrieved duck better than a Labrador. This combination of hunting and show qualities is all in the Lionheart tradition.

Big Ernie is owned by Denise and Michael Tobey, and his son Jack Flash, bred by Connie Brown, started his career under the ownership of the Tobeys, but eventually he acquired additional owners, making him almost syndicated, the other two being Milt Schmidt and the Stone Ridge Kennels. Jack Flash also won, and retired the Steve Woods Memorial Trophy. This becomes an unexpected tie-in with his relative

102

Ch. Jerilee's Jumping Jericho (Ch. Geoffrey Earl of Stratford ex Flintkote River Princess), owned by Jerry and Leslie Rosenstock and bred by Paul W. Hellman, is one of the top-winning Airedales of the 1970s. He is a Specialty and Westminster winner and is shown here winning BB at the Beverly Hills KC under judge Grace Brewin, handler Clay Coady. *Yuhl*

103

Ch. Buckshot III, or at least that dog's owner. This dog has had many Group wins and placements and as of mid-1977 has won two Bests in Show. His latest Specialty triumph is that of the California Specialty. So you see, this branch from *Liontamer* does make a specialty of Specialties. With three crosses to Ch. Town Girl's Challenge, Jack Flash has tripled this lineage back to the first PNW Specialty winner, "Brassy" and of course to *Liontamer*.

The second main branch from *Liontamer* is through "Coppercrest" breeding. This comes down via Coppercrest Brandy, then Souixaire's Chief Duff, to *Ch. Love's Stoney Burke*. One of Stoney's seventeen champions is Elinor Hellman's Ch. Geoffrey Earl of Stratford, a big winner in his day, as was Stoney, and he sired the full brothers Ch. Jerilee's Jumping Jericho and Ch. Coppercrest Contender, among others.

Jericho, owned by Leslie and Jerry Rosenstock, was three times Best of Breed at the prestigious Beverly Hills (California) show, but added to his national image by going BB at Westminster in 1974 and 1975 and was Group fourth there in 1974. The 1974 Garden placing made Jericho the first Airedale in many years to even get close to the top four. He also won the Great Lakes, SCAA and CATC Specialties. Proving he is a "laster," Jericho topped a record number of 130 Airedales at Montgomery County in 1976. This was a double Centennial show—since it was the Bicentennial Year celebration of American independence, but it was the 100th year of the Airedale breed, an event celebrated in England also. I'm not sure how the exact year, 1877, was decided upon, since at that time there was still arguments about a name for the breed, or even what sort of classification it should have. However, now it's settled, and that's that.

Jericho seems to enjoy doing things in duplicate and this time he did it through a son. Ch. Jamboree Don Diego was Winners Dog at Montgomery 1976, apparently finishing with this major. Exclusive of a few absentees, there were 40 other dogs competing for those five points. This was an entry of size and quality.

By early 1977, Jericho had won around 100 Bests of Breed, and 20 Group placements. He was high-scoring in the various rating systems, as already mentioned. Like Ch. Ernie's Jack Flash, he has three lines to *Liontamer* through his sire, two via Ch. Town Girl's Challenge, which brings in the other line, but nevertheless the third one is the tail-male tracing as already shown. The distaff side of his pedigree is all English, through Ch. Talyn's River Rogue and Mex. Ch. Siccawei Gypsy, the latter by Eng. Ch. Bengal Fastnet.

The same breeding of course applies to his younger brother, Ch. Coppercrest Contender, owned by Gini Dreyfus and Leslie Rosenstock. Newer on the scene, this dog nevertheless wasted no time. He

Ch. Love's Stoney Burke.

Ludwig

At the ATC of New England Specialty in 1965 judge Frank Brumby awarded BW and BOS to Christopher's Lady Jean (left) owned and handled by Charles Foley and BB to Ch. Jokyl Bengal Figaro, handled by William Thompson.   *Shafer*

Ch. Anfealt I'm Terrific (left), owned, bred and handled by Charles and Regina Foley, was BW and BOS at the ATC of New England Specialty in 1975 under Mrs. Phyllis Haage enroute to the title. BB was Ch. Dandyaire Quickfire, handled by Peter Green.   *Gilbert*

won the Metropolitan Washington and the New England Specialties, and in his first five weeks of showing in the East he was entered in 18 shows, of which he was Best of Breed 16 times, along with a Group third and a fourth. These wins were made in the early part of 1977. The tally has subsequently increased.

Another branch from *Ch. Love's Stoney Burke* is through Ch. Geronimo of Indianaire, sire of the Group winner Ch. Moeson of Indianaire. There are other lines but the first two have proven the most sensational so far.

A *Liontamer* son, sire of three champions, is Ch. Lionheart Ajax. Since all three of these are bitches, there is no chance of a tail-male line through them. However as sire of Ch. Christopher's Rag A Muffin and Ch. Christopher's Lady Jean, he became part of the background of the Anfeald Airedales of Mr. and Mrs. Charles Foley. Ch. Anfeald Brandywine, winner of the Airedale Terrier Club of New England Specialty, although of the Eng. Ch. Barton of Burdale sire line, is "double Ajax", since he is out of Rag A Muffin and his sire is out of Christopher's Lady Jean. The latter was BW and BOS at same specialty six years earlier to that great international traveler, winner and movie star, Bengal Figaro. Ten years later, in 1975, Ch. Anfeald I'm Terrific won exactly the same succession of honors at Montgomery County to Ch. Ironsides Pacific Station under Thomas Gately.

Her dam is by Brandywine and her sire traces in tail-female to Rag A Muffin. While Ajax' name appears several times, the tail male line is to Ch. Bengal Leprechaun, and in fact the pedigree is heavy enough in Bengal lines, including another to Leprechaun, to outweigh all others. Terrific's dam, Ch. Anfeald Duende, was BOS at the New York Specialty to Eng. and Am. Ch. Optimist of Mynair, but earlier had come up through the classes to take the same honor at Montgomery in 1972, this time to Ch. Jokyl Prince Regent. It would seem that while the ladies of this clan are inclined to let the gentlemen take top honors, the males don't mind who or what they knock off on the way to the summit.

It was the unexpected death of *Ch. Studio Liontamer* that took the heart out of me for a while, and in the period since then I have become deeply involved with the horse industry, primarily Arabians. During this hiatus I lost track of Airedale bloodlines and accordingly was rather surprised to discover the almost complete take-over by "new English" (all Airedales trace to "old" English lines) sire lines at present. I did know that Simba (Liontamer) was represented through several producing (i.e. female) lines, such as the famous "Red" litter of Coppercrest (five champions) which accounted for many later champions too, but I did not know that a direct sire line back to him still existed. I've had some big thrills by Simba's wins, and possibly the greatest (next to the 1953 SCAA Specialty) was when he won the Long

Ch. Anfeald Brandywine, owned and bred by Charles (handling) and Regina Foley, was BB at the ATC of New England's 1971 Specialty under judge Anthony Stamm. *Gilbert*

Ch. Anfeald Duende, owned by Charles (handling) and Regina Foley, finished at the ATCA Specialty with Montgomery County in 1972 under Mrs. Charles W. Marck. *Gilbert*

108

Beach group, as mentioned earlier, but the thrill of discovering that several top-winning dogs trace directly back to him in tail-male, has to be of equal moment. For, you see, Simba was the light of my life. He was the great protector (and took this very seriously) the extrovert clown, the infallible mindreader, the heap big hunter (when he had the chance, as during his youth), and most of all he was my friend. As to his showmanship, Ric Chashoudian's kind comments about him in the Southern California Airedale Association's 1977 *Yearbook* tell it all, and to have Ric say that Simba was one of the few dogs he ever "begged to show" is a compliment beyond measure.

I should add that it is not just that there *are* direct sire lines back to Simba, it is that the situation is unique—the only American-bred line to make a dent in the almost all-English sire-line situation today. And among the breed's leading sires, *Ch. Love's Stoney Burke* of this line, is the only American-bred in the group of dogs having fifteen or more champions to their credit, as of early 1977 statistics.

It is entirely possible, in view of the past track records of imports and their sons, that this one sole surviving "American" line will eventually be wiped out also, although it seems to have come up with some mighty tough fighters which do not give up easily, even if only in combat for top honors in the show ring. Nevertheless it is here, *now,* and for that I am grateful. To me it is a living memorial to Simba, just as it is also to the Lionheart strain. As to the latter, that strain is carried on mostly through many branches of the Lionheart female lines—all tracing back to *Lou's Cross* regardless of any, or many, top crosses of the various male lines, whether "new English" or of other American strains.

Another branch of the *Walnut King Nobbler* line which accounts for a modern Airedale Bowl winner is that of *Ch. Walnut Clipper of Freedom,* via *Ch. Freedom Full Force.* Through Ch. Rek En Nad's High and Mighty of Freedom, down through Ch. Rek En Ad's Hitting Away, the Bowl winner Ch. Rek En Nad's Mainliner is descended. Winner of the 1968 Northern Ohio Specialty, he was owned by C. Z. Euga. A grandson of Full Force is Ch. Freedom Fighting Front, and although he may not have representatives in the sire line at present, he does have influence through the family line of his daughter Ch. Lionheart Holly, dam of eight champions and from which many branches now descend.

The *Walnut King Nobbler* branch via *Turkish Western Guard* still has mostly English-bred descendants except for the branch from *Eng. Ch. Barton of Burdale* through Ch. Sanbrook Senator. Otherwise his descendants are mostly through daughters, except for Australia, where the Aust. Ch. Mr. Smith of Burdale is very influential.

The line from Ch. *Lamorna Prince Nobbler* was very active for a while during the 1950s because of Ch. Elroy's Top Kick, winner of the 1958 SCAA Specialty and two Groups. He was bred and owned by Eddie and Bernice McElroy. At present this line is apparently dormant, or on its way out, like so many others.

Still another *Walnut King Nobbler* branch founder is Ch. *Llanipsa Toreador*. Some of this line's history is told in the previous chapter, when Ch. *Riverina Tweed* was just hitting his stride. This dog's son Ch. Riverina Tweedsbairn has been even more sensational than his sire. He was Dog of the Year in England in 1960 and 1961 by virtue of Best in Show wins at Windsor, Birmingham City, Ladies' Kennel Club and Birmingham National in 1960, climaxed by Best in Show at Crufts, Leeds, Belfast and the National Terrier Show, plus Reserve BIS at Cardiff. In acquiring his 23 challenge certificates and through never having been defeated in the breed, Tweedsbairn automatically closed out any other males which might otherwise have gained enough c.c.s. to have become champions at that time. I have a feeling that a number of exhibitors were glad to see him retire despite the great amount of publicity and glory he brought to the breed. This male line seems to have been overwhelmed by those of the *Mandarin* dynasty, but it has done very well in Australia, as will be seen in a later chapter. Referring back to *Turkish Western Guard*, Ch. Sanbrook Senturian, of the Eng. Ch. Barton of Burdale branch, also had notable influence in Australia through his son Ch. Mr. Smith of Burdale, the leading sire there at this writing.

The Clee Courtier Line

The line from Ch. *Matador Mandarin* is now the "champion of champions" sire line in the breed, mainly through the Ch. *Wolstanton Bostock* branch via *Berrycroft Atoppa* and the latter's son *Solo Aristocrat*. Reference to Chart I will show the line of descent to Ch. *Bengal Sabu*. From that point on the champion-siring lines exploded like shrapnel, but the effect was more like a star shell in the way it lit up the scene. The result of this as far as the upper strata of Airedale wins is concerned has already been touched upon. What it has done to the Airedale population as a whole can be easily guessed. The "banyan tree" simile in the previous chapter regarding the *Mandarin* branches, has now become a veritable forest. However mixed the metaphors may be about this line, what is obvious is that it has taken over the majority in the breed, there are no mixed views on that.

The leading *Mandarin* branch is now that of Ch. *Wolstanton Bostock*, which in any case was always the most numerous from any source. Just as the *Mandarin* line descends through only one son, Ch. *Stockfield Aristocrat*, so too does that of *Aristocrat* but the line here divides with his sons *Waycon Designer* and *Ch. Wolstanton Bostock.* Of the four *Bostock* sons listed in the chart in the 1966 edition of this book, only two are prominent today, but *how* prominent! So much so that the records of their champions and major wins tower over everything else.

In this connection it should be re-emphasized that while this domination of one or two lines may seemingly do away with others, usually there are plentiful crosses in the background to represent other important lines, quite often repeated through linebreeding. It is possible, but not likely, for a pedigree to have only the top line (sire line) trace back to that line's founder or at least branch founder, but usually there is sufficient crossing of popular lines to bring the relationship closer.

To digress even more and as an example, it is known that the famous Thoroughbred horse *Secretariat* traces back in tail male to the *Darley Arabian.* One gets the impression that there is just this one line to that famous Arab. However, thanks to the many crossings and recrossings in over 250 years, he has close to 115,000 lines back to the *Darley Arabian.* But there are even more lines to a horse which is never given any credit in the average literature on the breed, and that is *D'Arcy's White Turk.* He has no tail-male representation, such as that of the "big three" (the Darley and Godolphin Arabian and the Byerley Turk), so is quite literally ignored. Yet, through having been on the scene much earlier and already having descendants, his name is in the pedigree of *Secretariat* around 235,000 times. There are also more lines to the *Godolphin Arabian,* about 125,000, than to the tail-male founder, the *Darley.* All Thoroughbreds trace in tail male to one of these "big three," which is why most people have the impression there were no other Oriental horses in the breed. The third of these also has more representation than does the *Darley;* the *Byerley Turk* has 188,000 lines, So, although these other lines get no credit, *they are there.* Yet, because it is easy, sire-line tracing is standard, and after all it is from sire to son, and—assuming the sire to be extra good—it is expected that he should pass on his best attributes—either in conformation or performance. He may not do so always, but in potent lines he does.

To bring the subject back to Airedales but using the same type of reference and taking a pedigree I can trace far back, that of *Liontamer* is useful as an example. Although he is of the *Walnut King Nobbler* dynasty, he has only seven lines to that dog, but has nine to *Int. Ch. Warland Protector of Shelterock,* an important sire no one ever thinks of in Simba's breeding, since he represents the *Nobbler* line. And he has exactly as many lines to *Mandarin* as he does to *Nobbler.* But like the cigarette ads used to state, "It's what's up front that counts" and the sire line may not be exactly up front, but it definitely is *on top,* and that's the name of the game.

111

A male line can predominate in a pedigree if there is enough linebreeding to dogs of that line. This might be best shown again through horse pedigrees. With Arabian horses, for a while many breeders were obsessed with inbreeding to a certain stallion, the Polish-bred *Skowronek*. Whether scions of this line were any good or not (and many were excellent), they were bred to mares of the same breeding, resulting in pedigrees where every male in, say the fourth or even the fifth, generation was either *Skowronek* or one of his sons. I don't doubt that breeders using this close inbreeding were envious of certain flowers, such as iris, which could be bred to itself. Some dog breeders are fond of in-and-in breeding too, but usually bring in an outside line to refresh the line (or take advantage of the popularity of a great sire or winner) every once in a while. But in any case, a breeding program can be built which returns to the original line several times and yet is not so close (because of different routes back to the taproot sire) as to be extremely in-bred. By contrast there is the incest type, where sire is bred to daughter, or dam to son. In the first instance the sire line is automatically renewed, in the second it would not be unless the bitch were also of that line.

So much for another tanget.

For a while after the original text of *The Complete Airedale Terrier* was written, the *Waycon Designer* branch was in the ascendancy. *Eng. Ch. Son of Merrijack* acquired more champions of his own with a total of at least eleven, and his son *Ch. Aireline Star Monarch* had nineteen, but due to *Monarch* having very few sons to prolong the line for him, it was left to another *Son of Merrijack* dog to do the job for the latter. This was *Ch. Bengal Bahadur of Harham* and he made up for lost time by providing five sons to which many champions presently trace.

While *Star Monarch* was eclipsed by Bahadur in the matter of sons, he more than made up for it in providing daughters which were outstanding producers. True, his son Ch. Lionheart Hercules won the SCAA and Parent Specialties, but no sire line goes back to him—he is only in "the middle of the pedigree" of subsequent champions. However, Hercules' full sister, Ch. Lionheart Hobby also won the Parent Club Specialty, and made a name for herself as a producer. She had eight champions to her credit and set her daughters and granddaughters off as producers of quality, as will be detailed under the *Lou's Cross* family.

Possibly the most spectacular of *Star Monarch's* daughters was *Ch. Scatterfoot Tim Tam*. She won the SCAA Specialty from the classes in 1962, and her daughter (by Liontamer) Ch. Scatterfoot Sheba was BOS the next year, as was another daughter, Ch. Coppercrest Red Marvel, in 1970. Marvel was one of the five bitches of the famous

Ch. Lionheart Hobby, owned by Sarah Coleman Brock, was BB at the ATCA Winter Specialty in 1959 under judge Chris Shuttleworth (right). Hobby was handled to the win by Ric Chashoudian. Barbara Stebeigh, Club President, presents the Airedale Bowl.

Shafer

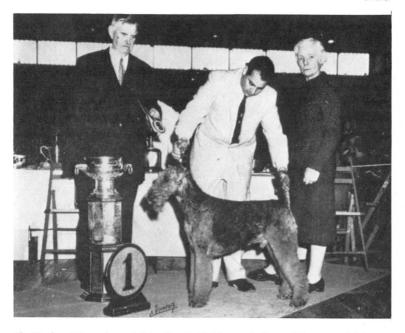

Ch. Lionheart Hercules, a full brother to Hobby, made it two Winter Specialties in a row for Mrs. Brock. Hercules triumphed in 1960 under judge Robert Floree.

Shafer

113

"Red" litter, of which one would finish, only to be followed by another sister, making rival owners wonder if there was no end. Another of these, Ch. Coppercrest Red Flare, produced *Ch. Love's Stoney Burke,* and is both dam and granddam of his (and her) son Ch. Geoffrey Earl of Stratford. Both of these dogs are previously mentioned as important links in the *Ch. Studio Liontamer* line.

Of the three champions *Star Monarch* sired in one litter, these were a "B" litter out of Ch. River-Aire Rock-C, UDT. Since Mrs. Schohner is much involved in obedience training, it is not surprising that most of her Airedales, including champions, have degrees. So one of the "B" litter, Ch. River-Aire Bonniroxie, has the CDX degree, and Ch. River-Aire Brisance, is responsible for two champions with Utility degrees, Ch. River-Aire Comus, UD, and Ch. River-Aire Cotoneaster, UD. And the beat goes on, nearly every generation of River-Aires includes at least one Companion Dog (CD).

Two *Star Monarch* sons with the Dandyaire prefix have done well, namely Ch. Dandyaire Cottage Commando and Ch. Dandyaire Friend Freddie, but the latter, like his sire, is represented more by daughters than sons.

The situation is far different with *Bahadur.* He, as was already indicated, has five major lines tracing to him via his sons. Of these the main contributor was *Aireline Hallmark,* to which at least 56 champions trace in direct tail-male. He himself sired five, but one of his sons was Ch. Wraggletaggle Checkmate, twice winner of the Northern Ohio Specialty and bred and owned by Mrs. R. N. Simonsen. Of his ten champions, Canadian and American Champion Dandyaire Cinnabar Gremlin is the most outstanding as to the number of champions sired, 13, and is himself a winner of the Pacific Northwest Specialty. He was bred and owned by Wilma Carter.

Other notable Checkmate sons are Ch. Lay-Dee-Ayr's Nicodemus (9) and Ch. Wraggletaggle Ebenezer (6), both with sons carrying on for them.

Second to the *Hallmark* branch is that of *Ch. Benaire Queen's Ransom,* son of the famous Ch. Aireline Storm Queen. This dog is himself the sire of ten champions and many of his sons have sired more than two, the whole branch giving him credit for 44 tail-male champion descendants. His son Ch. Erowah Crown Prince is a Bowl winner, and he in turn sired the Bowl winner and Best in Show winner Ch. Benaire's Sock It To Me. Dogs founding other branches of the *Queen's Ransom* line to which many champions trace are Ch. Buccaneer's Rocky Mount, Ch. Danrow of Farouk and Ch. Querencia's Bengal Diplomat. The Bowl winner Ch. Talyn's Man About Town is of the Farouk branch.

Another *Merrijack* son is Blackheath Exchequer. This has a direct

Ch. Geoffrey Earl of Stratford.   *Yuhl*

A trio of champion littermates are (from left) Ch. Wraggletaggle Checkmate, Ch. Wraggletaggle Chelsea and Ch. Wraggletaggle Cadence.

115

line of descent, with no branches en route, but at least one champion in every generation, to Ch. Pequod's Salt Horse, a dog whose name indicates he is a tough one indeed. Bred and owned by Albert and Janet Stevens (Pequod Kennels), he won the New King Bowl at the New England Specialty and was second-highest Airedale in 1973 in the Knight System and among the top five on the *Terrier Type* System. He in turn sired Ch. Pequod Blackbeard the Pirate, who was No. 1, all systems, in 1975, and continued as a top winner thereafter, with three Bests in Show in 1976, and ten Groups.

Successful as has been the *Waycon Designer* line, it now cannot approach that of *Ch. Wolstanton Bostock,* another son of *Ch. Waycon Aristocrat.* The majority of *Designer's* champion tail-male descendants trace through his son *Berrycroft Atoppa,* and of these most descend through the *Solo Aristocrat* branch. Of these the two with the largest following are *Ch. Rural Wyrewood Apollo* and *Ch. Riverina Siccawei Phoebus.*

The first of the latter duo has had astounding success, chiefly through his great-grandson *Ch. Bengal Sabu,* to which dog some four hundred champions trace in the male line alone, and countless others through daughters, granddaughters and so on. The greatest number by far trace through the English-bred son *Ch. Bengal Bladud of Harham* and the latter's son, *Eng. Ch. Bengal Kresent Brave.* At this point one could sing out *"Figaro, FIGARO!"*, for it is *Brave's* son *Ch. Jokyl Bengal Figaro,* whose title is not only American but also English, Canadian, Dutch and German, who is an important link in the chain, mainly through Eng. Ch. Jokyl Space Leader. *Figaro* was one of the Airedales used in the Walt Disney movie *The Ballad of Hector.* He had been purchased by the Disney Company at age sixteen months, after he had completed his English championship, then was taken with three other Airedales to Spain for work in the film. Afterward he was sold to a buyer in Germany where he gained additional titles. Finally he was imported to America by William Laffer, who set a goal of attaining not only American but also Canadian or Mexican titles for *Figaro.* He won his American title quickly, gaining one of his majors at the 1965 Illinois Specialty. In a litter sired by him in England was the aforementioned Space Leader and Ch. Jokyl Queen of Space, both BB winners at Crufts.

Although *Figaro* sired some notable champions in America, such as Ch. Reffal Prince Figaro, a Bowl winner, it was through the English-bred Space Leader that the main line descends, for that dog was the sire of the illustrious Am. and Eng. Ch. Jokyl Superman, sire of over 45 champions (the number increases steadily), among them the well-named Ch. Jokyl Supermaster (30 chs. and this number too is still fluid as this is written).

116

Ch. Pequod's Salt Horse, owned and bred by Albert and Janet Stevens, a consistent winner, is shown in a BB win at the Boardwalk KC under Mrs. John T. Marvin, handled by Roberta Krohne.

Klein

Ch. Pequod's Blackbeard the Pirate, owned by Albert and Janet Stevens and bred by John and Kathy McGoldrick. A BIS winner, he is shown winning BB at the Penn Treaty KC under breeder-judge Oresto Toppi, handled by Ronald Krohne.

Gilbert

117

Ch. Jokyl Superman, owned by Mr. and Mrs. Gilbert Morcroft, had a brilliant career in the United States, making many important wins and siring top winners in turn. *Tauskey.*

In 1969 and 1970 Superman led the breed on all systems, and included Best in Show Wins among his triumphs. His most important win in all-Airedale competition was at the 1970 Montgomery County show where he topped an entry of 108 dogs. This event was judged by Mrs. Mollie Harmsworth, well known for her "Bengal" Airedales, not the least of which was *Sabu* himself. He had won the previous year at the Montgomery Specialty.

So often great sires are relegated to kennel lives, a prisoner in a cage, so to speak, albeit a gilded one. It is especially cheering therefore to read the tribute paid to Superman by his handler William Thompson, as printed in *Terrier Type:*

> It is very difficult to put the character of a dog into words, especially one that is such a character! The obvious traits come easy—loving, playful, intelligent, noisy—but the subtle shadings are a little more difficult. Once you have been around him you fully realize what the ideal temperament really is—all business in the ring, but equally exciting to be around when he is just a dog. Perhaps the overriding thing about "Tom" and Airedales in general is the desire to please, whether you or himself. His great adaptability to all situations never fails to amaze me, whether he is asleep among the Christmas wrappings and debris on Christmas morning—in the Best in Show ring—or walking through an airport lobby, gently pulling a stuffed Teddy Bear out of a little girl's hand with that "I like to play with stuffed toys, too" look.
>
> I think I can honestly say that here is a dog whose record will long be remembered, but only by being around Tom can you fully appreciate what he is and what he is passing on to his get.

Superman was bred by J. E. Derrick and is owned by G. E. Morcroft. As the record indicates, he is the greatest sire in the history of the breed, succeeding *Sabu* for that title.

However there is also Supermaster to consider, for he too is going strong and of course is a year younger. This dog was bred by Olive Jackson and imported by Dr. and Mrs. F. Neal Johnson (Stone Ridge Kennels) in Illinois. He now lives with Bob and Beverly Talbert in Oregon. Mrs. Talbert tells this of Supermaster, better known as "Timmy":

> When Timmy first arrived he was quite the gentleman—maybe chasing one of our cats for fun—but no chewing or prankish escapades. Then one day, after coming home from his regular check-up and teeth-cleaning at the vet's the previous day, we discovered we were in for a surprise. Timmy greeted us in the morning on the front porch. Seems as though during the night he completely rennovated his new dog house to his own satisfaction, and being proud and wanting appreciation of his work, he strolled over, opened up the latch on his run, and came up on the porch. There he sat, proud and pleased, as only an Airedale can be, with a twinkle in his eye and a smile on his face knowing he had done a job well!

One can't help but wonder just what form this "renovating" took. He

Ch. Jokyl Supermaster came from the George Jacksons' well-known British Kennel to set his excellent stamp on many successful American Airedales.

dearly loves to go for a ride in the family pickup, where, as Mrs. Talbert says: "Sitting in the front seat he asserts his Kingmanship by peering down into cars as we go by, looking quite royal."

The pedigree of Supermaster could almost be called "three-fourths Space Leader" since his sire is by that dog and his dam is a full sister to Space Leader. This leaves only his paternal granddam as an outcross—she is by Eng. Ch. Searchlight Troubadore out of Suliston Victoria, both grandsires of the same sire line (*Ch. Rural Wyrewood Apollo*) but distantly. Supermaster is a Best in Show winner, and both he and Superman were high on the Top Ten lists in 1971, Supermaster being fourth in the *Terrier Type* rating and sixth in the Knight System.

His son Ch. Argus Stone Ridge Hunky Dory won the Illinois and New York Specialties. Another son, Ch. Eden's Spring Hepatica, has the California and Southern California Specialty winner Ch. Eden's Sal Sorbus to his credit; also Ch. Stone Ridge Gingerbred Man, whose daughter, Ch. Wagtail Woodbine, was first on the *Terrier Type* list of Top Ten Terrier bitches for 1976 and has always been on that list in the last couple of years. She is a multiple Group and Best in Show winner. Spring Hepatica had sired ten champions before his rather early death. One of Supermaster's strongest-winning sons was Ch. Harbour Hills Klark Kent owned by Mr. and Mrs. Gilbert Morcroft, a Best in Show winner and who twice took the Montgomery Specialty, one of these in 1973 in an entry of 120 Airedales. He won as far west as California (SCAA), and took the Illinois and Northern Illinois specialties too, going back East again to top the Washington event. The Eden prefix is that of Bob and Betty Hoisington.

Another Bowl winner by Supermaster is Ch. Dandyaire Quickfire, winner of the floating Specialty at San Francisco in 1974 where he also won the Group and later taking several other groups. Ch. Argus Stone Ridge Hunky Dory, mentioned earlier, won the floating Specialty, in 1975, and he was No. 1 in the Knight System that year. Klark Kent was No. 2, Knight and *Terrier Type* systems in 1972 and the next year went to the top of both.

Ch. Jokyl Prince Regent, owned by Mrs. R. V. Clark, Jr., is another Space Leader son, and in addition to having 13 champion offspring, twice won the Bowl and was also Best of Breed at Westminster. Among his champions is Ch. Talyn's Limited Edition, also a two-time Bowl winner. The Talyn prefix is that of James and Theresa McLynn.

Ch. Bengal Flyer, litter brother of *Figaro,* won two Bests in Show in 1962, and out of ten showings in America in that year he was Best of Breed nine times, with several Group placings. In 1963 he won the Montgomery Specialty and in 1965 he was Best of Breed at Westminster. He was imported by J.R.T. Alford, as was his half brother (both out of Bengal Chippinghey Fircone) Ch. Bengal Leprechaun.

Among *Flyer's* notable sons are Ch. Aristocrat of White House (11 champions) and Ch. Talyn's Yohorum. The latter was bred by Mr. and Mrs. James McLynn and brought to California in the ownership of Charles Marck and Sarah Coleman Brock. Mr. Marck was owner of Ch. Aireline Star Monarch, among others, and Miss Brock was then owner of the Lionheart Kennels after the death of Lou Holiday. Yohorum (pronounced by some YoHORum and by others Yo-ho-RUM, but known as Rummy) was the sire of 31 champions and became the top Airedale dog of 1967. He was a Best in Show winner and won the Airedale Bowl at New York. Yohorum has at least seven champion-producing daughters and of course his sons are doing well in carrying on his line. In reference Rummy daughters, it should be mentioned that *Figaro* too was effective as a brood bitch sire, since seven of his champion daughters were notable producers, topped by the phenomenal Ch. Reffal Quality Queen, dam of fifteen title-holders.

A third dog of the famous "F" litter by *Eng. Ch. Kresent Brave* is Eng. Ch. *Bengal Fastnet,* sire of the 1970 Crufts Best of Breed winner, Eng. Ch. Siccawei King's Ransom. The latter has, at this moment, only one less champion than his sire, namely eight.

In a later litter the *Kresent Brave*-Fircone combination produced the *English champion Bengal Gunga Din.* Several Crufts BB winners descend from him, starting with his son Eng. Ch. Searchlight Tycoon, also a Best in Show winner, and among whose get is Ch. Avaricious of Tanworth, owned by Mr. and Mrs. Ron Worthington (Canada). This fine, although rather greedily-named bitch won both the New York Specialty and Best of Breed at Westminster. Tycoon sired Just So of Tanworth (1 champion) and Ch. Searchlight Conquest (3 champions). The latter is an import owned by Karl Nelson's Flintkote Kennels. This establishment has Airedales of several lines and families with many champions to its credit. Mr. Nelson has been of great help to novices and everyone interested in training, showing and other useful activities.

The *Gunga Din* line at present is that of Eng. and Am. Ch. Bengal Mowgli whose son Bengal Buldeo sired Eng. Ch. Bengal Flamboyant, another Crufts winner, and already the sire of twenty champions. Among these is Eng. and Am. Ch. Jokyl Spic n' Span, owned by Elizabeth Hoisington and R. A. Hetherington. This dog is close on the heels of his sire, with nineteen champions so far, and is a Specialty winner. One of his youthful sons, Ch. Schaire's Ajax has scored well on the Knight and *Terrier Type* ratings.

Also by Flamboyant is Eng. Ch. Siccawei Galliard whose daughter Eng. Ch. Drakehall Dinah won the Airedale Centenary show in England in 1976.

Ch. Bengal Flyer, owned by J.R.T. Alford, shown winning Best in Show at the Eastern Dog Club under T.H. Carruthers, III, Tom Gately handling.   *Shafer*

Ch. Senator of White House.

Also among the Crufts winners tracing to *Gunga Din* is Eng. Ch. Jokyl Smart Guy, and he in turn sired the 1977 Crufts winner, Eng. Ch. Tanworth Merriment. "Guy" has won 19 CCs, 15 BB, a Group first and three Group seconds.

Ch. Bengal Nevasa is still another *Gunga Din* son, the winner of two Specialties, and has so far sired three champions. He is owned by Phyllis Beecroft, Tally-Ho Kennels. The announcement of the new champion Blackburn's Angelita Grande gives her sire, (who is by *Gunga Din*) Can. Ch. Bengal Badrudin, credit for 23 champions, but whether many of these are Canadian and/or English, as well as American is not stated. Angelita is out of Ch. Bengal Donna, giving Donna an even ten champions as of mid-1977.

The next line from *Ch. Bengal Kresent Brave,* is that of *Brulyn Baha'Dur,* two of whose sons were BB at Crufts, namely Ch. Taltaris Advocate and Eng., Am. Can. Ch. Optimist of Mynair. Optimist was subsequently acquired by Mr. and Mrs. R. Worthington, the owners of Am. and Can. Ch. Avaricious of Tanworth. He was owner-handled in Canada and was the Top Terrier in England for 1970. In England he won nine Bests in Show, three at National Terrier Association events, and collected thirteen Challenge Certificates en route. In 1973 Optimist won the New York Specialty and Best of Breed at Westminster. Twice he was Best of Breed at the Chicago International and in 1975 and 1976 was the top sire. At present he has sired thirteen champions.

Ch. Querencia's Suerte Brava, mentioned earlier in this chapter was a son of *Ch. Bengal Bladud of Harham,* and owned by Ercilia E. LeNy. Several champions descend from him, including the Bowl winner Ch. Ringtrue Mr. Wonderful. Along with his group win at Westminster, Suerte Brava won both the New York and Montgomery Specialties.

One of *Sabu's* American-bred sons, Ch. Talyn's River Rogue (11 champions) was one of the greatest winners of his day—another specialist in Specialties, it would seem. He won the New York Specialty three years in a row—1968-70, and by way of an afterthought snapped up a Westminster BB; he won the Montgomery affair in 1968 and this same Specialty was taken by his son Ch. Talyn's Ironclad Leave three years later. American-bred, the Rogue saw some of the country, so won additional Bowls at the New England and Southern California Specialties. He was owned by the Clairedale Kennels during these winning years.

Another Bowl winner by *Sabu* is Ch. Birchrun Bartender, whose son Ch. Blackburn's Baronof Brutus has already sired eight champions, six out of Ch. Bengal Donna. One of these is Am. and Can. Ch. Blackburn's Dyan, No. 8. Airedale bitch in the U.S. for 1974.

Ch. Avaricious of Tanworth, owned by Mr. and Mrs. R. Worthington, was BOS at the ATCA Specialty with Montgomery County under the noted British authority Molly Harmsworth of the Bengal prefix, Mr. Worthington handling. *Shafer*

Ch. Bengal Nevasa, owned by Phyllis Beechcroft, shown in a win under judge Langdon Skarda, handler, Brenda Feik. *Cauldwell*

The second main line from *Solo Aristocrat,* is that of *Ch. Riverina Siccawei Phoebus.* As it now turns out, the most important of this branch by far, and the one to which the major winners of this dynasty trace, is through his son *Ch. Lanewood Lysander.* In addition to English champions he sired dogs of such far-separated regions as Australia and Norway. One of his English champions produced the 1971 English Best in Show winner, Ch. Lanewood Royal. Still farther afield was *South African champion Bengal Skipper of Limebell,* who sired Ch. Bengal Leprechaun, Bengal Leander and Eng. and Am. Ch. Jokyl Bengal Lionheart before leaving for the sunny south (of Africa).

Of these, it is Ch. Jokyl Bengal Lionheart to whom most champions of the *Phoebus* line do trace. He sired at least 27 champions, some top winners among them. But before that he had indulged in a foray of trophy-hunting and usually came up with the silverware. He is a Best in Show winner, and won the Airedale Bowl twice—at New York and Southern California, and had won about everything in England before his importation (on the advice of Ric Chashoudian) by Mr. and Mrs. Marck and Miss Brock. The story of the "near miss" with "Skipper" at New York is told in lively fashion by Ric in the 1977 *SCAA Yearbook.* It seems that the dog was in absolutely top condition—ready to take Best in Show, with luck, when he quite literally tanked up with water, not only gurgling like a water tank, but having the same amount of apathy. Needless to say the judge was not impressed by "Skipper's" sodden imitation of a water-filled balloon, so the dog barely managed to get third in a class Ric was confident would be just a stepping stone to BB and hopefully higher. Such are the vagaries of showing! The fact that Lionheart was Best Terrier in the U.S. the next year proves that Ric kept him away from the water hole at crucial times.

The Lionheart sons which have carried on for him with the most success at present are Ch. Lionheart Gladwyn (17 champions) and Lionheart Ute (7 champions) who sired Ch. Lionheart Factor credited with the same number, and he in turn is followed by Ch. Ironsides Pek's Bad Boy, also with seven—so far. The latter's son, Ch. Ironsides Pacific Station, won the CATC Specialty and the 1975 Montgomery Specialty. A son of Ute which did not play follow-the-leader with a seven nevertheless came up with a winner. That son is Ch. Briardale Charlie Brown who sired Ch. Briardale Kung Fu, a dog which, after warming up at Westminster and the New York Specialty with WD and gaining his title therby, won both the SCAA and the Floating Specialty a few months later. Kung Fu is owned by Patricia and Stanley Schwartz and Grace Bullwinkel. From Lionheart's last litter came Ch. Cyrano Apollo C.D., who came up from the classes to win Best of Breed at the SCAA Specialty in 1975 thereby also winning the Airedale Bowl, and then on to New York for the Specialty and

Ch. Optimist of Mynair, owned by Mr. and Mrs. R. Worthington. *Wibaut*

Ch. Briardale's Kung Fu, owned by Patricia L. and Stanley Schwartz and Grace Bullwinkel, was BB at the ATCA floating Specialty at Beverly Hills under judge Ernest Schache of Australia. He was handled to the win by Michael Nemeth. *Yuhl*

127

Ch. Bengal Donna.

Westminster in 1976 taking BOW and WD, respectively. Thus he set the stage for Kung Fu the next year, only he did it in reverse—ending up with the SCAA win. A second champion from Lionheart's last litter is Cyrano Admiral's Alert.

Bengal Leander was sold to Europe but had sired Ch. Bengal Havildar (9 champions) who has several sons working for him, and also Eng. Ch. Bengal Begum, who is dam of the famed Eng. and Am. Ch. Bengal Springtime.

Ch. Bengal Leprechaun has a several-branched line, dominated by Ch. Bitmar Bengal Fere of Barbate, whose two sons continued the pace. The line from Barbate Chorister winds up at present with his grandson Ch. Barbate Henchman, with six champions to date.

Lysander's son Kresent Golden Boy sired Ch. Kresent Red Ribbons, a Best in Show dog and winner of the Bowl at Montgomery. He was imported by J. R. T. Alford, who also brought over Leprechaun. Red Ribbons was later owned by Mrs. Garloch. Nine champions are credited to this dog, and a grandson. Ch. Reffal Gallant Guy, is already aiming at that number with six.

The third line from *Lysander* is that of Ch. Winstony Exceptional (10 champions). Among his sons is the Bowl winner Ch. Copperdale Ramrod. Another line descends through Ch. Sierradale Warbow to Ch. Sierradale El Jefe. Another is a full brother of Ramrod, Ch. Copperdale Rifleman.

Foundation Tail-Female Families Since 1960

In Chapter 4 the leading brood matron families were detailed in a fashion similar to the tail-male lines. These are of course the female equivalent, the tail-female lines—that is, the tracing along the bottom of the pedigree—from dam to daughter, or going at it from the other direction, back to the taproot family founder, or at least to the main branch (or known, traceable founder). Unless one has all the early stud books it is impossible to go all the way back for a hundred years, nor is there need to.

Just as the male lines have faded out or disappeared in many instances, so too have some of the female families. And again in the same fashion, some have developed strong branches which have proliferated to an amazing degree. The families will be taken in the same order as in Chapter 4 but those now dormant have been eliminated.

The Ch. Fiesolana Family

Of the branches previously ascribed to this family, apparently the only one still producing many champions is that of *Aireline Symbol*, through *Aireline Elegance II* and *Aireline Ruth*.

Elegance produced Woodsman Blazing Star, dam of Peg o' My Heart (2 champions) and here the line divides, through Ahl's Blissful Bridget of Em and Ch. Courtney's Sweet Samantha (2 champions).

Aireline Ruth is the taproot bitch of the highly successful Wraggle-taggle Kennels of Marion Simonsen. Wraggletaggle Cinderella, out of *Ruth* produced six champions, no small feat in itself, but this number included Ch. Wraggletaggle Checkmate (10 champions) whose line of descent is shown in the Bahadur tail-male chart, through Aireline Hall-mark. A litter sister to Checkmate, Wraggletaggle Cinderella, was bred to him, producing Wraggletaggle Effervescence, C.D., and Wraggletaggle Ebenezer (bowl winner and sire of 6 champions). Effer-vescence became the dam of Barbate Indecision (dam of Ch. Anfeald Duende) and Barbate Faretheewell, whose son, Ch. Barbate Hench-man (of the Leprechaun branch from Lanewood Lysander), sired six champions. Duende's daughter Anfeald I'm Terrific was BOS to Ch. Ironsides Pacific Station at Montgomery County in 1975 and Duende herself was BOS at the same show three years earlier to Ch. Jokyl Prince Regent. I'm Terrific was also BOS to Ch. Dandyaire Quickfire at the ATCNE Specialty in 1975. The Anfeald prefix belongs to Regina and Charles Foley.

A second *Aireline Ruth* bitch is Ch. Wraggletaggle Cadence (2 champions) from whom a line descends through Ch. Wraggletaggle Lorelei, Wraggletaggle Sassafras and Ch. Wraggletaggle Tivoli.

Ch. Lou's Cross

This was originally called the *Ch. Lionheart Comet* family but since another line traces back to *Comet's* dam, *Lou's Cross*, it is divided here. Some of the ancestry of *Lou's Cross* is given in Chapter 3, but taken farther back her pedigree brings in many of the breed's greatest old-time dogs, such as *Int. Ch. Warland Ditto* twice, close up, *Ch. Soudan Swiveller, Ch. Crompton Oorang, Midland Royal, Eng. Ch. Bolton Woods Royal, Ch. Cragsman Dictator* (sire of *Ditto*, but also through another line), *Ch. Clonmel Monarch, Ch. Master Briar, Ch. The Gamecock, Ch. Dumbarton Vixen, Ch. Cragsman King* and *Ch. Red Raven.* Although the line goes a few generations farther back, it is simpler to start with *Lionheart Queen*, dam of *Lionheart Cross*, down through the generations previously sketched, to *Lou's Cross.* The *Comet* lines have two main divisions, No. II and No. III. Represent-ing *Ch. Lionheart Comet II* now is the descent through *Ch. Lionheart Baroness*, and this has two branches. First is that of Ch. Lionheart Hagar, the generations from her being Breezewood Baguette (3 cham-pions), Ch. Lavender Hills Heather (1 champion) and Ch. Talyn's Black-eyed Susan (2 champions). Right here this line starts to make history, for Susan's daughter Ch. Talyn's Tuppence produced eleven champions, one of which is Ch. Talyn's Yohorum (31 champions), whose record is given in this sire-line section of this chapter. Of her daughters, several have founded branches with champion-producing daughters of their own. These are Ch. Talyn's You Betcha, dam of Talyn's River Rogue; and Ch. Talyn's Prom Date, dam of Ch. Talyn's Ironclad Leave. Ch. Talyn's Deed I Do has produced four champions and her daughters and granddaughters are carrying on for her.

The other line from *Baroness* is through Ch. Lionheart Kootenai, whose granddaughter Lionheart Beryl is the dam of Ch. Lionheart Joker and Ch. Lionheart Ute. A daughter, Ch. Lionheart Joy, has produced two champions.

A full sister to *Ch. Lionheart Comet II, Mary Jane Dale* was evidently a pet, for it is not until four generations later that a producer of champions shows up. This is Blossom Hills Queen Mother, dam of two champions, one of which was Ch. Will-Lyn Dale of Blossom Hill, a Bowl winner. She followed her mother's example, and one of her daughters is Ch. Ironsides Fire One, whose nautical name continues with her daughter, Ch. Ironsides Scrimshaw.

Lionheart Enchantress is now the main contributor to the *Ch. Lionheart Comet III* line. She is of course the dam of *Ch. Studio Liontamer*, founder of the only "all American" sire line which has taken BB at major Specialties and Westminster against the formidible "new English" competition. She also produced five other champions, among them Ch. Lionheart Starlight (full sister of Liontamer) dam of Ch. Lionheart Hobby, who won the New York Specialty in 1959 and Ch. Lionheart Hercules, who made the same win in 1960. Hobby's five champions include Ch. Lionheart Holly (8 champions), and Ch. Lionheart Hobby's Jill, U.D. (2 champions) who went BOS from the classes to Ch. Querencia's Suerte Brava at Westminster. Three daughters of Holly carry on that branch, namely Ch. Lionheart Winsome (2 champions), Ch. Lionheart Fortune (6 champions) and Ch. Lionheart Penny (2 champions). Fortune in turn is represented by two daughters of which Ch. Rachdale Atlantis (3 champions) is in the lead at present. Penny produced Ch. Lionheart Gaymond (3 champions) whose brother Ch. Lionheart Gladwyn sired 15 champions. Gaymond's line branches out further, with Ch. Lionheart Ydanda (2 champions) leading.

As would be guessed by the U.D. suffix for Jill, her owners, Mr. and Mrs. W. A. Nesbitt, were strong advocates of Obedience training. Mr. Nesbitt recently succumbed to a long illness but his widow continues the interest. The names could be confusing in this line, for the daughter of Hobby is Ch. Lionheart Hobby's Jill, U.D., who produced Ch. Ttibsens (Nesbitt, spelled backward) Jill's Hobby C.D. From here the names differ. One of her five champions is Rum N' Ginger, dam of one champion so far. Another Jill's Hobby daughter is Ch. Ttibsen's Mickey Finn, whose name indicates she is a knock-out. A son of Jill's Hobby is Ch. Ttibsen's Rum N' Spice, C.D. He is by Ch. Talyn's Yohorum who won the 1968 SCAA Specialty. Jill's Hobby was BOS to him on that occasion.

The branch from *Comet III* founded by Lionheart Irene, U.D. was mentioned in the Chapter 3, but now there are more statistics. Irene produced two champions, and her daughter Ch. River-Aire Rock-C, U.D.T. produced three. One of these was Ch. River-Aire Brisance (2 champions), and she in turn produced River-Aire Chrys o'Bris, U.D. The daughter of Bris is River-Aire Lark, C.D.X. whose daughter, River-Aire Pine Cone was RB at the CATC Specialty but was killed by a car shortly thereafter. Also out of Lark is River-Aire Proud Piper, dam of three champions, one of which is Ch. Marble Mountain Aire Rusty, American and Canadian C.D. Another is Ch. Sundale's Holliday (2 champions), whose line already has three branches. The River-Aire prefix is that of Marjorie Schohner, who is also an obedience devotee and maintains records on all champions and their ancestry (as far as traceable without having all the early stud books, or foreign lines unrelated to most American breeding). She has furnished most of the material for bloodlines given here. Without her help it could never have been done.

Another River-Aire line is from Ch. Lionheart Starlight, through Jill of River-Aire C.D., dam of Ch. River-Aire Flying Feather, U.D. She in turn produced River-Aire Natoma, C.D., dam of Ch. River-Aire Roca of Tarawood (1 champion).

Lionheart Comet IV is, as might be expected, still another daughter of "III." This branch has not produced a large number of champions, but has a fair number even so. Her greatgranddaughter Ravenaire Spicy produced three champions but two non-champions carried on the line with at least one champion in every generation, ending—as of the moment (through Sternick Notaword, and four generations later) with Mexican and American Champion Berry's Big Bertha, C.D.X. who also has at least one leg on her U.D. degree.

The final Lou's Cross line is through *Lionheart Carry On*, and one gal in this line sure did carry it on! This is Ch. Burnweel Bessie, the family heritage descending from *Carry On* through Vasona's Relion Daisy, Vasona's Liberty Bell (1 champion), Cinnabar Imp, and Cinnabar Almaden, dam of Bessie. The latter, bred by Sam Williston, became the foundation of the Dandyaire Airedales bred by Reg and Wilma Carter. Bessie was a Ch. Murose Replica daughter, and she produced seven champions. Moreover they bred on in both directions—that is, her sons did as well as her daughters. She produced three

Ch. Ttibsen's Rum N' Spice, C.D., a homebred of Mrs. W. A. Nesbitt, shown in a win under Nick Calicura, handler Ric Chashoudian. *Yuhl*

Ch. Burnwheel Bessie (Ch. Murose Replica ex Cinnabar Almaden)

133

Ch. Dandyaire Kaniksu (Ch. Bengal Flyer ex Ch. Carryall of Dandyaire) is a successful matron with some 11 champions to her credit.

Bennett

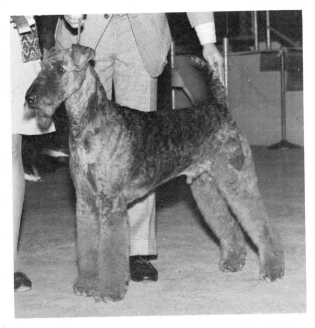

Ch. Dandyaire Oil Producer (Ch. Dandyaire Monarch ex Ch. Dandyaire Expresso), owned by John Hawkins. *McMillan*

Ch. Dandyaire Quickfire, owned by Mr. and Mrs. (handling) R. H. Carter was first in the Terrier Group at the Sir Francis Drake KC under judge William L. Kendrick following a BB win at the ATCA floating Specialty in 1972. He was also BB at the New England Specialty the following year. *Francis*

champions each in her two litters by Ch. Aireline Star Monarch. A brother-sister mating produced Am. and Can. Ch. Carryall of Dandyaire, and she, bred to Ch. Bengal Flyer, produced the phenomenal Ch. Dandyaire Kaniksu, a Specialty winner, whose record of twelve champions has been topped by very few bitches. At this point five of her daughters are following the family tradition, all of them champions themselves. Of these the leader is Ch. Dandyaire Miss Bristol (6 champions) Tidying up "shipshape and Bristol fashion" she too has a several-branched family of champion-producers.

Bessie's call name was "Coffee" so her champion daughter Ch. Dandyaire Last Cup of Coffee indicates her place in the succession. She produced two champion bitches, but the beverage-named line from Dandyaire Java is the longest, through Ch. Dandyaire Expresso (2 champions) with the most recent being Ch. Dandyaire One For The Road, a name with a bit more zap than mere caffeine. A Group-winning son of Expresso is Ch. Dandyaire Oil Producer.

The Dandyaires have done everything from taking the points at Specialties to topping the lot—up and down the Pacific Coast, several times taking the Pacific Northwest Specialty. The most recent is Ch. Dandyaire Quickfire, winner of the California Specialty and the Floating Specialty—thereby winning the Bowl. He also took a jaunt East where he topped the New England Specialty.

The Ch. Ridgemoor Sweetberry Family

This family, via *Ch. Eleanore's Sweetberry*, is now represented mostly by the Harbour Hills Airedales. This branch comes down through Ch. Seaward's Hobby, then Seaward's Cinnamon Bun, to Cinnamon Sal, dam of three champions, two of which form branches which produced many of the Harbour Hills champions through two or three generations.

The second branch from *Sweetberry* is one which ends with Ch. Whistle Towns Lara's Theme, one of her dam's two champions.

The Rockley Glitter Family

The leading branch of this family is that of *Can. and Am. Ch. Tedhurst Pin Up Girl*. The last of the *Ch. Raylerock Mica* line mentioned in Chapter 3 was Ch. Foxglove Studio Joye. This now continues from her to Dandyaire Enjoyment, one of whose daughters, Scarlett's Miss produced two champions. The other, Chahoudi's Boom Boom La Rue, also produced two, and one of these, Ch. Briardale's Miss Bertha CD is the dam of Ch. Briardale's Charlie Brown, sire of the "giant-killer" Ch. Briardale Kung Fu whose name may be an indication of his tactics, for at the SCAA and Floating Specialties in Los Angeles in 1977 he knocked off many of the breed's greatest winners in going Best of Breed at both.

136

The second branch from *Pin Up Girl* is through Tedhurst Jet, but the third has the most daughters. This is through Tedhurst Lucky Star, with three champions producing one champion each and of these, Ch. Meadowaire Magna produced Ch. Meadowaire Belle Star, dam of three champions.

The Tridwr Milady Family

This family has switched emphasis from *Eng. and Am. Ch. Westhay Fiona of Harham* to several others, all stemming from her daughter *Ch. Riverina Bewitched.* The current leading brood matron in the breed is of this family, tracing back to the Reffal Kennels' import *Riverina Winter Wanton* whose daughter, Ch. Reffal Humdinger, produced Ch. Reffal Quality Queen, a matron who can add "quantity" to the "quality" for she has an all-time record fifteen champions to her credit. She was owned by the Lay De Ayr Kennels, but was bred by Martha Burns and William Laffer (Reffal is through-the-mirror Laffer). Her sire is Ch. Jokyl Bengal Figaro.

The *Bewitched* daughter *Eng. Ch. Riverina Diana of Siccawei* produced five champions, among them Eng. Ch. Siccawei Artemis (4 champions) whose imported daughter Ch. Siccawei Princess Pat founded a branch for Reffal; and another, Eng. Ch. Siccawei Princess Pam, in the dam of Eng. Ch. Impudent Miss (dam of Eng. Ch. Siccawei Galliard). Impudent Miss also produced Eng. Ch. Siccawei Ruby (4 champions). A *Diana* son, Ch. Siccawei Remus, is a prominent sire in Australia.

Two other *Diana* daughters have founded many-branched families of their own. One is Siccawei Rosalie, dam of Mex. Ch. Siccawei Gypsy Flintkote. The latter produced Ch. Fleetwood Sassy Flyer (1 champion) whose line continues this work; also Flintkote River Princess, two of whose five champions include the top winners Ch. Jerilee's Jumping Jericho and Ch. Coppercrest Contender; and Flintkote Bengal Tigress. Tigress' daughter Ch. Flintkote Red Sensation has already produced three champion daughters, two of which have in turn produced two champions each.

The second of these two *Diana* matrons is Ch. Siccawei Moonlight (7 champions). Of her two champion daughters one, Ch. Jackson's Astral Amber, has outdone all others of this matriarchy by producing eight champions. Of these, Ch. Jackson's Dazzling Diana (4 champions) is the dam of Ch. Jackson's Lucy Locket. The Jacksons are Alice and Charles A. Jackson, the latter, as he says "retired and gone to the Dogs" handling his own winners to their titles. Lucy Locket was 1974's No. 2 Airedale bitch, making a jump of two places from the previous year, when she was 5th. Her daughter, Ch. Jackson's Peggy O'Neal was No. 5 Airedale Bitch, 1976, on the Knight system.

The branch from *Eng. Ch. Riverina Westhay Flayre* has declined in numbers in contrast to other *Bewitched* daughters, but there is still a line from the famous *Fiona*—two, in fact. One is Harham's Fiona Flirtatious, with three daughters to carry on for her, but best known for her son, Ch. Querencia's Suerte Brava. The other *Fiona* daughter is Harham's Fiona Fashion Plate (4 champions). A second *Flayre* branch is through *Noire of Hawthorne* whose granddaughter Windessa of Whitehouse (2 champions) produced Ch. Picadilly Tia Juana Brass (5 champions).

To return to other daughters of *Bewitched*, there is *Eng. Ch. Braknight Riverina Garnet* and *Riverina Danaides*, with the latter having more branches. Also her granddaughter Eng. Ch. Siccawei Humdinger, is the dam of Eng. Ch. Siccawei King's Ransom.

Going clear back now, to *Tridwr Milady*, there is another important daughter, Riverina Vogue (1 champion) with the line of succession going through Riverina Exclusive, Suliston Solitaire and Suliston Victoria to Siccawei Psyche (3 champions) whose son Ch. Jokyl Superman (45 champions) of the *Sabu* dynasty is the breed's greatest sire. Psyche's daughter Eng. and Am. Ch. Bengal Suliston Merrie Maid is the dam of the fine sire Bengal Buldeo and Eng. and Swedish Ch. Bengal Mogul, and is a full sister to Eng. Ch. Searchlight Tycoon, a Best in Show winner in England. Tycoon is the sire of Am. Can. Ch. Avaricious of Tanworth, a Bowl winner and also a Best in Show Airedale.

Although Merrie Maid may have gained much acclaim through her son and brother, it was another daughter of Psyche who apparently has carried on the family line with greatest emphasis. This is Suliston Rowena, who produced Bengal Sundari, dam of Ch. Bengal Donna, whose latest champion brings her score to ten. Donna is also the dam of the Australian Best in Show winner Aust. Ch. Bengal Valley Forge.

It is obvious that this is an extremely strong and productive family, containing not only the dams of numerous champions, but also great sires, with more than mere numbers to speak for them, but the quality of their wins as well. The totals increase constantly, so the numbers of champions given are minimum, except for those of many years ago. This is also true of all other lines and families coming under review.

The Eng. Ch. Kresent Sincerity Family

All this family is through *Kresent Model Maid* (11 champions), dam of the great sire Ch. Bengal Kresent Brave. Her daughter Eng. Ch. Bengal Kresent Ballerina (3 champions) is represented by two lines, the one with the most numerous champion-producing matrons is that of Eng. Ch. Bengal Begum, and in turn the latter's most successful daughter was Eng. and Am. Ch. Bengal Springtime, winner of 17 c.c.'s, 14

BBs, and Best Terrier Bitch at Crufts in 1969. Her son Eng. Ch. Bengal Flamboyant is not only a "flamboyant" winner, but is now a leading sire in England. Springtime produced five other champions, three of which are daughters already having two champions as has also a granddaughter. Another son is the American bred Ch. Eden's Spring Hepatica (10 champions) by Supermaster.

Eng. and Am. Ch. Bengal Kresent Duchess of Harham has one more champion than Ballerina and was also a Best in Show winner in England and a winner of the Airedale Bowl at the Illinois Specialty. As the suffix indicates she was imported by Harold Florsheim's Harham Kennels. Two lines descend from her, the longest starting with Ch. Querencia's High Stepper, the other also through a Querencia bitch, Ch. Querencia's Duchess Pride (2 champions).

"Meanwhile, back at the ranch" in England, another line descends through Loudwell Kresent Karousel, then to Loudwell Mother of Pearl whose daughter Loudwell Quest has three champions as does Quest's daughter Eng. Ch. Loudwell Starlight.

The Onyx of Joreen Family

It is through *Chippinghey Briar Rose* that this "semi-precious" line changes from a gem to an earthly-then-arboreal context and becomes very precious indeed. As far as super-sires and super-producers go, along with the highest-quality wins, this family has no equal. And quantity gets into the picture also.

Although there is another branch from *Briar Rose* (through Ch. Chippinghey Indian Princess) it is short, and all of the great Airedales of this fantastic family trace back to *Chippinghey Deep Loam*. Just as in agriculture the term "deep loam" is indicative of richness and fertility, so it is with this well-named matron. It was not she herself who proved unusually fertile, but instead it was her daughter *Bengal Chippinghey Fircone*, dam of ten English and/or American champions. Another daughter, *Eng. Ch. Jokyl Top of the Form* has only four, but they include two Crufts BB winners—Ch. Jokyl Queen of Space, Ch. Jokyl Space Leader and Ch. Jokyl Goal Keeper. Not included in Top of the Form's number are an Irish and a Norwegian champion. Whatever else Queen of Space may have done, she did her share in producing Ch. Jokyl Supermaster, a leading sire of the *Sabu* line. Her family line is continued through Jokyl Hera (1 champion) whose daughter Eng. Ch. Jokyl Elegance (3 champions) produced Ch. Jokyl Sweet n' Sour, sister of Ch. Jokyl Spic n' Span and Eng. Ch. Jokyl Smart Guy. Sweet n' Sour is dam of Ch. Springfield Maude.

And now to *Fircone,* who somehow makes you think of Christmas trees, but to those in the know, her name means super-champions and super-sires. For in one litter alone—the famous "F" litter—she produced the Bengal champions Figaro, Fastnet and Flyer, by Eng. Ch. Bengal Kresent Brave, and a repeat breeding resulted in Eng. Ch. Bengal Gunga Din. Bred to South African Champion Bengal Skipper of Limebell she produced Eng. and Am. Ch. Jokyl Bengal Lionheart and Bengal Leander (sire of Ch. Bengal Havildar and Aust. Ch. Bengal Jemadar).

Just to have such outstanding sires on her honor roll should have been enough—although that would have stopped the family line right there. So, to continue on with her good name and producing qualities, *Fircone* provided posterity with six branches of the family tree. These descend through Ch. Bengal Chi Chi (3 champions), Bengal Freya (1 champion), Bengal Fantasia, Ch. Bengal Carousel (1 champion) and Bengal Frigga. The greatest of these is Chi Chi. In addition to champion sons of the Erowah prefix, she also had producing daughters bearing that prefix, namely Benaire Erowah Cha Cha (5 champions), Ch. Erowah Electric (1 champion) and Ch. Erowah Aur A Lee. Electric started a current with her daughter Ch. Triumph's Singleton Queen, for of the latter's three champions, one was Ch. Triumph's Benaire Daffodil C.D., dam of thirteen, which puts her mighty close to Quality Queen on the Top Producer list. Her daughter Ch. Eden's Simply Smashing (2 champions) produced the big winner Ch. Eden's Sal Sorbus, but the family is carried on through his sister Ch. Eden's Sal Sophoro. Two other Daffodil daughters are Ch. Eden's Super Satisfaction (2 champions) and Ch. Eden's Jokyl Sunpiper, U.D. A Chi-Chi son is Erowah Checkmate, sire of the top-winning bitch Ch. Erowah Indian Ginger. (See Kewi Kwendreda family).

Those just mentioned as founding branches of the *Fircone* family, but which had no champions indicated, are nevertheless the dams of champion-producers. For instance Bengal Frigga produced Bengal Thunderbird, whose two champions are Ch. Bengal Maharawi and Am. and Eng. Ch. Bengal Mowgli, a notable sire. Bengal Freya is the dam of Toryaire Tova, whose son Blackburn's Baronof Brutus is a Canadian and American champion, and sire of Blackburn's Dyan, with the same dual championships and No. 8 Airedale bitch in America for 1974. The Carousel line produced several White House champions including the outstanding sire Ch. Aristocrat of White House. The line down from Fantasia shows Eng. Ch. Loudwell Folly as dam of the English Best in Show winner, Eng. Ch. Loudwell Regal. And the beat goes on, for the branches from *Fircone* are flourishing and still comparatively young.

The Kewi Kwendreda Family

This family is English and possibly more easily traceable in that country. It is not so from this side of the Pond. At any rate it branches

140

Ch. Erowah Indian Ginger, owned and handled by Park Peters, shown in a Terrier Group win at the Pontiac KC under judge Henry Stoecker. *Norton of Kent*

Eden Jokyl Sunpiper, U.D., one of many that have enjoyed good success both in the show ring and in obedience. She is shown winning under Mrs. Tom Stevenson, handler Ric Chashoudian.

141

out quickly from *Kwendreda's* daughter *Kewi Fantasy* through three branches. These are from Rietbok Kewi Ondine (2 champions) whose daughter Ch. Bengal Olympic produced Ch. Sweet Hills Cousin Echo, dam of Ch. White Rose Eroica (2 champions); and Sunset Hills Sabrina (2 champions) also with a champion-producing daughter. Another *Fantasy* daughter is Lanewood Kewi Oriole, dam of the noted dog Ch. Lanewood Lysander (Ch. Riverina Siccawei Phoebus line) to whom many great winners trace.

However the main producing branch is through Rietbok Kewi Naiad, via three sources. Bengal Kiki of Limebell produced the imported Ch. Bengal Seaweed of Limebell and Seafern of Limebell, dam of Ch. Brunells of Siccawei, also imported here. The second line is that of Bengal Khana Kha whose daughter Bengal Charlotte is the dam of Ch. Searchlight Conquest (3 champions), owned by the Flintkote Kennels. He is of the Gunga Din sire line.

The top brood matron of this family is Naiad's daughter Bengal Katerina (6 champions) who produced Ch. Erowah Indian Ginger, a multi-group winner, with an American Best in Show added plus three more in Canada. She won the Illinois Specialty and was BOS at the Northern Ohio event. What adds significance is the fact that she was owner-handled by Park Peters, of the Suzark Kennels. It is said there have been only two owner-handled Best in Show Airedales, so obviously this is quite a feat. Ginger completed her Canadian championship with four consecutive BBs, a Group second, two Group firsts, and two Bests in Show. She was a Top Ten Airedale for four years, and was No. 1 Airedale and No. 10 Terrier in Canada in just eight showings in 1967. She produced only two litters, but of the nine puppies in all, six are champions. One dog is Ch. Suzark Open Sesame, an owner-handled Group and Specialty winner. Of Ginger's five champion-producing daughters, the untitled Suzark Tain't Proper has the most at present.

The Sally of Llanipsa Family

This family traces down without branches four generations to *Siccawei Preses* (3 champions) whose daughter, Eng. and Am. Ch. Siccawei Ideal produced the great sire Siccawei Phoebus and two other champions. One of these is Ch. Siccawei Vanessa, imported by the Reffal kennels. Her daughter Ch. Reffal Royal Mary (6 champions) is represented by seven branches, two of them by non-champions, and another non-champion holds a C.D.X. degree. The branch from Ch. Reffal Keepsake is at present most prolific regarding champions, for along with one from Keepsake herself are five from Reffal Zsa Zsa, and one from Reffal Zither.

Ch. Golliwog's Gidget, owned and handled by Margaret Hochstetler, shown in a win at the Redwood Empire KC under the late breeder-judge Charles W. Marck.

Bennett

At the 1975 Specialty of the California ATC Ch. Golliwog's Gidget was selected as the winner of the brood bitch class by Mrs. Charles W. Marck. Gidget (extreme left) won the class on the merits of Ch. Golliwog Anastasia, Ch. Golliwog Annie Laurie and Ch. Golliwog Obeah pictured with her. *Yuhl*

143

The Ch. Birchrun Richochet Family

Stockton Victory Lass is actually the founder of this family, but there are no branches leading to *Richochet,* so it's just as well to start with her. She is the foundation bitch of Barbara Strebeigh's Birchrun Kennels. Dam of five champions, *Richochet* includes three among the branches tracing to her. Needless to say, this family beginning nicked extremely well with *Ch. Bengal Sabu,* whose lineage—to and from—is already traced. The longest lines are via *Ch. Birchrun Essie Extra* (2 champions), dam of Birchrun Sabette (4 champions). The latter's two daughters Ch. Birchrun Sonata (2 champions) and Ch. Birchrun Sass 'Em (6 champions) really started something, for Sonata's daughter Ch. Birchrun Ragamuffin (2 champions) is represented by none other than Ch. Golliwog's Gidget, dam of twelve champions, and one of the leading producers in the breed. Since she still has several more youngsters to keep up the good work, she can very well go to the top, for a couple already have 14 points at this date, and others have similar aspirations. Golliwog is the prefix for the Airedales of Margaret (Straub) Hochstetler.

Now back to Ch. Birchrun Sass'Em, among whose six champions are Ch. Birchrun Lucretia (dam of Ch. Trevorwood Aurora); Ch. Birchrun Sassylass and Ch. Trick of Little Cherry (1 champion) who produced Pilgrim's Princess Indianaire, C.D. (3 champions). But it is the non-titled Treat of Little Cherry who has three daughters which produced the most, two of them champions themselves, but again the "stay-at-home" came up with the most, this is Deepwood Baba au Rhum (3 champions), one of the champion daughters of Rhum being Deepwood Mira who also produced three champions, but it is her non-champion daughter Arrowwood Storm Cloud who came up with a pair of champions.

Next to the previous line in length and divisions is the *Richochet* daughter *Ch. Birchrun Lulu Belle,* dam of Ch. Dellaire Wirecrest Sabella. Here the line branches out through Ch. Wraggletaggle Gypsy-O into those of Ch. Barbate As You Like It (1 champion), and Barbate Dorchester, C.D. (dam of Ch. Cyrano Apollo C.D., a Bowl winner of the Lanewood Lysander line). Barbate is the prefix of Paul and Mary Lanken. The third is Ch. Barbate Daisy Clipper, dam of Ch. Barbate Jasmine.

The second Sabella line is that of Ch. Wraggletaggle Airelane Coquette (3 champions). The most notable of these at present is that of Ch. Laneaire Pequod's Flying Jib (1 champion) granddam of Ch. Pequod's Blackbeard the Pirate, a Best in Show winner and No. 1 Airedale, all systems, in 1975. Flying Jib is dam of Ch. Pequod Salt Horse, the Pirate's sire.

The Ch. Cyndale's Shawney Sabu, C.D. Family

This is another family which goes back several generations but without branches, so it will be taken from that dividing point. *Shawney Sabu* is another leading producer, her champions numbering an even dozen at the moment. She is by Ch. Benaire Crown Prince who is by Ch. Benaire Queen's Ransom out of Ch. Bengal Chi Chi of the *Fircone* family. *Shawney's* dam is Gypsy of Zebu, whose sire is by *Sabu*. Leading the current five lines from *Shawney* at present is that of Ch. Cyndale's Brass Onyx, which combination of stone and metal came up with Ch. Stone Ridge Brass Tacks, with two others less suitably named (as to family tradition) Ch. Stone Ridge Bell Tam and Ch. Stone Ridge Space Queen who has produced Ch. Stone Ridge April Love. Ch. Cyndale Ebony Bronze, another good producer, is the dam of three champions, one of which also has the title in Sweden, England and Finland—Ch. Bodelm Barnacle Bill, a BIS winner overseas and a top sire in Sweden.

The Ch. Scatterfoot Tim Tam Family

There are a few generations behind *Tim Tam* without any branches, so to all intents and purposes, it is best to start with her.

She is by *Int. Ch. Aireline Star Monarch* of the *Waycon Designer* line, out of Scatterfoot Lady whose great-grand-dam was Lady Sparkle. Much of the *Tim Tam* story is given under *Star Monarch's* heading, but to recap, Tim Tam herself came up from the classes to win the 1962 SCAA Specialty, and her daughter Ch. Scatterfoot Sheba was BOS the next year. Then there was the famous "Red" litter of five bitches. As soon as one talented sister attained the title another would be ready to take the next points. Frustrated competitors thought the "Reds" would never end. One of these was Ch. Coppercrest Red Flare who produced Ch. Love's Stoney Burke, and in a son to dam mating, produced Ch. Geoffrey Earl of Stratford. Both of these are mentioned in the *Walnut King Nobbler* material under the *Ch. Studio Liontamer* branch. Love's Gabriel of Coppercrest, brother of the Earl, was Winners Dog at the New York Specialty in 1970. Ch. Coppercrest Red Rocket and Ch. Coppercrest Red Queen each produced a champion, as did a daughter of Queen, but it was "Margay", Ch. Coppercrest Red Marvel, who topped the lot with nine champions. Among them are Ch. Coppercrest Royal Rendition, owned by Lynn Donaldson, winner of the 1969 New England Specialty. Five of Red Marvel's champions—among them the "Royals"—were by Ch. Love's Stoney Burke, and four were by the English import Ch. Winstony Exceptional. Among these are the littermates Ch. Coppercrest Ramrod and Ch. Coppercrest Rifleman. At the 1975 Beverly Hills show, Ramrod pulled a double win by himself going Best of Breed and his daughter Ch. Coppercrest Santana taking Best of Opposite Sex. The Coppercrest Kennels are owned by June and Robert Dutcher. Along with breeding consistently good Airedales they have always helped novices and anyone else interested in anything to do with Airedales in particular or any Terrier breed in general. The Dutchers have been a major force in putting on Specialties and all the work they involve. Their dogs have met with great success, and several important winners, such as Ch. Jerilee's Jumping Jericho and his brother Ch. Coppercrest Contender (bred by Elinor Hellmann) bear Coppercrest antecedents in their pedigrees.

A non-champion daughter of Red Marvel also produced two champions, and two other untitled daughters of *Tim Tam* produced one each, as did a couple other of the "Reds." Ch. Coppercrest Hummingbird produced Haywire's Highland Heather, dam of three champions.

Ch. Scatterfoot Tim Tam (center) was the dam of the celebrated Coppercrest "Red" litter. She is seen here winning the brood bitch class at the Southern California Airedale Association with two members of that litter, Ch. Coppercrest Red Flare (left) and Ch. Coppercrest Red Marvel. The judge was Ellsworth C. Gamble. *Ludwig*

Ch. Coppercrest Rifleman (Ch. Winstony Exceptional ex Ch. Copper-crest Red Marvel).   *Ludwig*

Ch. Coppercrest Ramrod, a full brother to Rifleman.   *Ludwig*

147

The Rocklege Dodi's Echo Family

This is another line which could be extended farther back, but the main branching is with the daughters of *Dodi's Echo*. She produced three champions, one of which, Ch. Harbour Hills Princess, produced ten champions, nine by Ch. Aristocrat of White House—five in the first litter, four in the next. Two of her champions daughters have already contributed to future generations, one is Ch. Harbour Hills Imogene, C.D. (1 champion) and the other is Ch. Harbour Hills Miss Comanche. This prefix belongs to Sarah and Carl Macklin.

There are many other promising families now, but which are not easily traced back many generations to see is they tie in with others, further back. Some go back to Oorang breeding, although top-crossed every generation with dogs of show, rather than hunting, background. This is true of several of the top-winning, or top-producing, bloodlines. However the Oorang, and other "hunting" strains, all go back to English breeding, taking the "Oorang" from Ch. Crompton Oorang, Ch. King Oorang, and others of that famous name.

Ch. Dandyaire Cinnabar Gremlin (Ch. Wraggletaggle Checkmate ex Ch. Dandyaire For Cinnabar), owned by Mr. and Mrs. R. H. Carter, is a Specialty winner and the sire of 13 champions. He is shown here with Mrs. Carter.

Roberts

Chart I
Direct tail male line of descent from the founder of the breed:

Airedale Jerry 1888
  Ch. Cholmondeley Briar
    Briar Test
      Ch. Master Briar
        Ch. Clonmel Monarch
          Clonmel Chilperic
            Ch. Master Royal
              Ch. Midland Royal
                Midland Rollo
                  Requistion
                    Wadsworth Royalist
                      Cragsman Dictator
                        Eng and Am. Ch. Warland Ditto 1919
                          Ch. Moorhead Marquis 1921
                          Ch. Warland Whatnot 1921
                                Ch. Warland Waterman 1924
                                Clonmel Monarque 1921
                                Ch. Clee Courtier 1925
                                        Ch. Junemore Bonnie Boy 1929
                                        Ch. Matador Supreme
                                        Ch. Warbreck Eclipse
                                        Walnut King Nobbler 1930
                                        Ch. Matador Mandarin 1929

Only two of these lines trace down to major winners and sires today although the others from *Ditto* are still represented in other descent than direct tail-male (from sire to son), or, to make it easier to visualize, along the top line of the pedigree. Other descent would be through the middle of the pedigree. The main branches from Walnut King Nobbler and Ch. Matador Mandarin are shown on the following charts. Once important lines which now are sparsely represented or have died out entirely are indicated through the branch founder only, without subsequent get. However some of these are strongly represented in other countries. A case in point is Eng. and Am. Ch. Murose Replica (by Ch. Holmbury Bandit, Atoppa branch of the Madarin line) whose dynasty is flourishing in Australia.

Chart I - A

Walnut King Nobbler
  Tri. Int. Ch. Cotteridge Brigand
    Ch. Rockley Robin Hood
    Ch. Fallcrest Harry
    Eng. Ch. Monarch of Tullochard
    Ch. Rockley Roasting Hot
        Ch. RoyEl Hot Rock
        Ch. Eleanore's Brigand
        Ch. Eleanore's Royalty of Lionheart
            Ch. Lionheart Copper
              Ch. Studio Top Brass
                Ch. Studio Liontamer   (Chart II - A)
  Eng. and Am. Ch. Cast Iron Monarch
  Ch. Walnut Clipper of Freedom   (Chart II - B)
    Ch. Freedom Freelance
      Ch. Freedom Full Force
  Ch. Lamorna Prince Nobbler
  Turkish Western Guard   (Chart II - C)
  Ch. Llanipsa Toreador   (Chart II - D)

149

Chart I - B

Ch. Matador Mandarin
    Ch. Stockfield Aristocrat (Eng.)
        Ch. Waycon Aristocrat (Eng.)
            Waycon Designer (Eng.)
                Can. Ch. Murraysgate Monty
                    Holmbury Murraysgate Merrijack (Eng.)
                        Eng. Ch. Son of Merrijack (Chart III)
        Ch. Wolstanton Bostock (Eng.)
            Berrycroft Atoppa (Eng.)
                Ch. Wyrewood Aristocratic of Harham
                Ch. Holmbury Bandit (Eng.)
                Solo Aristocrat
                    Ch. Rural Wirewood Apollo (Eng.)
                        Ch. Searchlight Defiance
                        Ch. Collipriest Stormer (Eng.)
                          Ch. Bengal Collipriest Diplomat (Eng.)
                            Ch. Bengal Sabu   (Chart IV)
                      Ch. Riverina Siccawei Phoebus (Chart V)
                Ch. Broadcaster of Harham
                Chathall Wostan (Eng.)

SIRE

DAM

Chart II - A

Ch. Studio Liontamer
  Ch. Hilltop's Rocky Top Notch
    Hilltop's Blitzkrieg
      Ch. Town Girl's Challenge
        Ch. Buckshot III
        Ch. Thunder's Playboy
          Ch. Airewyre's Big Ernie
            Ch. Ernie's Jack Flash
  Coppercrest Brandy
    Siouxaire's Chief Duff
      Ch. Love's Stoney Burke
        Ch. Coppercrest Ringleader
        Ch. Geoffrey Earl of Stratford
          Ch. Jerrilee's Jumping Jericho
          Ch. Coppercrest Contender
        Ch. Geronimo of Indianaire
          Ch. Moeson of Indianaire

Chart II - B

Ch. Walnut Clipper of Freedom
  Ch. Freedom Freelance
    Ch. Freedom Full Force
      Ch. Rek En Nad's High and Mighty of Freedom
        Ch. Rek En Nad's Hitting Away
          Ch. Rek En Nad's Mainliner
        Ch. Rek En Nad's Sir Richard

150

Chart II - C

Ch. Turkish Western Guard (Eng.)
Turkish Western Dictator (Eng.)
Talena Majestic (Eng.)
Cont. Ch. Brineland Bonny Boy
Lineside Marquis of Burdale (Eng.)
Ch. Barton of Burdale
Ch. Kresent Samuel (Eng.)
Brunel of Mynair (Eng.)
Eng. Am. Ch. Sanbrook Sandpiper
Sanbrook Senator
Ch. Sanbrook Senturian
Anfeald Grundy's Britt
Aust. Ch. Mr. Smith of Burdale

Chart II - D

Ch. Llanipsa Toreador (Eng.)
Westhay Alliance (Eng.)
Ch. Riverina Reunion (Eng.)
Ch. Riverina Tweed (Eng.)
Ch. Riverina Tweedsbairn (Eng.)
Aust. Ch. Riverina Mandarin
Aust. Ch. Siccawei Remus

Chart III

Eng. Ch. Son of Merrijack
Ch. Bengal Bahadur of Harham
Ch. Danhow Farouk
Ch. Talyn's Tom Tom
Ch. Talyn's Man About Town
Ch. Buccaneer Rocky Mount
Aireline Hallmark
Ch. Wraggletaggle Checkmate
Ch. Wraggletaggle Ebenezer
Ch. Dandyaire Cinnabar Gremlin _DAm
Ch. Lay de Ayr Niccodemus
Ch. Benaire Queen's Ransom
Ch. Benaire Courtney's Duet
Ch. Benaire Argus Blackjack
Ch. Argus Checkmate
Ch. Benaire Argus Atlas
Ch. Erowah Command Performance
Ch. Querencia's Bengal Diplomat
Blackheath Exchequer
Ch. Toprock Blackwood
Ch. Glenaird Alister
Ch. Pequod Sea Bird
Ch. Pequod T'Gallant
Ch. Pequod Salt Horse
Ch. Pequod Blackbeard the Pirate
Can. and Am. Ch. Aireline Star Monarch
Ch. Dandyaire Cottage Commando
Blackheath Inquisitor
Ch. Dandyaire Friend Freddy

Chart IV

Ch. Bengal Sabu
> Ch. Bengal Bladud of Harham
>> Eng. Ch. Kresent Brave
>>> Eng. Ch. Bengal Fastnet
>>>> Eng. Ch. Siccawei Ransom
>>>> Eng., Am. Can. Ger. Dutch Ch. Bengal Figaro
>>>>> Ch. Reffal Prince Figaro
>>>>> Eng. Am. Ch. Jokyl Supreme
>>>>> Ch. Wraggletaggle Marksman
>>>>> Eng. Ch. Jokyl Space Leader
>>>>>> Eng. Am. Ch. Jokyl Superior
>>>>>> Eng. Am. Ch. Jokyl Kenlucky Sam
>>>>>> Jokyl Chippinghey Kestrel
>>>>>> Ch. Jokyl Prince Regent
>>>>>>> Ch. Senator of Whitehouse
>>>>>>> Ch. Talyn's Limited Edition
>>>>>> Eng. Am. Ch. Jokyl Superman
>>>>>>> Ch. Lay de Ayr's Wakanda
>>>>>>> Ch. Marydale's Headliner
>>>>>>> Ch. Suzark Open Sesame
>>>>>>> Ch. Harbour Hills Klark Kent
>>>>>>> Ch. Dandyaire Quickfire
>>>>>>> Ch. Jokyl Supermaster
>>>>>>>> Ch. Eden Spring Hepatica
>>>>>>>>> Ch. Eden Sal Sorbus
>>>>>>>>> Ch. Stone Ridge Gingerbredman
>>>>>>>> Ch. Argus Stone Ridge Hunky Dory
>>> Brulyn's Baha-Dur
>>>> Eng. Am. Ch. Optimist of Mynair
>>> Ch. Bengal Flyer
>>>> Ch. Talyn's Yohorum
>>>> Ch. Aristocrat of Whitehouse
>>> Eng. Ch. Bengal Gunga Din
>>>> Ch. Bengal Mowgli
>>>>> Bengal Buldeo
>>>>>> Eng. Ch. Bengal Flamboyant
>>>>>>> Eng. Ch. Siccawei Galliard
>>>>>>> Eng. Am. Ch. Jokyl Spic n' Span   SIRE
>>>>>> Eng. Ch. Jokyl Smart Guy
>>> Ch. Bengal Nevasa
>>> Eng. Sw. Ch. Bengal Brulyn Sahib
>>> Ch. Searchlight Tycoon
> Ch. Querencia's Suerte Brava
>> Ch. Ringtrue Mr. Wonderful
> Ch. Talyn's River Rogue
> Ch. Birchrun Barmaster
>> Ch. Blackburn's Baronof Brutus
> Ch. Buccaneer's Copper Crown
> Ch. Birchrun Bash'em
> Ch. Birchrun Prizefighter

152

Chart V

Ch. Riverina Siccawei Phoebus (Eng.)
Ch. Mayjack Briar (Eng.)
  Ch. Lanewood Lysander
    So. Afr. Ch. Bengal Skipper of Limebell
      Ch. Bengal Leprechaun
        Ch. Jackson's Conquistador
        Ch. Bitmar Bengal Fere of Barbate
      Bengal Leander
        Ch. Bengal Havildar
      Eng. Am. Ch. Jokyl Bengal Lionheart
        Lionheart Ute
          Ch. Lionheart Factor
            Ch. Ironsides' Pek's Bad Boy
              Ch. Ironsides Pacific Station
        Ch. Briardale Charlie Brown
          Ch. Briardale Kung Fu
        Ch. Cyrano Apollo
        Ch. Lionheart Gladwyn
        Ch. Flintkote Jokyl Krackerjack ___ DAM SIDE
      Ch. Winstony Exceptional
        Ch. Coppercrest Rifleman
        Ch. Coppercrest Ramrod
        Ch. Sierradale Warbow
      Ch. Kresent Golden Boy
        Ch. Kresent Red Ribbons
        Reffal All American
          Ch. Reffal Gallant Guy

Ch. Dandyaire Cinnabar Garm, BB at the 1965 Pacific Northwest Specialty.
Roberts

153

Ch. Wait N' See of Jokyl.

Roslin-Williams

6

The Airedale in
Great Britain

THERE ARE two modern English books on the
Airedale, both of which name most of the successful breeders of this
and earlier eras, and there is no need for duplicating such information
here, except where it applies particularly to American Airedales, or
where it concerns a later period than covered in *The Airedale Terrier*
(1948), by J. L. Ethel Aspinall, and *Airedales* (1950), by Aylwin
Bowen.

Male Lines

From 1901 to 1958 only 341 Airedales (164 dogs and 177 bitches)
have won the title of champion in England. The war years (1915-1919
and 1938-1945) prevented the holding of championship shows, so cut
down materially on the total, just as they did the hopes for the title of
the dogs left with one or two c.c.s when the restrictions went into effect. Modern English champions are preponderately of the Int. Ch.
Clee Courtier branch of the Warland Whatnot line from Ditto, just as
in the United States, but are divided almost equally between Walnut
King Nobbler and Ch. Matador Mandarin.

The *Mandarin* line has already been traced down through Can. Ch.
Murraysgate Monty and Berrycroft Atoppa in Chapter 3, but here it
develops other branches. The main one is that of Atoppa's grandson
Ch. Rural Wyrewood Apollo, a good winner sired by Solo Aristocrat

and himself a sire of several champions in other countries as well as in England. His most noted son is *Ch. Riverina Siccawei Phoebus,* but he sired others of outstanding quality including Ch. Collipriest Stormer, Ch. Searchlight Defiance, and Cont. Ch. Searchlight Sequence. Two untitled sons of note are Rural Paladin of Joreen, sire of Ch. Bengal Newydd Bonny Boy (sire of Am. Ch. Bengal Bazar of Harham); and Tregarthen Happy Lad, sire of Am. Ch. Tregarthen Falcon. Several champion daughters of Apollo are carrying on as producers, too; two that upheld the family honor in early postwar shows were Ch. Phoebe of Joreen and Ch. Penelope of Joreen, litter sisters.

Following World War II, Apollo was the second Airedale dog to become a champion—Holmbury Bandit being the first. In bitches Foxdenton Topscore was first—and was the only Airedale champion made in the first year after championship shows were resumed.

Another Atoppa line already mentioned as contributing to American Airedales is that of *Eng. and Am. Ch. Murose Replica,* sired by another Atoppa son, Ch. Holmbury Bandit. Replica sired no male champions in England, but his son *Tycroit Hilsam Highnote* sired two, and Replica's daughters Wonder of Joreen and Carol of Joreen each produced two champions. Riverina Vogue, dam of the leading bitch c.c. winner, Ch. Riverina Encore, is also by Replica. In fact Replica's name appears with increasing frequency in the distaff side of pedigrees both here and in England. Highnote's sons, Ch. Tycroit Tosca and Ch. Tycroit Tulyar, were both exported to the Continent, with Tulyar winning the *Siegerklasse* at the 1956 Dortmund show in Germany where Cont. and Eng. Ch. Tycroit Glenbina was *Weltsieger* (world champion) in an entry of 98 Airedales. A litter brother of Tulyar, Tycroit Toreador, remained in England to carry on the line. Another Bandit son was Ch. Chip of Lancooross, sire of a number of champions, including Searchlight Pride of Gwen.

Going back to Atoppa's sire, Ch. *Wolstanton Bostock,* we find another of his dynasty who founded a strong branch. This line starts with the Bostock son, Chathall Wolstan, who sired Chathall Newsboy, in turn the sire of the very influential Ch. *Murraysgate Minstrel,* runner-up for Best in Show at Edinburgh in 1948 but best remembered now as a sire, having nine English champions to his credit as well as a Swedish champion. Two of these were litter brothers, Rob Roy of Joreen and Hamish of Joreen, while Cardinal of Joreen was exported to France. Southkirk Monarch is another of Bostock's champion sons, and he sired Ch. Gosmore Attack, a dog subsequently sold to Germany where he lived up to his name as a police dog, passing all tests with honors. A son of Attack is Ch. Gosmore Talked About, a Crufts winner and sire of a Swedish champion.

A strong Minstrel line is that which produced Ch. Tycroit Tempo.

Tycroit Hilsam Highnote.

Ch. Tycroit Tempo.

Ch. Riverina Encore.

Ch. Braknight Riverina Garnet.

157

This line starts with the Minstrel son Ch. Murraysgate Maestro, who sired the littermates Tycroit Tomkins (sire of Tempo) and Ch. Tycroit Tinkabell. A very famous daughter of Minstrel is Ch. Mellish Melody.

Two lines from *Walnut King Nobbler,* distinct from those so familiar in the United States, have contributed greatly to the roster of English winners. One of these Nobbler branches is that of *Ch. Llanipsa Toreador,* whose son Westhay Alliance sired Ch. Riverina Reunion, a noted winner and sire of winners whose progeny is breeding on with great success. The dam of Westhay Alliance was a granddaughter of Walnut King Nobbler, as was also Reunion's granddam, since she was by Toreador. Another sizzler of the line is Reunion's son, Ch. Riverina Tweed. The Atoppa lines also are represented here, as Tweed's dam is Riverina Vogue by Replica, and Vogue's dam (Tridwr Milady) was by Atoppa. Another Reunion line is that of Siccawei Jester, sire of Siccawei Marquis. The latter's son, Krescent Mariner, unfortunately died shortly after winning Best in Show at Bath. He had sired one litter, however, and two puppies from this lot seem destined to carry on the line: Kresent Consolation and Kresent Caress. Reunion is another dog whose value is seen in the produce of his daughters and granddaughters, as will be shown in delineating the family of Ch. Riverina Bewitched a little later.

Among present winners in England, the longest and most multi-branched line from Walnut King Nobbler is that having its start through his son *Turkish Western Guard,* whose son Turkish Western Dictator sired Talena Majestic, a victim of the wartime blackout on championship shows. However, at the resumption of such shows after the war, seven out of the eight c.c.s won the first year (1946) were awarded to dogs and bitches sired by Majestic. Two litter mates, Talena Britannia and *Brineland Bonny Boy,* were major winners in that first year—Britannia becoming the first postwar international Airedale champion by qualifying in Ireland also. Bonny Boy, a great success as a sire, had been sold immediately after winning his second c.c., but in his new home quickly became a Continental champion. Bonny Boy's dam traced to Ch. Waycon Aristocrat and Ch. Aislaby Aethling in the second generation, and the dam of Majestic, Princess Catherine, was by Bostock out of a daughter of Aristocrat. Bonny Boy sired *Lineside Marquis of Burdale,* sire of five champions. Of the dogs, *Ch. Barton of Burdale* is undoubtedly the best-known—a great show dog who toppled from their thrones such kings as Replica and Wyldboy. Barton sired three champions: Kresent Sincerity, Hamish of Glenbeth, and Kresent Samuel, the latter a Best in Show winner. Highfield Brian, by Barton, sired Sanbrook Senator, sire of Ch. Sanbrook Sandpiper.

Two other champion sons of Marquis are Haldys Field Marshall and Bertram of Burdale. Another dog by Marquis, Boris of Burdale,

Ch. Barton of Burdale.

Ch. Sanbrook Sandpiper.

Barclay of Burdale (at one year of age).

159

sired Ch. Radcliffe Celebrity. Eng. and Cont. Ch. Tycroit Glenbina, one of Marquis' daughters, however, has earned the most fame. She won the "World Title" at the huge Dortmund show already mentioned, beating 300 other Terriers in the Group. Glenbina was best Airedale every time exhibited in Holland, and had won Best of Breed at Crufts shortly before being exported.

Going back again to *Talena Majestic* we encounter another champion son, Siccawei Wizard, and an international champion, Talena Statesman, sire of Ch. Bamfylde Knight. Knight's dam, Springtime Enchantress, is by Westhay Alliance, sire of Ch. Riverina Reunion. Knight is another destined to be remembered through his daughters, the 1956 Ch. Quayton Cherie being out of Ch. Quayton Adorable, who was sired by Knight, and the granddam of Ch. Tycroit Tosca was also by Knight.

Bitch Lines

There have been many influential bitch lines—such as the family founded by Mrs. Plant's *Ch. Little Varmint,* which produced the Wolstanton champions Duchess and Superb, and Duchess' daughters, Ballet Girl, Peach, and Belle. This family also produced other "Wolstantons" of international fame, such as Ch. W. Flush, Ch. W. Ideal, Ch. W. Pam, and the great sire Ch. W. Bostock. Besides these there were certificate winners exported before gaining their English titles, and other bitches from the family that were sold by Mrs. Plant and that produced champions for other breeders.

The most fabulously successful family at present is that founded by *Tridwr Milady,* foundation bitch of the Riverina Kennels of Miss Mc-Caughey and Mrs. Schuth. Tridwr Milady, a daughter of Berrycroft Atoppa, founded two strong branches through her daughters by Replica: *Riverina Vogue* and *Ch. Riverina Bewitched.* The former produced Ch. Riverina Encore, a beautiful Airedale who collected twelve certificates before she was retired. Encore was sired by Ch. Riverina Reunion, and her younger brother Riverina Tweed was one of 1957's first champions. Bewitched, mentioned earlier in this chapter, produced Ch. Riverina Dryad (by Phoebus) and her sister Ch. Riverina Diana of Siccawei; Ch. Braknight Riverina Garnet (by Siccawei Jester, who was by Reunion); and *Ch. Riverina Westhay Flayre* (by Apollo), dam of Eng. and Am. Ch. Westhay Fiona of Harham, sired by Jamus. Still another daughter of Bewitched is Riverina Galena (by Riverina Yorik).

The Murraysgates, already touched upon in reference to two different sire lines, are tied together by a strong family strain. Mr. Kerr rarely keeps more than three adult bitches at a time, and these trace in tail-female to *Murraysgate Merry Mascot,* foundation bitch of the ken-

Ch. Murraysgate Minstrel (Chathall Newsboy ex Murraysgate Winniedale).

Tithebarn Tycroit Tandit

161

nel. Mated to Warland Warboy, she produced *Murraysgate Merriment* and *Chathall Miranda*. Miranda was the dam of Ch. Chathall Caliban, while Merriment produced Can. Ch. Murraysgate Monty (by Waycon Designer) a dog that founded a highly successful line, as shown in Chapter 3; and Ch. Murraysgate Mustang (by Chathall Newsboy). Since this branch has wound up in the sire line department, we will now refer back to Merry Mascot again. Bred to Waithland's Warlock (another who did not attain his championship because of the war) Merry Mascot produced the South African Ch. Murraysgate Merriboy and the fine brood matron *Murraysgate Winniedale*. Warlock was by Int. Ch. Shelterock Merry Sovereign, as was also Merry Mascot. The many "Merries" of today trace in the main to this source. This family is also dealt with briefly under the Warland Sprite tail-female line in Chapter 4, and shows further branches. Winniedale, through her progeny, is one of the most influential of matrons. Bred to Chathall Newsboy, she produced Ch. Murraysgate Minstrel, whose accomplishments—on the sire line basis—already have been recounted. However, this left out his daughters, the Champions Tycroit Caprice of Joreen, Mellish Melanie, Mellish Melody, and Lass-o-the Man. The latter is tied in through another line from Winniedale also, her dam being Murraysgate Waydonna (ex Winniedale). The two branches again meet in Southkirk Monarch, for he is a son of Lass. Waydonna was a litter sister of the ill-fated Merrijack, a dog that met an untimely death but did found the strong Merrijak (no "c") line through his son in the United States. Ch. Murraysgate Merrijoe is another from Winniedale, and sired by Merry Mascot's son Bring Luck (by Warboy).

The foundation of Miss A. M. Jenkinson's Tycroit Kennels was *Ch. Tycroit Caprice of Joreen*, sired by Minstrel. Her dam was Wonder of Joreen, by Replica ex Ch. Penelope of Joreen (by Apollo). Bred to Ch. Murraysgate Maestro, Caprice produced Ch. Tycroit Tinkabell and Tycroit Tomkins (sire of Ch. Tycroit Tempo). Bred to the Replica son Tycroit Hilsam Highnote, she produced Ch. Tycroit Tulyar and Toreador and the brood matron Tearose. Highnote's dam is a Minstrel daughter sired by Merriboy. Another good producer from the Tycroit Kennels was Tycroit Treble, whose dam, Tycroit Tenderness was a litter sister of the Weycroft champions, Wyldboy, Wondrous, and Wishful. Treble (by Highnote) was the dam of the handsome Ch. Tycroit Tempo, biggest winner of his day. Since Tempo was by Caprice's son Tomkins, this united the two families. Another producer was Coronation Princess, whose sire, Ch. Cardinal of Joreen, was a litter brother of Caprice. Princess' dam brings in the Talena Statesman and Apollo lines, and another generation back in direct tail female line is found Westhay Alliance, sire of Onyx of Joreen, whose daughter Ch. Phoebe of Joreen is the granddam of Princess—the connecting link being Gay of Joreen. Princess was the dam of Ch. Tycroit Tosca. Onyx, as the dam of Phoebe's sister Penelope, was also greatgranddam of Caprice.

So far as the bitch line is concerned, the Siccawei Kennels of Mrs. C. M. Halford were founded by *Llanipsa Peach of Siccawei.* Peach was a daughter of Ch. Aislaby Aethling and Eng. and Am. Ch. Llanipsa Princess Pam, who was sired by Walnut King Nobbler. However, the first bitch actually was Tsarina of Siccawei, a granddaughter of Brownfield Brigand, but as she died after whelping, leaving only one puppy—Siccawei Singleton King—the tail female family ends abruptly there. Nevertheless, Tsarina does figure in the present family line of the Siccaweis, for her son King, when mated to Peach, sired *Siccawei Patrician,* now foundation of the homebred line. This combination also produced Am. and Eng. Ch. Rural Rhapsody, while Peach in addition produced the good sire Rural Defiance, whose sire was Ch. Monarch of Wyndhurst, by Cotteridge Brigand.

Patrician's daughter, Siccawei Psyche (by Turkish Western Dictator), produced Siccawei Preses when bred to Defiance, thus doubling up the original bloodlines. Preses was the dam of Ch. Siccawei Wizard, by Talena Majestic, and Wizard's name can be found in the pedigrees of such winners as Ch. Kresent Sincerity, Ch. Kresent Samson, Ch. Acter of Mynair, Ch. Riverina Celebrity, Ch. Alexia of Yellowhills, and Kresent Mariner. A daughter of Preses was Ch. Siccawei Zarina, by Apollo, and she became the dam of another good sire, Siccawei Jester (by Reunion). Siccawei Marquis, sire of Kresent Mariner, was by Jester out of Siccawei Iolanthe, a daughter of Preses by Reunion.

Ch. Siccawei Ideal was by Reunion out of Preses, and Ch. Riverina Siccawei Phoebus, already referred to in the sire line section, was a son of Ideal. Zarina also contributed to the list of winning Airedales, mainly through her son Siccawei Jester, who sired Riverina Yorik, sire of the sensational bitch Ch. Braknight Riverina Garnet and her full sister Riverina Galena. The direct line from Zarina, however, is continued through her daughter, the obedience-trained Ch. Siccawei Olympic. Another Siccawei bitch, Wyrewood Siccawei Pictorial (ex Patrician), was the dam of the famous Apollo as well as Ch. Wyrewood Aristocratic of Harham, a dog whose line in America came down through Ch. Aireline Apollo II and Harham's Beaming Boy. The latter sired Ch. Sundown Serenade, a fine winner and producer in the United States already mentioned in the section on American tail-female families under that of Lionheart Comet. The great sire Am. Ch. Squire of Siccawei was, of course, Siccawei-bred throughout, being the tail-male line of Rural Defiance (ex Peach of Siccawei) and tail

163

Ch. Siccawei Ideal.

Ch. Riverina Diana of Siccawei.

Siccawei Singleton King.

female to Siccawei Patrician, going back to both foundation bitches—Peach and Tsarina.

The Joreen bitches of Mrs. Coghlan are featured in the distaff side of many champions and sires, and served as the foundation of many strains, the Tycroits being one notable example. The Joreen sires also contributed to Airedale excellence, and Mrs. Coghlan bred seven champions in all. Although *Riverina Encore* holds the record for c.c.s won by an Airedale bitch, it is *Int. Ch. Tycroit Glenbina* who holds the world's record—fourteen c.c.s in a row, in Britain, Holland, Belgium, France, and Germany. Her titles include International Champion, British and Dutch, and *Weltsiegerin* (World Champion) won in 1956 and 1957. Glenbina, although of the Tycroit prefix and by a Burdale sire (Lineside Marquis of Burdale), was out of Carol of Joreen. Carol had a champion in each of her two litters, the second being Hamish of Glenbeth, by Barton of Burdale, and these were bred by J. Speed. Another that was Joreen in tail female was Motto's Maid Marian (dam of the police-trained Ch. Gosmore Attack), her great-granddam being Jane of Joreen. Onyx of Joreen, prominent in the background of the "Tycroits," was the dam of the South African Ch. Poseidon of Joreen and the fine sire Rural Paladin of Joreen, as well as the champion bitches Phoebe and Penelope.

Outstanding Kennels to Mid-Century

Lineside Marquis of Burdale, by Cont. Ch. Brineland Bonnie Boy, was the "father" of the Burdales of Miss E. M. Jones. Marquis, of course, was the sire of Ch. Barton of Burdale, whose Best in Show win at the National Terrier championship event made headline news, since Miss Jones at that time was a novice—and so was Barton. Miss Jones was the first amateur in sixteen years to make an Airedale dog a champion. Marquis earned his claim to fame in Barton and Glenbina alone, and was certain proof of Miss Jones' "eye" for an Airedale.

The great Clonmel Kennel of Holland Buckley continued to contribute to Airedale improvement as late as the 1930s, with the majority of today's winners in all countries tracing to Clonmel Monarque, a grandson of Ditto. Sam Bamford's Walnut line, Major J. H. Wright with his Holmbury prefix, George Oliver's Brownfields, the Cragsman strain of E. T. Tree, the Warlands of J. P. Hall, and the Waycons of J. Lang are familiar to anyone studying modern pedigrees. A. J. Edwards' Towyn prefix was another that was well known, although his most famous dog was Ch. Mespot Tinker. The Stockfield prefix of E. Grice is another that appears frequently in famous sire lines and families, with Aristocrat probably the best known of his dogs. Stockfield Nina is one of the few West Coast imports to live on in today's pedigrees, and this she does through the Comet line bitches of Lionheart fame, this family again tying in with the Stockfields through the Ridgemoor Sweetberry family of Royalty's dam.

Others of special note are the Berrycrofts of Jean Hopwood, the Rural Kennels of Mrs. Anna Care, and the Raimons of Nan Haslam. William Burrow, the well-known judge, was the breeder of Ch. Newsgirl Charming, while Leo Wilson, editor of *Dog World* (England), owned Leader Writer, maternal grandsire of Ch. Squire of Siccawei. The Flornell Terriers of Jim Parkington have also been featured through the years. In Scotland, the Murraysgate Kennels of Mr. Kerr maintained a high standard of excellence, and for many years the Glenmavis prefix of J. Williamson was very well known, the representative in the United States being the beautiful Eng. and Am. Ch. Glenmavis Solitaire. Tom Brampton is probably better known as a successful handler than as an exhibitor, but his is the Weycroft prefix that adorned quite a few famous Airedales, including the noted Wyldboy. The Quayton Airedales of W. F. Quick have also won high honors, with Cherie the 1956 title holder.

Although Llanipsa, the prefix of Mrs. Ethel Aspinall, is no longer in the news, many a dog with this prefix can be found in the best pedigrees. The Of the Edge Airedales also had a good run for a period, and are represented in the United States primarily via the Lamorna Kennels of Canada, the big winner Ch. Protector of the Edge being a leading sire there. The Ardross Kennel was a very big establishment and, in addition to the kennel itself, operated a training school for kennel maids. Ardross was the kennel of Mrs. Beamish-Levey, but was disbanded when Mrs. Beamish-Levey moved to France, though she still has some Airedales. Many Ardross dogs can be found in pedigrees of our Airedales, when traced back far enough.

The Tregarthen prefix of Mr. and Mrs. Garth Fowell is now familiar in America through the successes of Ch. Tregarthen Falcon; and the Tullochards of James Hardie are especially noted by students of pedigrees, with Ch. Squire of Siccawei having a Tullochard sire. Mrs. E. Halliday, breeder of the Bamfylde Airedales, had the rare thrill of bringing a seven-year-old dog out of retirement to win the largest Airedale specialty in years, when her Ch. Bamfylde Knight was chosen best at the National Airedale Terrier Association show in an entry of 112 dogs. The Searchlights of Mrs. M. F. Kington are as well known on the Continent as in England, having champions in both places. Mr. R. G. Bradley's Matador prefix is another well known in several countries, having lines in America from Mandarin and from Supreme, and a many-branched line in England from Mandarin, to which many Continental winners also trace.

Mr. and Mrs. George Dallison's Gosmore Kennels were originally all-Airedale but now contain top specimens of many breeds. Fred

166

Chatterton had a successful run with his Airedales, these being the Chathalls; his most noted bitch was Ch. Chathall News, sister of the famous Ridgemoor Sweetberry; and his Chathall Newsboy was an outstanding sire. The Aislaby Kennel of Col. and Mrs. Hayes produced some of the most influential dogs of their period, Ch. Aislaby Aethling, sire of six English champions, being one of them. Lawmer represents the Airedales of William Cookson, and the name of Lawmer Brigand is found in the pedigrees of a good proportion of modern Airedales. Doctor Bently owned the Covert prefix, one eminently respected by competitors of the beautiful Ch. Covert Dazzle—later the dam of the immortal Eng. and Am. Ch. Shelterock Merry Sovereign.

Among the many Airedalers who became noted judges is Tom Scott, whose "Cotteridge" prefix graces that eminent sire, Tri. Int. Ch. Cotteridge Brigand. The Collipriest Kennels of Mrs. William Pincott, though small, have contributed to some of the most noted lines, with Ch. Collipriest Stormer an outstanding sire. Mr. Probert's Radcliffe Kennels produced the 1956 champion Radcliffe Celebrity. And Mrs. I. E. Marshal, of the Sanbrook prefix, is one of the very successful breeders, with Ch. Sanbrook Sandpiper being an outstanding winner and Sinders following right on his heels for show honors.

Back in the late 1920s, the Moorhead Kennels of R. C. S. Wade were prominent, with Moorhead Marquis the premier sire. Another kennel dating back to the early days of the Airedale is that of J. E. Watson, whose Brineland stud dogs have had a great influence in the breed.

A prefix with Indian connotations is that of Mollie Harmsworth's Bengal Airedales. The litter brothers Bengali and Bahadur were both exported, the former to Sweden and the latter to America, and both made history in their new homes. Another export is Am. Ch. Bengal Bazar of Harham, who also had a good record. The Pottery Kennels of Harry Seabridge have produced many winners, one of this breeding being the Am. Ch. Cactus, a dog that gained fame for his fighting prowess against varied antagonists. The Thelwyn Kennels of C. Dew have sent some noteworthy exports to this country, mainly to the Harham Kennels, but should be mentioned especially for having housed Solo Aristocrat, sire of Ch. Rural Wyrewood Apollo, founder of a very strong line.

Breed Clubs

There are several breed clubs in the British Isles, the oldest being the Midland Counties Airedale Terrier Club in Birmingham, founded in 1907. The National Airedale Terrier Association could almost be called the Parent Club, as its purpose is to serve all areas as much as possible. To this end a newsletter was inaugurated in 1956, and since the newsletter was first published, membership in this club has increased 500%, with members from such far-away places as America, Australia, Denmark, Germany, Holland, India, Japan, Union of South Africa, Southern Rhodesia, Switzerland, and Sweden.

The North of England Airedale Terrier Club is another old one, with headquarters at Birmingham. The South of England Airedale Terrier Club (London) was founded in 1935, and was named after the club founded by Holland Buckley and his partner, Royston Mills. The newest club is the West of England and South Wales Airedale Terrier Club, and other clubs are in Ireland and Scotland. In fact the Ulster, Ireland, club is one of oldest, having been founded in 1910.

British Activity Since 1960

Since many of the Airedales mentioned earlier in this chapter are also included in the background of American lines, it seemed best to make reference to the greats of yesteryear, even though they are now so far back in pedigrees as to be "off the paper" in many instances.

The interesting part is the way they have bred on—almost a case of "the rich get richer" or at least the best get better. True, many of the famous prefixes are no longer seen due to the death or inactivity of their owners, yet the presence of those prefixes in the pedigrees of modern winners proves that, like "old soldiers," they never really die. But unlike the old soldiers of General MacArthur's famous quote, they do not even "fade away." The magic worked by those English breeders is still with us, whether they are living or not, and England remains the prime source from which breeders of all countries continually obtain or refresh their breeding stock.

For the last couple of decades it has been the Bengal Airedales of Mrs. Mollie Harmsworth that have been setting the style and the pace. One of her advertisements stated "Study the pedigrees of the top winners: there are not many that do not include the Bengal breeding lines." And that's the truth, *wherever* you are—especially in America at this time.

It is interesting to look back in the earlier reference to the Bengal Airedales and see that they were merely touched on, taking up only four sentences. A similar irony is seen in casually mentioning the breed in Australia in only one sentence! Now, as will be seen later, it is hard to cram all the "down under" information into a whole chapter.

Even when the first edition of this book was written the Bengal Airedales were making their presence known. Ch. Bengal Kresent Duchess in eight months during 1958 won six c.c.s and 4 reserves; ten Bests in Show, and was Best Terrier nineteen times. She was sold to Harold Florsheim that same year and the same advertisement that told of Duchess also mentions the "dog puppy, Bengal Sabu" was shortly

Ch. Bengal Leprechaun, owned by J.R.T. Alford and handled by Tom Gately, was another successful import of the 1960s. He is shown here in a Best in Show win under Alva Rosenberg. *Shafer*

Ch. Siccawei Galliard, owned by Olive and George Jackson and bred by Clare Halford, has sired many of the best British Airedales of today. One of his sons is Walter Troutman's Ch. Turith Adonis, a multiple Specialty and Group winner and BB at the 1978 Westminster show. *Anne Roslin-Williams*

169

to be shown and used at stud. Little did anyone foresee then what a revolution that "puppy" was to cause, bringing the name Bengal more fame than the original province's famous tigers.

As to Duchess, she produced four champions, among them Ch. Querencia's Bengal Diplomat (4 champions), and won the New York Specialty twice. Sabu came over the next year, and started his clean-up campaign at the shows and his revisions of popular sire lines in 1960. Duchess was bred by Mr. and Mrs. Tom Hodgkinson, whose Kresent strain was already well established, but Sabu was Bengal-bred though both were by the same sire. Several Bengals were originally Kresent with the Bengal prefix added later, just as many Jokyl and other lines start out as Bengal only to add thier own prefix when obtained by new owners.

The Jokyl Airedales, owned and bred by George and Olive Jackson, came into their own in this same period. One need only look at the pedigrees of current top dogs to see the influence of the Jokyl breeding program. Mr. Jackson bred *Ch Mayjack Briar,* sire of *Ch. Lanewood Lysander,* and started quite a ball rolling, right there. However it is through the combination of several other noteworthy lines as well—especially the nick with *Sabu* descendants—that this successful strain evolved. Ch. Jokyl Smart Guy is the present No. 1 Jokyl, with 19 c.c.s, 15 BB and a Group first.

Siccawei, mentioned earlier was the third of the three main lines since 1950, and in fact this kennel pre-dated that period. Many great ones have come from this kennel, not the least of which was *Ch. Riverina Siccawei Phoebus,* mentioned among the prominent sire-lines. One of the younger dogs of this prefix is Aust. Ch. Siccawei Remus (15 champions) and another "Down Under" resident is Aust. Ch. Chancellor of Siccawei (16 champions).

Contributing to the winning ways of Airedales of the 1960s and 1970s was the Suliston line bred by Mr. Derrick, (the dam of Superman is of this family); and the Chippinghey family from Briar Rose. The Chippingheys, bred by Mrs. Monica Gibbons, are said to be well known for their performance in working trials, at least originally.

The Tanworth line is another which started in the 1950s, and owned by John and Barbara Holland. An excellent example of this breeding is Mr. and Mrs. Worthington's Am. and Can. Ch. Avaricious of Tanworth, BB at both Westminster and the New York Specialty. Only Me of Tanworth is a Best in Show winner in England. Can. Ch. Kerworth Chagren of Tanworth and Can Ch. Kerworth Keswick of Tanworth are also owned by Mr. and Mrs. R. Worthington.

Arthur Lodge, who judged the Australian Centenary Airedale Specialty in 1976, owns the Mynair prefix, the best known dog being Eng., Can. and Am. Ch. Optimist of Mynair, Top Terrier in England in

1970, winning nine Bests in Show including the National Terrier Show. Although this last might be compared with a Group win, to top the lot in the home of Terriers is quite a feat.

The Loudwell Kennels are comparatively new, yet this prefix is found in several imports of recent years. Ch. Loudwell Kommando and Ch. Loudwell Folly provided their owner, Mrs. Jean Campbell, the unique experience of winning both c.c.s at the Leeds championship show in 1965.

Ch. Bengal Kresent Brave.

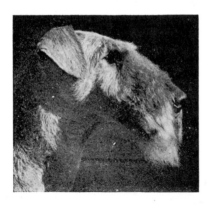

Ch. Riverina Tweedsbairn, a BIS winner at Crufts.

English, Swedish, Danish Ch. Bengal Bengali (Sweden).

Ch. Southkirk Monarch (left) Ch. Gosmore Attack.

172

7

The Airedale in Foreign Lands

THE FIRST Airedale sent to Sweden was from England and took part in a show in Stockholm in 1894. For several years progress was comparatively slow, but from 1920 until about 1940 the breed developed rapidly in Sweden as the result of the importation of German and English Airedales.

Up to the early 1940s, Airedales belonged to the Swedish Working Dog Club, and a number were well known for their outstanding working ability. In 1923-24 an Airedale by the name of Ragg, owned by O. Björklund, proved to be a very successful working dog, especially as a guard and messenger, becoming so adept at the work that a book was written about him. Vinland Vixen, owned by Mr. Sundquist, was another good working dog that also excelled in messenger work. Many Airedales showed exceptional talent for the work, but breeders who stressed show points rather than working qualities won out, and in 1943, Airedales withdrew from the Working Club. However, they can still gain army certificates, and nowadays Swedish Airedales are listed in the so-called *National Book of Breed,* which means that Airedales are considered useful for military service and can be entered in open competition with other working dogs.

The Swedish methods of judging differ from those in England and the United States, and there are only fifteen shows a year in Sweden, of which three are international. In the latter, a dog may win an International Certificate, known as a CACIB, but only on the presumption that he is of high international class. To become a champion, a dog must win three certificates (of which at least one must be in a Swedish Kennel Club show) and under different judges, with an interval of at least twelve months between the first and third certificates. Up to 1952 Airedales also had to pass a special trial of character before they could gain the title of champion, but since then it has been the responsibility of the judge to test temperament in the ring.

Mrs. Richardis Sörvik and her daughter Mrs. Aase Cornéer maintain the Roederich Kennel from which many champions have come. They have imported many of England's best, including Ch. Aislaby Bertric and Ch. Trottens Trubadur. The latter is one of the foundation sires of the breed in Sweden. Mrs. Carin Lindhé of the Mountebank Kennel also imported several dogs, among them Norwegian Ch. Billy Boy and Warland Tobasco, with the American-breds Shelterock Man o' War and Eleanore's Lucky Star augmenting the list. Mrs. Lindhé is an international judge and has officated in the United States on a number of occasions.

A few years ago the Trotten Kennel of Gunnar Arvidssen contained many top dogs, including the excellent stud Ch. Trottens Trots Allt, sire of the famous Ch. Burrens Black Baal, bred by Mrs. Anna Bergman and subsequently owned in Norway. Another sire in the Arvidssen Kennels was the imported Turkish Chieftan.

Emil Nilsson is another successful breeder, and one of twenty-five years' standing. His prefix is Önsvala. His Danish bitch Ch. Fureö Cilla has been an outstanding brood matron and his Ch. Önsvala Björn is a well-known stud dog.

Mr. and Mrs. Carl-Olof Jungfeldt, of the Jungfältets Kennels, have had a number of Airedales which were imported from England. The most famous of their imports was Eng. Ch. Bengal Bengali (brother of Bahadur). He quickly acquired Danish and Swedish titles also; although the Jungfeldts had the misfortune to lose him after he had been there only a year. He had shown great promise as a sire, and in one litter by him were five Airedales that won certificates. Another English dog Ch. Aislaby Magnus, sired Ch. Jungfältets Jolante (ex Ch. Gosmore Mellish Marigold) as well as many other champions. Talked Again of Joreen, a son of Ch. Gosmore Talked About, also became a champion.

Mrs. Ulla Thimander of the Memphis prefix bred two champions in the same litter, these being by Magnus and out of her imported bitch Ch. Riverina Remember.

The foregoing paragraphs on Airedales in Sweden have been left as they were, since no new information has been received from that country, and at least this serves to show the background of current

Airedales there although of course not indicating any new trend due to new importations. However, the winner of the Airedale Centenary show in England was a bitch being purchased by Stig Ahlberg of Sweden. This is Ch. Drakehall Dinah, bred by her handler Ernie Sharpe, and she won over an entry of 144 dogs, the largest entry ever (except Australia's Victoria Centenary) for the breed.

Two Swedish kennels advertised in the 1977 *Our Dogs* Annual, and they picture two magnificent Airedales. One is Int. and Nord. Ch. Tanwood Not In A Million (Eng., Swed., and Norw. Ch. Bengal Mogul ex Int. and Nord. Ch. Gay Gordon's Babycham), owned by the Gay Gordon's kennels (Mrs. Ingela Nilsson). Not In A Million was the top winning Terrier in Scandinavia in 1975. The other is also by Mogul and is Swed. and Nord. Ch. Pintos Polyglott. The kennel name is Pinto and the owners are Mrs. Pia Lundberg and Mrs. Ruth Rudenholt. So again the Bengal Airedales dominate the scene, for Ch. Drakehall Dinah too has that blood, for her sire, Eng. Ch. Siccawei Galliard, is by Eng. Ch. Bengal Flamboyant. Unfortunately I do not have the rest of her pedigree in order to check on further "relativity."

Denmark

In Denmark the first Airedales were imported in 1923, but the real start did not take place until 1926, when Captain Emil Soya-Jensen, of the Fureso Kennels, imported Airedales from England, including some of the famous Cragsman strain. In the ensuing years, stock sired by Ch. Fureso Björn and his litter brother Ch. Fureso Bum won consistently. A few years later Mrs. Helga Wunsch of the Solbakken Kennel imported some of the Wolstanton bitches as well as some from the Lawmer Kennels, and until World War II these two kennels did most of the winning in Denmark. During this period, Captain Soya-Jensen strengthened his kennel by importing several dogs and bitches from the Ileene and Of the Edge Kennels, among them being the beautiful Quality of the Edge. He also imported the great Brownfield Brigand, sire of six English champions.

After the war it became necessary to replenish the stock of both kennels, which Mrs. Wunsch did with the best blood she could obtain from Sweden's Roederich Kennels and from Norway; Captain Soya-Jensen imported Airedales from England, with the well-known Joreen, Gosmore, and Rural Kennels being well represented. At present two newer kennels are adding interest to the competition. They are the Jullinsehöi Kennels of Mrs. Kiaer Nielsen and the Sitka Kennels of Mrs. Biothe Bach, a daughter of Mrs. Wunsch. Notable winners in Denmark have been Ch. Solbakken's Catalina, Ch. Solbakken's Carissima, Ch. Jyllinsehöi Flot, Ch. Toreador of Joreen, and Rural Happy Wanderer.

Holland

In Holland the Airedale is one of the most popular dogs, and among the prominent breeders are C. Mutsaerts, G. H. Overdiep, and Peter Spierenburg. One of Mr. Mutsaerts' earlier stud dogs was Ch. Llanipsa Paladin, a fine sire who produced a dog that attained the score of 297 in working trials—the best ever acquired in Holland in police training. Mr. Overdiep has imported several Searchlight Airedales, all of which became Continental champions—among them Searchlight Maid Marian and Searchlight Sequence, a son of Ch. Rural Wyrewood Apollo and Ch. Searchlight Pride of Gwen. Two notable Airedales owned by Mr. Spierenburg were Ch. Tycroit Tulyar and Ch. Tycroit Glenbina, both of which won the title of *Weltsieger* at the 1956 Dortmund World Show in Germany.

Switzerland

Airedales are to be seen everywhere in Switzerland, but not until 1957 was a club formed in their interest. Otto Haefelin is the guiding spirit of the organization and is especially interested in the Airedale as a worker. He imported Ch. Tycroit Tosca and Jocular of Siccawei, as well as Gosmore Diamond, who passed the third test of the Police-Guard Dog Trials, obtaining the maximum points in seeking the "criminal" after tracking for two miles over rough country. Another breeder intensely interested in using the Airedale for this work is Hugo Zingg.

Germany

In Germany the Airedale is the most popular Terrier breed, and the very active *Klub für Terrier* has a membership of more than 3,000, with the magazine *Der Terrier* its official organ. Breed surveys are held regularly in order to ensure that dogs are in good condition both physically and temperamentally. Breeding regulations are very strict, with close inbreeding not permitted. An Airedale "specialist" comes to the breeder's kennel three to five days after a litter is whelped and checks each pup thoroughly, permitting the breeder to keep only those he believes to be best; all the others are destroyed at once.

Shows in Germany have heavy entries in Airedale classes, with few professional handlers. Not only are most dogs owner-shown, but most are also owner-trimmed and -trained. Because the dogs are usually guard-trained, judges do not object to aggressiveness in the ring. Continental dogs are taught to attack and are expected to do so. German judges dictate their critiques to a secretary, who accompanies them in the ring, and the reports giving good and bad points of each dog are published in *Der Terrier*. At the World Show in Dortmund the title of *Weltsieger* (World Champion) is awarded in both sexes. The title *Klub-Leistungs-Sieger* is awarded the highest-scoring guard-trained dog, whose rating is indicated by the abbreviation *Sch* followed by I,

Ch. Tycroit Glenbina.

A team of Airedales at a show in Amsterdam Holland.

Ch. M. Bengal Brownfield Briar (France).

177

Ezza v.d. Klappergasse, Sch. H III, a German Airedale owned and trained by Marga Swoboda. In the top photo she is shown taking a jump from the top of a nine-foot wall and in the lower photo she sails through double hoops held out by her owner.

178

II, or III. *Sch.* is the abbreviation for *Schutzhund,* or guard dog (actually police dog in some cases), and the numerals denote years and degrees of training. In Germany more importance is given to temperament and trainability, plus soundness, than to minor beauty points, and German breeders, like those in most Continental countries, place more emphasis on complete dentition than do breeders in England and America.

One of the leading breeders of Airedales in Germany dating back many decades was Herr Cuppers, who had imported several Airedales from England, including Cont. and Eng. Ch. Gosmore Attack, Sch. III. A daughter of Attack was brought to America, at 6 yrs, by Trevor Evan, then in the Army. Although she, Cupper's Kostprobe, had only one litter she has many champion descendants here, including some of the Bryn Hafod and Pendragon prefix. Kostprobe's dam, to show the international travels of show dogs on the Continent, was German, Swiss and Italian Ch. Cupper's Grille. The many Airedale clubs in Germany are more of a "get-together with your dogs" type of club than social or political gatherings as some clubs seem to be here, with training part of the picture.

The pictures of Ezza v.d. Klappergasse Sch. III and F.H. show only two of her accomplishments, for the Sch. III as already seen, means the highest grade of police (guard) training, while the F.H. is the tracking dog degree. This bitch was very famous in Germany and other countries as was her son Arco von Schloss Solitude who had earned the same degrees. They were owned and trained by Marga Swoboda, one of the best-known trainers in Germany.

Recent copies of *Der Terrier* show the Von den Schönen Bergen kennels to be among the most successful of late, with Sarah, Mecki, Remus, Scout and Wotan, all with the foregoing suffix, taking many top championships in 1976. These include *Europasieger* and *Klubsieger* won by Remus, and KFT *Jugendsieger* won by Wotan, who also won the youth title of *Europa-Jugendesieger.* Sarah, Mecki and Remus won several *Vorzüglich* (Excellent) ratings. Incidentally the next rating *Sehr gut* (Very Good), is not to be sneezed at either.

The vom Stammhof Kennels too have won many championships, with Lord vom Stammhof taking international as well as German honors. He too is Sch. III and has the RH, FH and AD traing degrees as well. Most of the von Stammhof dogs have at least the guard dog degree and several others are also international as well as German champions.

A most attractive picture of five Airedales looking out the back of a station wagon and titled *Eine hundfamilie mit sympathischer ausstrahlung!* shows the "dog family" of most attractive Airedales of Dr. Rolf and Waltrud Weckmuller (v.d. Burg Ludwigstein Kennels).

Ch. Stockfield Aristocrat was one of England's earliest exports to Japan. Prior to his expatriation he won BIS at the Kennel Club show at Olympia in 1934. He is shown here with his handler, A. E. Sheldon (left) and his owner in England, Frederick Peake. The 100 Guinea Challenge Cup in the center was Aristocrat's prize at Olympia.

English Ch. Junemore Bonnie Boy, an early export to Japan.

These include Isis, Clochard, Bengal Brilliant Star, Datscha, and Kandy, most of them have the foregoing suffix. And their titles include two world champions, one European champion, two junior (*jugend*) world champions, three international champions and four from several individual European countries as well as Germany. So this handsome carload has good reason to be so eye-catching. Wenke v.d. Neidenburg Sch. H. I is the 1976 German National Champion bitch and Vidor v.d. Neidenburg, Sch. H. III won the dog title. They are owned by F. Frevart and W. Dammeier, respectively.

This just touches upon the top winners of 1976, and there are many other kennels also represented in well-illustrated ads—the dogs shown "as is" yet well trimmed and appealing. Although the parentage on most of the Airedales does not strike a familiar note in those cases where several generations are German or at least foreign-bred, there is one whose immediate family is well known in England and North America indeed. This is Impressionist Rusty-Dusty, owned by Friedel Michaelis. The sire of this dog is Int. Ch., Ital. Ch., *Hauptzuchtschausieger* (Specialty BB) 1970 *Schweizersieger* (Swiss Champion) 1971 Oscar of Mynair. The dam of Rusty-Dusty is by Int. Ch. Jokyl Bengal Figaro. I am sure that equally familiar ancestry would also be found on the other German Airedales a few generations back. From illustrations in *Der Terrier,* one gets a highly favorable impression of the German Airedales, and the various degrees held by most of them makes their qualifications rate even higher.

Other Continental Activity

Madame Sulser is the leading Airedale breeder and exhibitor in France, her dogs (Airedales and Lakelands) often winning highest honors in French shows. In Italy the Airedale is not classed as a Terrier but is grouped with the Guard Dogs. Belgium and Portugal also have their Airedale fanciers, with several English-bred dogs going to these countries through the years. Even Hungary, despite its many adversities, still keeps up its Airedale interest. An enthusiastic owner is Frau Rojos, who writes that the Airedale formerly was used chiefly for hunting wild boar in Hungary, but that in the circumstances prevailing now, the Airedale is mainly a companion and watchdog. In Budapest there are three training schools for Airedales where owners meet and train their dogs each Sunday morning. Eventually the Airedales undergo obedience tests and if they meet a certain standard, their tax is reduced and they are allowed to travel free on streetcars and trains—a privilege accorded all "useful" dogs in contrast to the "pet" variety.

Japan

The following text was supplied by Mr. Haruki T. Endoh of Tokyo, and is not only concise and factual, but also, in view of the quality of in-

181

dividuals imported to Japan, shows that the Japanese are as discerning in their selection of high class dogs as they are in the purchase of superior Thoroughbred horses. The comments on the use of English-bred Airedales (or of that breeding) for obedience work, a sideline apparently not stressed for the breed in England, is also of interest. You will find the ancestors of many English and American Airedales among those sent to Japan, including some of the breed's greatest dogs.

The first Airedale Terrier was sent to Japan in 1920 and some more came from the United States in the latter half of the 1920s. This stimulated the establishment of the Japan Airedale Terrier Society in January 1930 by those who were eager to study and foster the breed. In the same year, Baron K. Iwasaki imported Whitchurch Workman and Cotsford Lassie and Mr. K. Nakamoto purchased a bitch, Ardross Angeline, from England, thus they established the foundation breeding stock.

In the following ten years, Airedales became one of the most popular breeds in Japan, and about forty fine Airedales were imported from England and other countries in a steady stream. Among these were the dogs Ch. Stockfield Aristocrat, Ch. Junemore Bonnie Boy, Ch. Ensign of the Edge, Ch. Warland Mascot (full brother of Int. Ch. Warland Protector), Ch. Warland Radio and Kresent Brigand. Bitches imported were Ch. Cranfield Charm, Ch. Easthorpe Anne, Ch. Charm of the Edge, Ch. Brigands Belle, Ch. Towyn Topflight, Dunwood Baroness and Aislaby Guelda.

Owing to the outbreak of World War II, Airedale breeding declined almost totally, and less than thirty Airedales barely survived at the end of the War. Some breeding, involving these survivors was carried out just after the war. It was in 1951 that breeding resumed in earnest. Two dogs were influential at this time. One was Fancy Boy (grandson of Am. Ch. Freedom Foresight), who was brought by an American soldier and stayed in Japan and the other was Corriedale Sonny (Aust. Ch. Omuka Flash, of the Eng. Ch. Waycon Aristocrat line), who was accompanied to Japan by an Australian diplomat.

Jupiter of Copperdale (by Flashlight Prince, and grandsire of Am. Ch. Peppertree Major) and Am. Ch. Aireline Blockbuster (Am. Ch. Aireline Bombsight ex Aireline Symbol) were imported from the United States and Gosmore Sensation (by Eng. Ch. Bengal Bengali) was also imported from England in succession. In 1954 Ardendale Busy Body II (Eng. Ch. Son of Merrijak ex Ardendale Top Me) was imported from the United States after being bred to Am. Ch. Ardendale Trouble's Double. Shortly after this, Boulder Gulch Painted Lady was shipped from the United States to Japan after breeding her back to her sire, Am. Ch. The Shiek of Ran-Aire. These two were excellent producers and had a great influence on the Airedale's future in Japan.

The Nippon Police Dog Association, established in March 1947, National Airedale Terrier Club of Japan, formed in 1959, and the Japan Airedale Terrier Society which is the oldest Specialty club in Japan all endeavored to improve and promote Airedales in Japan. As a consequence, the Airedale became more popular than before the war, dogs of excellent quality appeared, and the number of fanciers increased.

Since the 1960s, many stud dogs and bitches have been imported from England. This includes the dogs Ch. Riverina Balquhider Bairn, Siccawei Premier (full brother of Am. Ch. Siccawei Prince Peter), Bengal Beau Brummel (Aust. Ch. Siccawei Sunday ex Am. Ch. Bengal Basket), Mollygray Cavalier (by Tycroit Rameses), Ch. Jokyl Eagle (by Jokyl Chippinghey Kestrel), Bengal Chippinghey Nomad (by Eng. Ch. Bengal Gunga Din), Wynadale Worldcap (by Wynadale Wishaw, of the Int. Ch. Jokyl Bengal Figaro line), Bengal Rough Diamond (by Eng. Ch. Lanewood Lombard) and Robton Abel (by Eng. Ch. Kresent Token). Brood bitches brought to Japan include Bengal Glamour Girl (litter sister of Eng. Ch. Bengal Gunga Din), Raimon Rig (by Eng. Ch. Raimon Robert the Bruce), Tycroit Charmer (by Eng. Ch. Tycroit Tempo), Bengal Kora (by Ch. Bengal Gunga Din), Bengal Maiko Girl (Bengal Buldeo ex Ch. Bengal Begum), Bengal Bathsheba (Ch. Kresent Token ex Ch. Bengal Suliston Merry Maid) and Jokyl Kenlucky Carmen (Eng. Ch. Bengal Flamboyant ex Kenlucky Latona).

In the 1970s, importation from England continued and from Germany came two dogs and three bitches. From the United States Ch. Coppercrest Royal (Ch. Winstony Exceptional ex Coppercrest Pro-Tec-Tor) and Coppercrest Lady Helen (Ch. Geoffrey Earl of Stratford ex Flintkote River Queen) were imported. By the decade of the '70s over 50 Airedale Terriers had been exported to Japan.

From the end of the War until April 1977, 83 Airedales became Japanese champions. The representative bloodlines and families of these champions are as follows: ten champions descended tail-male from Am. and Jap. Ch. Aireline Blockbuster and Am. Ch. The Shiek of Ran-Aire on the Int. Ch. Cotteridge Brigand line. Eight Champions were from the line of Jap. Ch. Gosmore Sensation who was the grandson of Eng. Ch. Son of Merrijak. Seven champions came through Jap. Ch. Bengal Beau Brummel, who was a grandson of Eng. Ch. Bengal Fastnet. Six champions were from Am. Ch. Ardendale Trouble's Double, who was a grandson of Am. Ch. Harham's Rocket. Six champions trace to Eng. Ch. Mayjack Briar, who was bred to Raimon Rig, before she was shipped to Japan. Five champions, which include those of 1977, came from the line of Jap. Ch. Jupiter of Copperdale.

But most of champions and other prize winners who have won in recent years were the progeny of Ch. Bengal Fastnet, Ch. Jokyl Bengal Figaro and Ch. Bengal Gunga Din, full brothers sired by Eng. Ch. Bengal Kresent Brave.

Another of the major producing families is that of Dunwood Baroness (grand-daughter of Ch. Little Varmint). From this family line, thirteen champions came from bitches owned by Mr. S. Shioda, Mr. and Mrs. A. Mori, Mrs. T. Satoh and Miss N. Takahashi. From the family of Ch. Cranfield Charm (Beechcroft Madcap family, the same family as Fiesolana in the United States and Riverina Bewitched and Riverina Vogue in England) Mr. K. Katoh, Mr. R. Sakagami and Mrs. S. Katoh bred 11 champions. These two families are the oldest in Japan.

From the family of Ardendale Busy Body II (Ridgemoor Sweetberry family), came 22 champions, the largest number from one family. These came from bitches owned by Mr. K. Sheba, Mr. Y. Bushizawa, Mrs. Y. Sekido and Mr. T. Hashimoto. Tycroit Charmer (granddaughter of Ch. Tycroit Tinkabell, Onyx of Joreen family) produced five champions as did Mr. N. Kawai's Bengal Kora (great-granddaughter of Suliston Psyche, dam of Int. Ch. Jokyl Superman and Ch. Searchlight Tycoon, Vogue family). Miss K. Takagi's Bengal Glamour Girl (Onyx of Joreen family) is the dam of three champions and granddam of one champion.

According to the Specialty club, the number of entries for the championship show range from twenty to fifty dogs, however, in obedience competition for Airedales alone thirty to fifty dogs are usually entered. In all-breed obedience competition Mr. A. Kutsukata's Annie of Glorious Aria (by Jap. Ch. Bengal Chippinghey Nomad, bred by Mr. I. Ishikawa) is an example of Japanese Airedale fanciers' enthusiasm for obedience competition. Mr. I. Takahashi's Jap. Ch. Rose von Senshinsow has the conformation championship as well as the title for obedience.

Airedales in Japan are actually serving as police dogs in various areas. Several are also serving as guide dogs for the blind. Ch. Jokyl Eagle, Jap. Ch. Bengal Beau Brummel, Siccawei Premier, Ch. Riverina Balquhider Bairn and other distinguished imports are in their backgrounds. Most of these Airedales were imported from England where training is the secondary object, and it is interesting that their descendants have adapted so well to various forms of training.

Airedales have been reputed to be superior to all other breeds in Japan for hunting wild boar. During the four-month hunting season, Andy of Creation, a typical Airedale, helped capture eleven wild boars. The pedigree of this dog is the same as that of most champions or trained dogs in Japan. He could probably be a winner if he were allowed to participate in championship shows.

184

Attack of Golden-Aire (Japan)

Japanese Ch. Bengal Beau
Brummel.

Japanese Police dog show, November 1955

185

Puppies in Japan

Japanese Airedale fanciers for many years are, in addition to the persons mentioned earlier, Mr. S. Akimoto, Mr. and Mrs. H. T. Endoh, Mrs. N. Fujioka, Mrs. M. Hanamura, Mrs. M. Higashida, Mr. R. Kawakami, Mr. and Mrs. S. Kohsaka, Mr. S. Ohori, Mr. S. Takagi, Mr. H. Takamiya, Mrs. J. Tsunashima and Mrs. K. Wakai. These and others are devoting themselves to the improvement and continued development of Airedale in Japan.

The Globe-Trotting Airedale

In India the Anglo influence is felt strongly and dog shows are popular, with the Airedale holding his own. South Africa is another area where Airedale activity has been high.' Germiston, Transvaal, is headquarters for the Airedale Terrier Club of South Africa, which publishes yearbooks as well as *The Airedale Record.* The title of champion is not easily acquired in South Africa, for the dog must win at least four challenge certificates in not less than three centers of the country, under at least three different judges. Shows are hardly numerous and entail a good deal of travel in most cases—even to Southern Rhodesia. Imports are made fairly often, with most of England's major kennels being represented. A. D. McLaren, of the Brenwood prefix, is one of the most prominent breeders and a hardworking club member, as is D. E. Cox, whose Caradoc Airedales are, high in the winning lists. Mrs. J. K. Charles' Sandown prefix figures in the show news, and the imported dog Ch. Sandown's Rural Poseidon of Joreen belongs to this kennel. The Buffalo Airedales of Mrs. N. Cook are prominent, and George Lane, of the Forward prefix, has exhibited and bred Airedales in Africa since 1904. A dog whose name is familiar in America is Ch. Murraysgate Merriboy of Bridgebank, owned by V. C. Trollope. Miss E. A. Slingsby (Farnhill), Mrs, A. C. Durham (Fairbridge), and Miss J. M. King (Marshallwick) are other successful exhibitors.

Mexico also has Airedales, as do the Latin-American countries. Canada has worked so closely with American Airedale breeders that the bloodlines are intermingled—both ways—and of course the influence of the Rockleys alone has been tremendous. Among present breeders in Canada are Dan Hargreaves, whose imports of the Murraysgate strain have already been mentioned; and Ede Ross, whose Can. and Am. Ch. Ross' Kontica Patience traces to Ch. Freedom Foresight in tail-male. The Milroy Kennels of Roy Black are one of Canada's oldest, and the Milroys are well known in the United States since they are consistently exhibited on this side of the border.

Ch. Moylarg Mohican, owned by Geisla Lesh and bred by Pauline Lewis, a well-known winner who numbers among his triumphs BB at the 1971 Melbourne Royal.

188

8

The Airedale Boom
in Australia

IN EARLIER editions of this book Australia was given only a casual reference and in just one sentence at that. Since the later 1950s however, coincidental with the boom in the breed in America, there has been an almost unbelievable quickening of Australian interest in the breed, resulting in many new breeders and importers, and consequently a whopping increase in exhibitors (both show and obedience).

The three Australian Airedale clubs have furnished more material than can be utilized, and despite the amount, it was in a concise and easily-followed form. About all that has been deleted was some of the earliest history in order to concentrate on those to which present Australian Airedales trace.

Prevailing Conditions

The clubs are Victoria (the largest and oldest, founded 1929); New South Wales, about twenty years old; and Queensland, whose club "The Queensland Airedalers" is five years old. Although there are Airedales in other states too, these are at present the only clubs, and they stage their own Specialties.

Due to the Commonwealth Quarantine Act of 1908 it is very difficult to import any kind of animal to Australia. Even from England the imports have to spend a quarantine period in Australia, but those from

Ch. Burfield Mr. Smith.

Ch. Foxfern Ariel.

190

other countries would have to be in quarantine six months in the United Kingdom first, and then the additional time in similar detention in Australia. It's too much to expect of an anxious owner to have his dog spend a year of his life in quarantine kennels. That is why most imports to Australia are from England (which would probably be the case anyway, that being *the source*, so to speak), with the resultant shorter period in limbo.

Although the Australian data was obtained through several sources, most of it was through the work of a committee of experienced members, mainly of the Victoria club, and was submitted by Marie Langdon, Hon. Secretary of that club.

The final section of this chapter is from that same committee but written by Keith Lovell. There is of course some repetition but that was necessary in bringing the notes up to date in "wrap-up" style.

I feel sure that most Americans will be surprised to know of the increased Airedale enthusiasm there, and pleased to see the close relationship with our winning lines. You will note that the leading sires are all from lines on the various American sire-line charts. This fact isn't too surprising since they too are "new English" of background or are themselves imported from England.

Despite the great expanse of inner Australia the population is concentrated in urban centers and surrounding areas, with most dog fanciers also being in or near such centers. Consequently the state of Victoria leads in interest and in number and size of dog shows. The first Airedales were imported to Victoria in 1890 by E.A. Edmonston (Thorpe) and A. Addy whose kennel was founded on the imports Yeadon Ring and Rosebud. By the turn of the century W. W. King's Queensbury prefix was well known and in 1899 the imported champion Accrington Rough was owned by T. S. Smith. There were several kennels in the next decade, many of which were founded on their own imports. In the 1920s the number of breeders had grown, and the increased interest led to the formation of the Airedale Terrier Club of Victoria, the oldest Specialty club in the state. This club held its first championship show in 1931.

Airedale Development in the Southern Continent

There were many "UK" (we call them English imports) imports to Australia of that period, and of prefixes very well known in England and America. The largest kennel of the era was that of N. A. Whiting (Marydale), and another great kennel was Stoneleigh, owned by W. H. Brilliante. Outstanding dogs of this kennel were Ch. Stoneleigh Stormer and Ch. Stoneleigh Solario. Many of Australia's best homebreds trace back through Stormer to Monarque of Cannon and Clonmel Monarque. At this time New South Wales, which had been im-

191

porting and breeding good Airedales since the early 1900s, got into the picture with a financial bang when Dr. Sparkes of that state imported the best dog brought over to that point, namely Ch. Ilan Flyaway, which in itself was news, but the price paid would have made a thump even today—it was £1000, at that time the equivalent of close to $5000. Translate that amount to today's inflated dollars, and you have a super price! Eng. Ch. Ilan Queen (dam of Eng. Ch. Little Varmint) was imported soon afterward, and presumably this well-known charmer was not obtained cheaply either.

The first Airedales to be shown trimmed were at Government House in 1918 by L. Latchford; and this created quite a buzz, pro and con. Up to that point Airedales had been shown "as is," but since in those days coats were usually fairly hard and furnishings not too profuse, it would not have made quite as much difference as it would today. The Latchford prefix was Aerial. N. Myers imported Walnut Brian and Easthorpe Jupiter, and his Austral prefix can still be found in Victorian Airedale pedigrees. H. E. Rhodes (Rhodesia) had a successful kennel, and won outright the Eileen O'Connor Memorial Trophy. The Hillmere Kennels were founded in the early 1930s and are still active in shows and obedience. They imported one of the early Bengals, among others, this being Ch. Bengal Boatswain, credited with bringing correct size and conformation to the breed in Australia in that period.

A "syndicate" of sorts was formed by Hillmere, Moylarg and Darrele kennels in 1971 to import Ch. Siccawei Baronet from the late Clare Halford. A top sire of both show and obedience winners, this dog was said to have been among those giving the breed a boost, although this was a period when many good ones were being shown and/or imported.

The Wolstanton prefix of England is well known in America, while Australia became even more aware of this line when Miss E. K. Garrard (Omuka), whose foundation bitch was Australian, brought over Ch. Wolstanton Rocket and Eng. Ch. Wolstanton Pam, the latter was the first English champion bitch ever imported to Victoria.

Australian Airedale Breeders

Mrs. Platt's Exmoor kennels were founded by an Omuka dog, but she subsequently brought over many English Airedales, among them Ch. Kresent Admiral, Ch. Bengal Jemadar, Ch. Bengal Crusader and Ch. Jokyl Leader's Legend. Jemadar made Airedale history in Australia by being runner-up for Dog of the Year in 1966. The latest import of this kennel is Ch. Bengal Valley Forge, who sired the Best Exhibit, Ch. Tjuringa Hurrah, at the Centenary show of the Victoria Club over 174 dogs in competition.

Ch. Loudwell Promise, an import owned by Mrs. D. Bywater,

Ch. Siccawei Baronet (Ch. Bengal Fastnet ex Siccawei Firelight), owned by Lorna Schuster, Pauline Lewis and Ray Stewart, won the ATC of Victoria Specialty in 1972 and became one of Australia's most significant stud forces.

Ch. Burfield Beau Benjamin.

was another big winner, one of her triumphs being Best Opposite Sex in Show at the Adelaide Royal. Although she had only one litter, one of her sons, Ch. Aasleagh Ambassador, was the founding father of the Kellington Kennels, later the importers of Lanewood Lovelight.

The Moylarg Kennels of Mrs. Pauline Lewis were founded in 1960. The foundation bitch was of the Exmoor prefix, sired by Ch. Augustus of Murlite out of Ch. Exmoor Eminence. Bred to Ch. Kresent Admiral she produced three champions in this first litter, one of which, Ch. Moylarg Sheba, became the foundation of the highly successful Strongfort Kennels. Mated to Ch. Siccawei Remus she produced Ch. Strongfort Stromboli, who in turn became the foundation bitch of the Rangeaire Kennels. Still another cornerstone was produced when a Sheba granddaughter bred to the English import Ch. Mr. Smith of Burdale, produced Tjuringa Kennels' Ch. Strongfort Samantha Jo.

A tie-in with the English Centenary show was made when the Moylarg and Hillmere Kennels imported Ch. Drakehall Dragoon, a litter brother of the aforesaid show winner, Ch. Drakehall Dinah. Two other champions in this litter are Drakehall Derby Day and Drakehall Delight. Dragoon quickly gained his title and was the top-winning Airedale in Australia in 1976 (an award of that year only—the Centenary). He already has sired five champions—all Group winners at Championship shows.

The Strongfort Kennels of Mrs. Geisla Lesh was founded on Ch. Moylarg Sheba. The important sire Ch. Siccawei Remus was a Strongfort import, and his line is one to be reckoned with in Queensland and New South Wales in addition to Victoria. This kennel moved to Sydney (New South Wales) from Victoria and became a dominant force there. A puppy by Ch. Moylarg Mohican (by Ch. Bengal Jemadar) was Best Puppy, All Breeds, at the Sydney Royal in 1973 under the American judge Derek Rayne, thereby making breed history. This is an unexpected tie-in to my own memories, for Derek Rayne judged the first Pacific Northwest Specialty, and selected my Ch. Studio Top Brass (sire of Liontamer) as his main winner.

Bob and Jane Harvey's Rangeaire Kennel has become one of the most influential in the country. Their foundation bitch was Ch. Strongfort Stromboli whose dam was Ch. Strongfort Sheba, but what was not brought out was that Remus (sire of Stromboli) was of the famous *Tridwr Milady* family, since his dam was Eng. Ch. Riverina Diana of Siccawei, a granddaughter of Milady. Mrs. Harvey had been greatly impressed by Ch. Siccawei Tyffany (imported from England with Ch. Chancellor of Siccawei, a son of the great winner Ch. Riverina Tweedsbairn) when she visited Mrs. D. Netherton's kennels in South Australia. Tyffany's sire was also a full brother to Tweedsbairn. Her dam was Int. Ch. Siccawei Artemis, also of the Riverina Diana family.

Ch. Drakehall Dragoon, imported from England and owned by Pauline Lewis and Lorna Schuster, won the ATC of Victoria 1975 Specialty show. Bred by Ernest Sharpe, he was sired by Ch. Siccawei Galliard out of Ch. Siccawei Ruby. In 1976, the Airedale Centenary, Dragoon was the top winning dog of the breed in Australia and the top sire in Victoria. *Robinson*

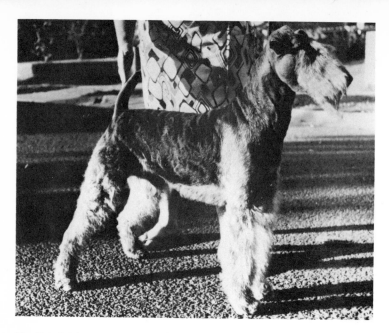

Ch. Brentleigh Ben Nevis, C.D., owned by Jean Harvey and bred by Mrs. Netherton, established an outstanding record in the ring. He made his presence felt even further by siring many good winners in turn.

Ch. Rangeaire Ringo Starr (Ch. Brentleigh Ben Nevis, C.D. ex Ch. Rangeaire Rangitaiki) sired the well-known Ch. Rangeaire Ramsey.

Mrs. Netherton sent the Harveys a son of Tyffany, Ch. Brentleigh Ben Nevis, C.D., by Chancellor, and three years later, Ch. Brentleigh Barbarell by Ch. Siccawei Sunday, a royally-bred dog by Ch. Bengal Fastnet out of Int. Ch. Siccawei Artemis.

The show record of Ben Nevis is outright fantastic. As one writer put it, he won enough challenge points to qualify for fifteen Australian championships. To boil this down to the actual number of c.c.s won, the total was 146, including three in consecutive years at the Royal Melbourne show. The record also included 44 Group placements. No other Australian Airedale has come near this accomplishment. He also attained the first obedience degree to be awarded to an Airedale in Victoria. To do all of this you would have expected he lived to be about fifteen, but instead he died prematurely before his eighth birthday. He sired only twelve litters, but still had eighteen Australian champions to his credit (eleven for Rangeaire and seven for Tjuringa). Two of his sons hold the only C.D.X. degrees in Victoria to this date. Stromboli produced eight of these champions in two litters. All eight won at least one Group placement. From Barbarell there were four champions one of which is Ch. Rangeaire Raggity Anne, winner of 73 c.c.s. She was Best Bitch in Show four times and had twenty-two Group placements. One of the first group, Ch. Rangeaire Rangitaiki, was bred to her sire, producing Ch. Rangeaire Ringo Starr. He was a champion at one year of age, with three Best Puppy in Show wins, and eventually had fourteen Group placements and fifty c.c.s before virtual retirement to make way for his son Ch. Rangeaire Ramsey, owned by Mr. A. C. Owens. This dog, though still young at this, has already gained 25 Group firsts, including the Royal Adelaide (4,159 entered) and the Royal Melbourne show in 1976, the largest dog show ever held in the Southern Hemisphere, with an entry of 6,216 dogs. In addition he was Best Exhibit in Show at the Sporting Terrier Club of Victoria's Specialty 1977. He has five Bests in Show, all breeds. All the BIS wins have been at championship shows. (Unlike American shows, points, or in this case c.c.s, are not available at all shows, only those designated championship affairs). Ramsey's litter sister, Aust. and New Zealand Ch. Rangeaire Ring a Bell, is owned by the Harveys. She is the first Airedale to have the title in Australia and New Zealand.

I have given this kennel's wins in some detail since the records are so remarkable, and also the entries at some of the shows indicates the tremendous interest taken in purebred dogs in Australia. It also shows that good Airedales can go far.

The acquisition of the foundation bitch of the Tjuringa Kennels makes a humorous story as told by Mrs. Keith Lovell. It seems that when the Lovells moved from an apartment to "the bush," she and her husband decided to buy a dog. She wanted a Dalmatian, but their first "port o' call" was the Strongfort Kennels. Mr. Lovell's father had had

Ch. Tjuringa Chancellor, owned by Mr. and Mrs. Keith Lovell, won the Terrier Group at Melbourne Royal in 1972—his first show. He subsequently was BB at this show on two other occasions.

Ch. Tjuringa Cactus Flower, owned by Wal and Myra Brown and bred by Mr. and Mrs. Keith Lovell, is a litter sister to Chancellor and has been a consistent winner through much of the 1970s.

Airedales and this was the only breed *he* had in mind. It was understood that they would "just look" and not buy anything until they had looked at some Dalmatian puppies too. Somehow it did not work out that way—they went home with an Airedale puppy—Strongfort Samantha Jo (which everyone thought was a "he" named Joe). Jo had been bought as a pet but they had thought of allowing her to have one litter. They took her to a training class bathed and clipped, in what must have looked like a pet Poodle clip. The clippers were purchased just two days before, and the only assistance the Lovells had was a couple of pictures of more-or-less trimmed Airedales to copy from. Amazingly, the judge recognized Samantha Jo as an Airedale, and she won. And they were hooked. They met Mrs. Harvey who "set them right" about trimming, and about showing too, apparently, for Jo became a champion, topping her career with the c.c. and BB at the Melbourne Royal in 1970. Her lasting importance is as foundation of the very successful Tjuringa Kennels, and, needless to say, the Lovells did not stop with that "just one litter." Two of her five litters were by Ben Nevis, and resulted in five champions. Samantha Jo is the dam of eight champions at present with several other sons and daughters on the way up.

An unshown Ben Nevis son spent his life as a fox hunter, but was a sire of show stock. One of the champions, Tjuringa Fair Dinkum won the c.c. at Melbourne Royal twice, and in obedience, Ch. Tjuringa Tarzan, C.D.X. was Best in Trial at the Melbourne Royal in 1972. The next litter was by Moylarg Brant, unshown because of a car accident. Two became champions. Ch. Tjuringa Cactus Flower was purchased by Mr. W. Brown, and was his first show dog, winning the bitch c.c. at Melbourne Royal, where her brother, Chancellor, unshown until he was fourteen months old, took the dog c.c., BB and first in the Group.

The Lovells then moved back to Melbourne and the next mating of Samantha Jo was to her own son, the "fox hunter." This produced Ch. Tjuringa Dinky Di, who, true to family custom, won the c.c. at Melbourne Royal, and at the Ladies' Kennel Association of Victoria show also going first in the Group and Best Opposite Sex in Show. Moreover she produced Ch. Tjuringa Hurrah, winner of the bitch c.c. at the 1975 ATC of Victoria Specialty, and the following year was Best in Show at the Centenary championship show. Jo's last litter was another repeat to Brant. To recap—from 1970 through 1975 Samantha Jo or her progeny won seven out of ten available c.c.s at the Melbourne Royal, plus winning one Group, one Best in Trial, and two final placings in the KCC Guineas Final at the Royal. Such is the history of one "family pet." Cactus Flower, by the way, is foundation of the Glenfailte Kennels of Wal and Myra Brown, and, as noted, she was their first show dog, and was still winning in 1977.

Jan and Peter Hatton, started their Bushveldt Kennels with Ch. Rangeaire Rani, and in turn champions of their breeding have become foundation bitches for other kennels. They owned Ch. Chancellor of Siccawei in his later years, and his influence is seen even through the third and fourth generation among Victoria Airedales.

The Old Iron prefix belongs to Ann and Ron Sorraghan, and despite the name is comparatively new on the scene. The most successful litter was by Ch. Siccawei Baronet out of Moylarg Salareana. Ch. Old Iron Son won "Victoria Airedale of the Year" in 1975 although only campaigned from April to November. In that period he won ten Best Terrier awards, Best of Breed at the Brisbane Royal and the c.c. at the Adelaide Royal. Old Iron Outlaw has consistently won in ATC of Victoria championship shows; 1974 1st Junior, 1st KCC Guineas; 1975 Intermediate in Show and 1976 c.c. and Best in Show.

The Windview Kennels of Mr. and Mrs. Wishart drew attention through three champions in one litter. Ch. Windview Wesley was Top Airedale in Queensland in 1976 and Ch. Windview Wonderful is a top-winning bitch in Victoria.

When the Strongfort Kennels moved to New South Wales in the 1960s, this naturally served to increase interest in the breed in that area, and needless to say it also saw a sudden increase in major wins of N.S.W. Airedales. Ch. Siccawei Remus not only took top honors in the show ring but also was an impressive sire, as already indicated. Also a Ch. Bengal Crusader daughter, Ch. Kiamaire Yarra Lass, bred to Ch. Bengal Valley Forge, produced Ch. Strongfort Sexpot, who was Top Terrier of the Year in 1974 and 1975 and runner-up to Best in Show at the Sydney Royal in 1975, having already won the Terrier Group. She won many c.c.s and was eight times Best in Show. Strongfort imported Ch. Loudwell Nice Girl and Ch. Jokyl Cinella, both successful for these kennels.

John Ellem, Carmarna Kennels, has had good results in producing champions with homebred bitches mated to Bengal imports, or to be more specific, to the champions of that prefix, imported to Australia.

Founded on Strongfort stock are the Midstream Kennels of Cavil Carter, using Ch. Bengal Crusader and Ch. Bengal Valley Forge as subsequent crosses.

An important dog which has founded a strong sire line in N.S.W. is Ch. Mr. Smith of Burdale, brought from England by Mrs. J. Woodburn of Gundowringa, along with Joy of Burdale. A son and two daughters of Mr. Smith were sent to Mr. Swabey in New Zealand, helping the breed to be re-established there. Since then breeders in that country have brought in a variety of bloodlines from Australia and have now formed their own breed club. A Jokyl bitch and a Sulliston bitch have been imported from England.

200

Ch. Old Iron Outlaw (Ch. Siccawei Baronet ex Moylarg Salareana), owned by Ann Sorraghan, was BOS at the 1976 ATC of Victoria Specialty.

Ch. Windview Wonderful (Ch. Tjuringa Chancellor ex Windview Wise One), owned by Geraldine McNamara, a strong winner in the late 1970s.

201

The effect of Ch. Mr. Smith of Burdale has been likened to that of his forebear, Ch. Brineland Bonny Boy in Europe. He is the foundation sire of Gundowringa, Adoah and Camarna Kennels in N.S.W., Sanaire in Queensland, Qualep in Western Australia and Tjuringa in Victoria, all of whose champions trace back to him, and PiHanz in New Zealand. Mr. Smith emerges as the top sire in Australia, and his daughter Ch. Forsvar Future Shock was top bitch in Australia and top Airedale in N.S.W. in 1976.

In 1968 Prenton Attila joined Gundowringa (Eng. Ch. Searchlight Tycoon ex Eng. Ch. Bernice of Burdale). He is a litter brother of Searchlight Prenton Amelis, owned by the Flintkote Kennels in the United States. Attila's daughter Ch. Gundowringa Hi Flyer is the foundation bitch of the successful Burfield Kennels in Queensland; Ch. Gundowringa Flash Lite, top Queensland Airedale of 1975 and winner of the Royal Brisbane Centenary International Sweepstakes; and Gundowringa Fire Eater, foundation bitch of Crieff Airedales in North Queensland.

The first championship show of the New South Wales Airedale Terrier Association was held in 1968. This is a growing club actively promoting the breed in both the show ring and obedience.

In the Australian Capital Territory the Forsvar Kennels have been noticeably successful, although comparatively new. This kennel, owned by Sue Matthews and Wayne Kelly was founded on Ch. Tjuringa Fair Go, who, mated to Ch. Mr. Smith of Burdale, produced Ch. Forsvar Future Shock, C.D. This young bitch has won ten Terrier Groups. She was best Terrier Bitch at Brisbane Royal 1976 and Best in Show at the Queenland Centenary show, among other notable wins. She was also Best in Trial at the Australian Capital Territory Club Trial in completing her C.D. degree. Two of her littermates also gained this degree. Forsvar Airedales also imported Ch. Loudwell Venus from England.

South Australia has never been an Airedale stronghold although there had been prominent breeders there in the 1920s, and a few up to the 1940s. At that time the Brentleigh Kennels of Mrs. D. Netherton and her late husband John were well known. They had shown several Exmoor Airedales before registering the Brentleigh prefix in 1940. A number of Siccawei Airedales were imported by this kennel, of which Ch. Chancellor of Siccawei (by Ch. Riverina Tweedsbairn) is best known. He was a fine show dog, with several Bests in Show to his credit. Moreover he is sire of 23 champions. His influential son, Ch. Brentleigh Ben Nevis, C.D. (11 champions) has already been mentioned in connection with Tjuringa Kennels. Ch. Siccawei Tyfanny, also mentioned earlier, was imported in 1963, and made a spectacular debut by going Best in Show. Another already mentioned was Ch. Sic-

Ch. Rangeaire Rangitaiki (Ch. Brentleigh Ben Nevis, C.D. ex Ch. Strongfort Stromboli).

Ch. Bushveldt Bewitched (Ch. Siccawei Baronet ex Ch. Rangeaire
Rani).

Ch. Bushveldt Bethesda (Ch. Siccawei Baronet ex Ch. Rangeaire
Rani).

203

cawei Sunday, a class winner at Crufts, and imported by Mrs. Netherton in 1965. When he retired five years later he had seven Best Exhibits to his credit. In 1973 Mr. Jim Bathgate became a partner in the Brentleigh Kennels. When he made a trip to England in 1973 the new partnership purchased Ch. Siccawei Kassel, the last of this prefix to go to Australia. Kassel is also a Best in Show winner.

Western Australia apparently was fifty years behind the rest of the country, as far as having any Airedale kennels is concerned. However records are incomplete. The "Tobias Honk" prefix belonged to Col. and Mrs. H. Van der Sluys who started in 1958 with Exmoor Airedales. Mr. and Mrs. Scull founded a kennel on Ch. Tobias Honk and Gundowringa Rebekah, a bitch of Burdale antecedents (by Mr. Smith and out of Joy of Burdale, both imported). This produced Ch. Qualep Raymonde, already a sire of two champions to this date.

An interesting sidelight on one of these last, Ch. Qualep Gay Minx, is her addiction to gate-opening. "Even a lock requiring three individual movements doesn't deter her in the slightest." Thereafter all gates were chained. Qualep Colstan, the second of these champions "can be very gentle when the mood takes him; he loves carrying frogs in his mouth, with their back legs hanging out either side, he looks a bit like Fu Manchu. He releases them unharmed and goes on his way. Probably his greatest delight is fishing around in the river, head under water (seemingly forever) looking for crabs, fish and sometimes old boots." This last sounds like regular "fisherman's luck," with more boots (or tires) than fish. It also shows the heritage from the old "waterside Terrier."

Queensland Airedales have been touched upon several times in relation to those of other areas, and also regarding the state club, "The Queensland Airedalers."

The Queenslander Bill Dorr, an international judge, says that he remembers large classes of lively and high quality Airedales battling it out for honors in the ring in Queensland in the 1920s and 1930s. However, as elsewhere, the number dropped to its nadir in the 1950s, with the later 1960s showing the interest that soon blossomed into participation in Australia's current Airedale boom. At this time most of the dogs were brought up from the southern states.

Mrs. Dorothy Hall (Rameses Kennels) had foundation stock of several N.S.W. and Victoria prefixes, including Winnear, Exmoor and Strongfort. The Tadjoe Kennels of the Vliegenthats used dogs of the N.S.W. lines of Gundahl and Strongfort, as did the D'Andreas (Rhanie Kennels), mainly from Ch. Siccawei Remus.

More recently, dogs from basically Burdale background (Lou Endean's Burfields, the Kuipers' Sanaires, and the Gundowringas of the Woodburns) have monopolized the wins, and have made Airedales

Gundowringa Busybody at six months.

Ch. Siccawei Kassel (Ch. Siccawei King's Ransom ex Siccawei Garnet), owned by D. Netherton and J. Bathgate. *Robinson*

forces to be reckoned with in Group and Best in Show competition. Additionally McQuires Woods Ch. Exmoor Lord Chester, a son of Ch. Bengal Valley Forge, and Mrs. Hall's Ch. Windview Wesley, have also made their mark.

The following comment, made regarding the judging of the Queensland Centenary show, will be of interest:

> The Queensland Airedalers brought up Mrs. Jane Harvey, (Victoria), Airedale breeder and "A" class terrier judge, to officiate at their 1976 Centenary show. Mrs. Harvey was impressed with the general quality of the entry, particularly with the heads and toplines. Of an entry from 10 different sires, all of the entry being dogs she had never seen before, Mrs. Harvey did an amazing piece of type judging, awarding every class in show to offspring of the one dog...(Ch. Mr. Smith of Burdale, imp. U.K.), and putting up that grand old dog himself as Best Veteran, at the age of twelve years.
>
> Of recent years two Queensland Airedales have gained obedience titles—Tadjoe Oscar his CD and CDX, and Ch. Kalliomont Karma her CD.

The "Ch." used in this chapter is usually Australian, and any English titles are so noted. It wasn't certain whether or not there were dual titles with some, but in most cases the material furnished was precise.

Background of the Top Producers

In order to tie in the leading sires and dams of Australia with those of America and England according to tail-male tracing, the following list refers to the charts according to Roman numerals in the left column:

Leading Sires

Chart	Name	Sire	# Chs.
II.D	Ch. Brentleigh Ben Nevis	Ch. Chancellor of Siccawei	17
IV	Ch. Siccawei Baronet	Eng. Ch. Bengal Fastnet	15
II.D	Ch. Siccawei Remus	Riverina Mandarin of Siccawei	15
I	Ch. Bengal Boatswain	Eng. and Am. Ch. Murose Replica	11
V	Ch. Bengal Jemadar	Bengal Leander	8
V	Ch. Moylarg Mohican	Ch. Bengal Jemadar	8
V	Ch. Kresent Admiral	Eng. Ch. Lanewood Lysander	7
II.D	Ch. Chancellor of Siccawei	Ch. Riverina Tweedsbairn	7
IV	Ch. Siccawei Sunday	Eng. Ch. Bengal Fastnet	5
II.C	Ch. Mr. Smith of Burdale*	Am. Ch. Sanbrook Senturian	5

(*the list for this dog is incomplete, and he has many other champions.)

Leading Dams

Name	Sire	# Chs.
Ch. Strongfort Samantha Jo	Ch. Mr. Smith of Burdale	8
Ch. Strongfort Stromboli	Ch. Siccawei Remus	8

Ch. Amberfold Gay	Ch. Bengal Boatswain	5
Ch. Hillmere Calypso, C.D.	Ch. Siccawei Chancellor	5
Ch. Rhodesia Revue	sire not stated	5
Ch. Brentleigh Barabell	Ch. Siccawei Sunday	5
Ch. Rangeaire Rani	Ch. Strongfort Stromboli	4

Australian Airedales in Obedience

There is a growing interest in obedience competition in the Australian Airedale fancy. At one Melbourne Royal two of the six final winners of the various classes were Airedales and in the play-off an Airedale was first.

At the Australian Capitol Territories trial in Canberra three young Airedales just out of the puppy class completed the requirements for their C.D. titles. One of these was a top scorer at a Saturday trial and a conformation winner in the show on Sunday. It has been performances like theirs that have convinced obedience judges how intelligent and trainable the Airedale really is.

To the credit of the Australian fancy, many of the best winners in the country have also done well in obedience competition. What follows is a resume of many of the best known obedience Airedales in the country.

Mr. Harry Lowe, of New South Wales, has done well with Airedales in obedience. His Ch. Fort Knox Commander, U.D. was the first Utility dog in the country and sired Wennair Doxo, C.D. He also trained Ch. Strongfort Calpurnia, C.D.X., her daughter Ch. Fortissimo Prima Donna, C.D., who got the obedience title at ten months, and Ch. Fortissimo Basso, C.D.

Brett Aristocrat, owned and trained by Mr. Gaywood, was the first Airedale in Australia to hold the C.D. degree.

Jean Harvey's celebrated winner and producer Ch. Brentleigh Ben Nevis had the C.D. degree and was, in fact, the first Airedale in Victoria with an obedience degree. He was trained by his owner, a qualified obedience instructor. Ch. Tjuringa Tarzan, C.D.X., owned and trained by Laurie O'Connell, and Ch. Rangeaire Rascoe, C.D.X., owned and trained by Mr. and Mrs. Horst Herter, were both sired by Ben Nevis. They also both contributed a share to the significant history of the breed as will be seen later. Another successful obedience Airedale that has also been outstanding in conformation competition is Ch. Forsvar Future Shock, owned, bred and trained by Sue Matthews. Two littler brothers of Future Shock, Forsvar Fresco and Forsvar Fencer have both qualified for the C.D. degree. Sue Matthews also trained her Ch. Tjuringa Fine Fellow, C.D.

Other champions with obedience degrees are Ch. Hillmere Calypso, C.D., the first bitch in Victoria with an obedience title, bred, owned and trained by Lorna Schuster, Chs. Hillmere Gamecock, C.D. and

Hillmere Motto, C.D. (Ch. Siccawei Baronet ex Ch. Hillmere Calypso).

Darelle Duke's Day, C.D. (Ch. Siccawei Baronet ex Ch. Moylarg Lady Catherine), was the highest scorer at the obedience trial held with the ATC of Victoria 1976 Specialty.

Ch. Strongfort Sea Sprite, C.D.X., owned and trained by Cor Scholten, jumping through a burning hoop. "Sabra" is a true working Airedale, often accompanying her owner on patrols in Tamworth, New South Wales.

208

Hillmere Limelight, C.D. also bred, owned and trained by Mrs. Schuster, Ch. Strongfort Conqueror, C.D.X. and Ch. Camarna Hi Flyer, C.D., owned and trained by Mr. D. Hollett.

Of particular interest is Ch. Strongfort Sea Sprite, C.D.X. She is owned and was trained by Cor Scholten, a fully qualified obedience judge. "Sabra" has applied her education to actual working situations. Mr. Scholten, a resident of New South Wales, takes Sabra on regular patrols in Tamworth.

On one occasion this man-dog team worked continuous night shifts for 21 days guarding the new council building prior to its opening. This building was scheduled to be opened by Her Majesty Queen Elizabeth II, and the patrols were set up to discourage vandalism and sabotage attempts. After the council building was opened, burglar alarms and other security devices were installed, but it was partly due to a vigilant Airedale that the building was kept safe before its official opening.

Sabra provides sport for her owner by working with ferrets and as a retriever. She is also a very important member of the Scholten family, a role the Airedale is very well suited to.

Other successful obedience Airedales worthy of mention are Tremorne Coonilla, C.D., owned and trained by Dr. Wright, Hillmere Motto, C.D., owned and trained by Lindsey Henderson, Moylarg Maid O'Kerry, C.D., owned and trained by Barrie Whitebrook and Darrelle Duke's Day, C.D., owned and trained by Ann Kapoulitsa.

The Centerary club show featured obedience competition and this trial was only the third one granted to a specialist club. Thirty-one dogs competed, many of which were also entered in the conformation classes, with Best in Trial going to Darrelle Duke's Day, C.D.

Airedales in Australia Since 1969
by Keith Lovell

In 1969 the largest display of Airedales in Australia was at the championship show of the Airedale Terrier Club of Victoria. The judge that drew this entry was Miss Pat McCaughy. Known throughout the world for her Riverina prefix, this was her first judging appearance in Australia. Best in Show went to Ch. Bengal Crusader with the bitch challenge awarded to Ch. Loudwell Promise, both English imports.

Since that time Airedales have progressed dramatically in Australia. The Victoria Club's Centenary show (1976) drew 174 entries for Arthur Lodge, owner of Mynair Kennels in England. This time all the main winners were Australian-bred.

What Crufts is to Great Britain and Westminster is to the United States, the Royal Melbourne show is to Australia. The Royal Mel-

Ch. Rangeaire Rascoe, C.D.X., a full brother of Raggity Anne.

Ch. Tjuringa Tarzan, C.D.X., owned and trained by Laurie O'Connell, made himself a place in the Australian history of the breed by winning Best in Trial at Melbourne Royal 1973.   *Neilson*

bourne averages five to eight times the Airedale entry of any other Royal show or Specialty with the exception of the Victoria Club's. What follows will delineate the main winners at Specialties of the ATC of Victoria through 1976 and at the Melbourne Royal for the same period. This overview will give the reader an idea of breed growth in this country during the first half of the 1970s.

The 1970 Royal Melbourne show drew a total entry of about 4,200 with Airedales numbering 38. Mr. L. C. James of England was the judge and awarded BB to the Keith Lovells' bitch Ch. Strongfort Samantha Jo, bred by Geisla Lesh. Samantha Jo has had a strong influence on the breed and at this point has shown herself to be an outstanding producer as well as a noted winner.

Two weeks following the Melbourne Royal, the Victoria Club Specialty brought out an entry of sixty. Best in Show was Ch. Rockall Rachel (Ch. Hillmere Cardinal ex Ch. Hillmere Debonair) while the dog challenge went to the English imported Ch. Jokyl Leader's Legend.

The strongest winner in the breed at this time was the celebrated Ch. Brentleigh Ben Nevis, C.D., bred by Mrs. Netherton of South· Australia. He was totally of Siccawei breeding and his success, in no small way, was due to the skillful, long-term campaigning by his owner Mrs. Harvey, who also trained him to the acquisition of his obedience degree. Ben Nevis had the unique distinction of winning enough to qualify for *fifteen Australian championships*—if that were possible! His record also included three challenges at the Melbourne Royal.

The Sydney Royal show of 1971 had an entry of fifteen Airedales, eleven from Melbourne. The BB was Ch. Moylarg Mohican (Ch. Bengal Jemadar ex Ch. Rhodesia Revue), owned by Mrs. Lesh and bred by Pauline Lewis. Mohican was a large, richly-colored, showy stallion and added to his laurels of 1971 the BB at the Melbourne Royal over an entry of 37. Ch. Tjuringa Fair Dinkum, who won the bitch challenge the same day was a daughter of the previous year's Melbourne c.c. winners Ch. Brentleigh Ben Nevis, C.D. and Ch. Strongfort Samantha Jo. Fair Dinkum was a class winner at the Melbourne Royal and ATC of Victoria shows in 1970 and was to win yet another Royal Melbourne challenge in the course of her career.

The 1971 ATC of Victoria Specialty was also a well-supported affair. The top winner was Ross and Eve Brennan's Ch. Aasleigh Ambassador (Ch. Bengal Crusader ex Ch. Loudwell Promise), bred by Aileen Bywater. The winner of the bitch challenge was the popular and consistent Ch. Strongfort Serenade (Ch. Siccawei Sunday ex Ch. Moylarg Sheba) exhibited by Don Watkins.

Tjuringa Paul won Best Puppy in Show. He was another that resulted from the combination of Ben Nevis and Samantha Jo, surely a good niche. In 1971 Paul, owned by Dr. Pierre Gorman, was commencing a career that was to include many Group awards and would earn him great popularity among the fancy.

The Centenary of the Royal Melbourne show, 1972, could have been called the *Year of the Airedale* as it was a remarkable and richly rewarding occasion for the breed. The two main winners were both newcomers to the scene, both taking their first c.c.s this day. They were also litter mates! The dog was Tjuringa Chancellor (Moylarg Brant ex Ch. Strongfort Samantha Jo) and he went from BB to an impressive Best in Group win over some of the strongest competition in the land on the breed and Group level. It was believed that at the time Chancellor was the first Airedale to win the Group at the Melbourne Royal. Amazingly, this was his first show. The judge at the 1972 Melbourne Royal was Carin Lindhe of Sweden. Mrs. Lindhe is an international judge and was herself an Airedale breeder. This fact made the win even more significant.

Chancellor's sister and companion in the winners' circle was Tjuringa Cactus Flower, owned by Wal and Myra Brown. This first outing was a forecast of things to come as "Mandy" went on to win many awards for Best in Group and Best of Opposite Sex in Group. She has also done well as a producer, so has performed admirably on both fronts.

Chancellor, too, went on to make a great name for himself. His show career was to include three Bests of Breed at the Melbourne Royal.

As usual, the ATC of Victoria show followed the Melbourne Royal closely. Here the tables turned and the top winner was the imported Ch. Siccawei Baronet (Ch. Bengal Fastnet ex Siccawei Firelight), owned by Pauline Lewis, Lorna Schuster and Ray Stewart. "Barry" was to become one of Australia's all-time top producers, siring litters out of many of the best bitches in the land. The Royal Group winner had to be content with reserve challenge. The bitch challenge at the Specialty was also owned by Mrs. Lewis. This being Ch. Moylarg Maid of Jemadar, a full sister to Mohican.

An American judge reviewed Airedales at the 1973 Melbourne Royal. This was Isidore Schoenberg, and was the first American judge to draw this assignment in many years. From an entry of 53, BB was May Platt's import Ch. Bengal Valley Forge (Ch. Bengal Mogul ex Ch. Bengal Donna). Though he was a difficult dog to pose, he moved like a dream and established himself as one of the best yet imported to Australia.

The bitch challenge at the 1973 Royal Melbourne was Ch. Tjuringa Fair Dinkum, duplicating her win of two years before. She was out of competition with a litter during the 1972 show.

212

Ch. Rangeaire Raggity Anne (Ch. Brentleigh Ben Nevis, C.D. ex Ch. Brentleigh Barbarell).

Ch. Burfield Beau Geste.

Ch. Tjuringa Hurrah (Ch. Bengal Valley Forge ex Ch. Tjuringa Dinki Di), owned by Mr. and Mrs. A. Friedman and bred by Mr. and Mrs. Keith Lovell, won the 1976 Specialty of the ATC of Victoria under Arthur Lodge of England. The entry of 174 was the Club's largest to that time.

Ch. Rangeaire Ramsey (Ch. Rangeaire Ringo Starr ex Ch. Brentleigh Barbarell) owned by A. C. Owens and bred by Mrs. J. Harvey (handling), was selected as Best Terrier at the 1976 Melbourne Royal show. The judge was Jean Fancy of the United States. The total entry for the Melbourne Royal in 1976 was 6,216 individual dogs, making this the largest dog show in the Southern Hemisphere to that time. *Neilson*

The obedience trial at the 1973 Melbourne Royal provided the most memorable side to the show for the Airedale fancy. Best in Trial was Mr. Laurie O'Connell's Ch. Tjuringa Tarzan, C.D.X., making the first time an Airedale took so high an obedience placing at this show. What added even more to the win was the fact that Tarzan was the O'Connells' first dog and he was owner-trained. There was only one other Airedale entered in the trial—Ch. Rangeaire Rascoe, C.D.X.—and he won his class! Truly, it was a great day for obedience Airedales.

The specialist judge Peter Luyton did the honors at the 1973 Victoria Specialty. His two top winners were a repeat of the Royal a few weeks earlier—Ch. Bengal Valley Forge and Ch. Tjuringa Fair Dinkum.

Arthur K. Y. Zane journeyed from Hawaii to judge Airedales at the 1974 Melbourne Royal and was greeted by an entry of 56 specimens. Mr. Zane awarded Tjuringa Chancellor his second BB at this show while he made Mrs. Harvey's Ch. Rangeaire Raggity Anne (Ch. Brentleigh Ben Nevis, C.D. ex Ch. Brentleigh Barbarell) winner of the bitch challenge. Bob Crawford, a past president of the ATC of Victoria, judged the 1974 Specialty, and was honored with an entry of ninety. From this collection he seconded Mr. Luyton's opinion of the year before, giving BB to Ch. Bengal Valley Forge. Best of Opposite Sex was Sue Matthews' and Wayne Kelly's Ch. Tjuringa Fair Go (Ch. Siccawei Baronet ex Ch. Tjuringa Fair Dinkum). Fair Go subsequently removed to Canberra, producing one of Australia's top winners, Ch. Forsvar Future Shock by Ch. Mr. Smith of Burdale.

Yet another American judge, Mrs. Tom Stevenson, judged Airedales at the 1975 Melbourne Royal. Her entry of 63 typified the trend of growing interest in the breed. Ringsiders and exhibitors were impressed with Mrs. Stevenson's consistency for type as she chose Ch. Tjuringa Chancellor for his third Melbourne Royal BB and a breed record. Another Tjuringa entry took the bitch certificate. This was Ch. Tjuringa Dinky Di (Tjuringa Karawi Chief ex Ch. Strongfort Samantha Jo), marking the second time the Lovells scored the double at Melbourne during the decade of the 1970s.

Many people have remarked that the judging seen at the ATC of Victoria's 1975 Specialty was the best and most consistent to type they had ever seen. Mrs. Geisla Lesh of Sydney's Strongfort Kennels judged the entry of 76, finding her BB in Drakehall Dragoon, the new import of Mrs. Lewis and Mrs. Schuster. Dragoon was bred by Ernest Sharpe from Siccawei lines. This triumph marked the beginning of a highly successful campaign for this superbly-colored, compact dog of excellent breed type. The recipient of the bitch certificate was a youngster attending her second show, Tjuringa Hurrah (Ch. Bengal Valley Forge ex Ch. Tjuringa Dinky Di). Hurrah finished in her next five shows in rousing style with a Best Opposite in Show (all breeds) and three Groups.

The year 1976 was the Centenary Year of the Airedale. In Australia this milestone took on special significance by the achievements made.

The 1976 Melbourne Royal proved to be a breed celebration in itself and for the second time in history an Airedale led all the Terriers here. The winner, Ch. Rangeaire Ramsey, owned by Alan Owen, collected his honors to the applause of the fancy for so illustriously representing the breed in its Centenary year. The bitch challenge was won by Carmen Arbrew's Ch. Monnettdale Baroness (Ch. Siccawei Baronet ex Monnettdale Alert). The judge this year, Mrs. Glenn Fancy, was again from the United States.

The 1976 ATC of Victoria show, in keeping with Centenary celebrations, offered the best view of the Airedale ever seen in Australia. To judge this group came one of the breed's leading authorities, Mr. Arthur Lodge. As noted earlier, Mr. Lodge is the owner of Mynair Kennels in England. The Australian fancy had a first-hand opportunity to observe the depth of the man's breed knowledge. It was demonstrated in the way he judged the huge entry of 174 and also in the enthusiasm with which he lectured, helped, demonstrated, trimmed and quietly discussed the breed. The cost of bringing a judge to Australia is not small, but in 1976 it was certainly worth it!

The Specialty winner for the Centenary year was Mrs. Lesh's choice among the bitches in 1975, Ch. Tjuringa Hurrah. Hurrah's win was enormously popular with the crowd partly because of her delightful personality and individual quality. The other reason for the endorsement of the fancy was the fact that she is Australian-bred. Her sire, Ch. Bengal Valley Forge, and her dam, Ch. Tjuringa Dinky Di, have both been mentioned in these notes as Royal and ATC challenge winners. Reserve to Hurrah was Ch. Forsvar Future Shock. In dogs, the certificate went to Ann Sorraghan's Ch. Old Iron Outlaw with the reserve to Ch. Rangeaire Ramsey.

It is obvious that the Airedale Terrier has made a definite place for himself in the Australian show scene. We can look forward to more growth and even better specimens in the future. The combination of wise importing and wise use of those imports in our breeding programs have carried us a long way. We plan to continue this course for the future.

9

The Airedale Terrier
Club of America

THE OBJECT of the Airedale Terrier Club of America is "promoting the breeding of pure Airedale Terriers—and doing all in its power to protect and advance the interests of the breed." To quote from the 1950 *Yearbook*, "its aim in addition to the one expressed by its founders, is to define and publish a definition of the true type of Airedale, to urge this type upon breeders and judges, and to support shows and help other Airedale clubs whose purpose is similar to ours. As the Parent Club, its sanction is necessary when regional Airedale clubs wish to hold Specialty shows, and the delegate of the Airedale Club of America to The American Kennel Club is practically spokesman of the breed with that body."

History of the Parent Club

The Airedale Terrier Club of America was founded in 1900 by Messrs. A. D. Cochrane, J. L. Arden, James Mortimer, William L. Barclay and Russell H. Johnson, Jr., and the list of past presidents and other officers reads like the "Who's Who" of dogdom. Membership in the Club was largely confined to the East until Barbara Strebeigh became secretary in 1949, when interest in the monthly newsletters she edited drew in a great many more members. Miss Strebeigh was elected president of the Club in 1957, becoming the first woman in the history of the Club to hold this office, and it is through her lively reporting of the news each month that members have come to know each other, and to hear of the exploits of Airedales from one end of the country to the other.

Club Activities

The Winter specialty of the Parent Club is usually held in connection with several other Terrier Specialties just before the Westminster show. This date makes it possible for exhibitors from afar to show at both events without a long stop-over. The Summer Specialty is held in connection with the Montgomery County show in Pennsylvania, but may be held in any location that might at the time draw the most entries. *Yearbooks* have been published at intervals, giving the past history of the club and the breed; the officers; a discussion of the Standard—past and present; progress of the breed during the preceding years; a list of Bowl and challenge cup winners; etc.

Club Trophies

The Airedale Bowl is a perpetual trophy that has been in competition since 1910. Originally valued at $750 (when dollars were dollars), it is now assessed at $3500, but so great is its intrinsic value that it is on display only at the Parent Club Specialties or on special occasions, one of which was the twenty-fifth Anniversary show of the Southern California Club.

During the period that William E. Buckley (later president of The American Kennel Club) was president of the Airedale Terrier Club of America, it was decided to put the Bowl into competition in areas other than the East that have strong Airedale entries, but for a total of no more than five times each year, including the home Specialties. Southern California was chosen for the first of these "outside" events, with Ch. Lionheart Copper topping an entry of fifty Airedales. Besides Southern California, New England and Illinois have had the Bowl offered on a more or less permanent basis, with other regional clubs having it from time to time.

Regional Airedale Clubs

The Club gives all possible help to its regional and affiliated clubs—and the local clubs give closer contact among owners than is possible through the Parent Club.

Since the last edition of *The Complete Airedale Terrier* was written, many new regional clubs have sprung up in all areas of the country. With the more venerable clubs in New England, the Midwest and the Pacific coast, they offer Airedale fanciers in many places an opportunity for direct participation in club affairs.

They exist as avenues of education, with many publishing their own newletters and offering educational programs to those interested in the

218

breed. They conduct matches and Specialties, many of which are very popular and filled with quality entries from far and wide every year. These regional clubs perform a very important service and fill a definite need in the fancy.

Anyone interested in locating a regional Airedale club has only to contact the American Kennel Club, 51 Madison Avenue, New York, N.Y. 10010, requesting the name and address of the Secretary of the nearest one.

Ch. Breezewood Ballyhoo (left) and Ch. Blackheath Geisha Girl were BB and BOS winners at an earlier Specialty of the ATC of New England under Percy Roberts (extreme left). *Brown*

Ch. Axel's Columbus, owned by Mrs. W. H. Messeck, Jr., was a top winner during the late 1950s. He is shown winning BB at the ATC of New England in 1957 handled by the late Jimmy Butler. *Brown*

219

Ch. Blackburn's Baronof Brutus. The "King of Terriers" can clown with the best of them.   *Lindsey*

10

Character and Utility
of the Breed

THE AIREDALE has been honored with the title "King of Terriers," and taking into consideration his innumerable and varied talents, this is a birthright of high esteem. But the Airedale is not a snobbish, aloof royalist; he is a product of modern times with its handy-man trend; hence, he is not only Terrier Rex, but is also the Royal Huntsman, the Palace Guard, and the Court Jester, and holder of any other title that is required of him. He has an ebullient joy of life, yet has the calm dignity befitting his majesty.

General Considerations

There are Airedales that are superior big-game dogs, some make fine coon dogs, others are natural bird dogs, many make excellent police dogs, an occasional Airedale will prove adept at herding stock, and a good number have fine records in obedience—to select but a few of their vocations. It would be an injustice to the breed, however, to claim that every Airedale can do all these things. Specialist breeds are naturally superior at their own work, but individuals of the Airedale breed can do innumerable tasks well.

Many times it happens that a purchaser of an Airedale puppy, fired with the tales of the Airedale's courage and assorted virtues, takes the puppy directly from a kennel run and expects him to be everything that the breed's most enthusiastic admirers claim for it. If the puppy is not

221

The versatile Airedale boasts proven ability in many ways. Shown here are Hilltops' Arne of Oregon and Hilltops' High Noon. These dogs are competent retrievers and hunters of upland game.

Early Lionheart Airedales after an encounter with a porcupine.

A group of Dr. Deacon's Buckhorn Airedales with a bag of mountain lion.

an immediate success as a watchdog, if it backs up from strangers or canine bullies, it quite probably will be branded a lemon, and the novice owner will feel he has been gypped. Other green owners, hearing of the Airedale's use as a hunter, will turn a city-bred dog loose on a trail and expect it to turn up with a dead wildcat, or promptly tackle a bear. The very fact that some Airedales *are* naturals for certain types of work has given the impression that all of them are, when actually the majority need training just as every Pointer, Setter and Spaniel needs training for its work, as every working Terrier must be entered to fox and badger gradually, and as every Hound must serve an apprenticeship with older Hounds.

Retrieving

It is often stated that Airedales are natural retrievers; certainly most of them do love to carry things. In fact, some like to carry something nearly all the time.

Simba is one that simply had to carry something if there was anything to carry. He would carry the wastepaper basket out to the incinerator and laboriously carry it back up the stairs, although it hit on his legs at every step. He had a hard time carrying in the Sunday paper, as it was too large for him to get a good grip and was heavy enough to present a weight problem, but he always managed somehow.

It is said that Airedales normally have hard mouths, but we had one bitch that brought in a whole clutch of baby chicks stranded on high ground during irrigation of the orchard. She brought them in one at a time, the downy chicks neither damp nor worried, and none the worse for their experience. But we had quite a shock when she brought in the first one, for it was, so far as we could tell, completely inside her mouth.

Crosswind, a natural killer os such animals as opossum, brought in a very young live rabbit without so much as dampening its fur. So when an Airedale wants to, it can have as soft a mouth as any bred-for-the-purpose Retriever. But remember that phrase "when it wants to." And even in this line will be found the "refusers" who will not accept the dumbell in obedience work, or who will not be bothered even to bring back a ball.

Some Airedales, bored with kennel life, will think up ways to break the monotony. One of Lou Holliday's Comet bitches had a flair for opening gates or doors. She could unlatch almost any sort of fastening, including the hook type with a spring safety which many a human cannot figure out quickly. One day she really stirred up activity by unlocking all the kennel runs, letting all the dogs out, including the deadly fighter Cold Steel and several other stud dogs. Fortunately her escapade was discovered before much damage occurred. Another of this line, Enchantress, could open a bolt fastener as fast as you could close it. Another bitch would stand up and work the doorknob with her paws and thus open ordinary doors.

One of the Messeck bitches, German-bred, won the gratitude of a hysterical milk goat whose kids had become lost in the woods the day before. The goat herself had not been able to find the kids, so Cora, the Airedale, was put on their trail. Soon she returned, with the two kids trotting ahead of her. She had worked out the trail in spite of rain during the night and was very proud of herself, rushing to Mrs. Messeck and lifting her lips in a smug smile as she sat down to receive her reward.

Guard Work

As a watchdog and guard dog the Airedale has earned a redoubtable reputation, but he guards his adopted family and his home through a strong protective instinct, rather than because he has been bred for generations to attack man—as is the case with a few strictly guard breeds. Although formidable to face and imprudent to challenge, the Airedale is not by nature a "sharp" dog, easily triggered into attack. He can be made sharp by systematized aggravating, as in attack dog training for certain types of sentry and police duty, but ordinarily he cannot be rated high on aggressiveness as applied to man. While a dog with a naturally sharp disposition is dangerous enough as is, if a sharp dog is also shy, then he is dynamite. This is the type called "shy-sharp"—the fear-biters, the dogs that cringe and snap at anything that happens to frighten them, be it man or beast. In the Airedale shy-sharpness is practically unknown—in fact, I have never yet heard of a case in the breed. There are occasional shy Airedales, both the timid type and the man-shy type, along with a number that are bold enough in every environment except the show ring, to the acute embarrassment of their hopeful owners. Nearly every breed of Terrier should show like a fighting-cock, and when the biggest and best of Terriers wilts his way around the ring like an old banana peel, it is a sad reflection on the breed. This can happen without the owner having an inkling it might, for some dogs—of any breed—just do not like show rings, though in all other environments they may show like "a house afire." Some dogs that look miserable in a show may make their owners very proud of them in the right element.

Often an attitude that is mistaken for shyness is merely uncertainty, the "fish out of water" feeling that only needs experience and confidence to eliminate it. The city dog, or the kennel dog, can be at a loss in the woods the first time, while a back-country bumpkin, in spite of a fine record in big-game hunting, may be completely confused in city traffic, in crowds, or at a dog show—if he ever has occasion to attend

224

the latter. Most Airedales are brash and cocky under most circumstances, but there are some that need a good fight or more outings to instill confidence. For this reason, entering sanction matches is a wonderful way to bring confidence to a puppy or a young dog before trying it at championship shows.

Problems of Shyness

There is one trait of temperament that is rarely considered worthy of mention by show fanciers, but which is an extremely serious problem with enthusiasts or breeders of bird dogs—the field type that work for their existence. This problem is gun-shyness, which would not bother a show dog; but sound-shyness, the "father" of gun-shyness, has a decided influence on the reaction of the dog under some circumstances. While thunder used to be the most common villain in this respect, now in some localities the "sonic boom" has out-performed thunder, and can make the walls of the house feel like they are about to fall in—or out. Dogs subjected to the experience, if the type that would ordinarily have been frightened under the bed by thunder, are also the type that go gun-shy, as a rule. Starting with the noise of the sonic blast, the dog becomes increasingly conscious of lesser, but similar, noises until finally every little pop bothers him.

The best cure is to try to accustom the dog to sudden loud noises by showing him that he cannot be hurt because of the noise. With a litter of puppies, gun-shyness and sound-shyness can usually be warded off by firing a cap pistol to call them to feed, gradually increasing the noise by other bangs, or by using .22 blanks. This method, although good, is not completely foolproof, for a fool can ruin pups that way by not noticing reaction. The sudden stop, the strained look and pulling back of the ears as the pup comes to feed indicate he is a doubtful case and has to be taken more slowly, with less loud noise. Completely sound-shy dogs, which will refuse to eat rather than come to feed when a noise is made, are hardly worth trying to work with. Since Airedales are used both as gun dogs and as police dogs, their reaction to gunfire can be as important as in the specialist breeds of bird dogs, where it is all-important, and in the guard breeds, where it is also a factor. Gun-shy dogs quickly learn to associate a firearm of any type with a loud noise that hurts their ears, so the sight or smell of any sort of gun will make them cringe or run for cover. Even ordinarily staunch dogs can be made sound-shy by stupid handling, usually by firing a large bore shotgun too close and too early in the dog's career, as well as too often if the dog starts to notice the noise. In fact, a good proportion of gunshyness, and possibly sound-shyness, is due to a flaw in the mentality of the dog's owner or trainer rather than in that of the dog.

Another trait that can spoil a dog as a showman is flash-shyness.

225

This is of a cumulative nature, first caused by a dog's being blinded temporarily by staring straight at the camera when his picture is taken in the ring, then "shot" at other shows. Sometimes, if his win is a big one, he has a battery of flash bulbs to face, and anyone knows such a flare really hurts the eyes. Some dogs just cannot understand what hurt them, but they do not intend to have it repeated. The proud and hopeful owner, taking his winner to the next show, is suddenly horrified to see the dog crouch and flinch all at once, after entering the ring as happy and full of himself as ever. The reason for this could be the dog's noticing a flash from another ring where a picture was being taken. A flash-shy dog will start watching for flashes, especially in indoor shows where they are more noticeable, and the strained, apprehensive look will foretell what will happen when he sees the flash. This attitude usually snowballs until the dog associates the show ring with unpleasantness—first the hurt to his eyes, then his memory of fear or apprehension in the ring; finally he becomes shy the minute he approches the ring, although elsewhere he is entirely his old self. Both sound-shyness and flash-shyness are from a hurt that cannot be fought back, so neither is a reflection on the dog's real courage, especially as both can be caused through mishandling. As to whether gun-shyness is hereditary or not, this has been argued up one wall and down the other by gun dog people and is just as good for starting arguments as is "heredity vs. environment."

Fur and Feather

The use of the Airedale as a "varmint" dog (and in this country varmints include big game such as cougar) brought the breed much fame. With Lou Holliday and Dr. Deacon being among the prominent Airedale breeders who also enjoyed ample opportunity for big-game hunting, there naturally have been many incidents reported involving their dogs. These two breeders were also avid enthusiasts of "scatter gun" shooting and consequently used Airedales for upland game and waterfowl work.

An incident that shows why Airedale Terriers were more often known merely as bear dogs in the big-game country is this, related by Lou Holliday:

My partner and I were hunting in Idaho and we had coupled all the dogs except Boss, then only 10½ months old, and taken a walk up the creek, a raging torrent. Decided to watch the opposite hillside for bear out after roots, etc., so tied all the dogs except Boss to the bushes. Suddenly I heard Boss growl, and he took off down the slide rock, across the creek which took him 75 yards down to a sand bar and the next thing we knew he was fighting a big bear (500 pounds, hide measures over six feet, skull measured 34 inches) all alone. By the time we got the pack cut loose he had him out of the willows and was taking him up the hill-

Lionheart Congresswoman (Mountainview Rush ex Illuminator's Queen) after a successful big game hunt.

Lou Holliday was an avid and successful big game hunter. This 1922 photo shows the result of eight days' hunting in the Idaho-Wyoming border country. Holliday, some of his early Airedales and a couple of hounds are shown with their bag of two black bears, a grizzly and a brown.

227

side. One by one the dogs got to the bear and we had to take chances in shooting but finally got him down with a lucky shot. When we got there, Primary Dynamite, an 8½ month old son of Lionheart Primary, was froze on to one front toe. Just as far away as he could get and still have a hold, but when he turned loose the toe came with him and the missing part shows to this day on the rug made from the hide. Boss was a grandson of Earlwood Warlock and weighed 65 pounds.

Mr. Holliday was as interested in hunting feather as in hunting fur and trained his Airedales for birds too, with some lines showing a natural instinct for bird hunting and retrieving. One young dog was so fond of retrieving that he would catch the neighbors' pullets and proudly bring them into the house, causing embarrassment to the Hollidays when friends were present, since they would then joke about training dogs to "bring home the bacon" (or poultry) the easy way. The chickens would be promptly returned over the fence, none the worse for wear, but to the chagrin of the helpful Rip. This dog later became proficient on retrieving wild geese, and he would watch them on the way down after they were shot, so that his goose was immediately brought to Mr. Holliday, saving the day on a couple of occasions when other, close-by, hunters thought they would collect a free bird. Rip was of a line of Airedales with natural bird sense, his granddam Crosswind and great-granddam Lionheart Jill both being especially good on upland game. The former was even more unique in that she would actually hold a point, rather than merely flush birds. Another of this line, a Group and Specialty winner, Ch. Hilltop's Rocky Top Notch, was equally "birdy"—to the extent that his owner became very popular with other hunters during the pheasant season. This hunting line is also that of the greatest number of holders of highest obedience degrees in the breed—the Sierradales and the River-Aires with the tap-root bitch being Ch. Lionheart Comet. Thus Comet and her descendants, which also include a formidable array of bench-show winners, are in themselves irrefutable proof of the amazing versatility of the Airedale. The fact that one branch was especially noted (or at least used) for hunting and the other for obedience work, shows that environment, and the interests of the owners play a great part in the development of doggy talent, yet that the latent ability is still there.

The Airedale and Big Game

The Lionheart Airedales, better remembered now for their bench-show accomplishments, started their road to fame in the back country of Montana, with wild game of all sorts, especially bear, all around them. The foundation of the strain was old Lionheart Queen, a bitch of fashionable show bloodlines, tracing eight times, close up, to Ch. Clonmel Monarch—and a mighty tough old gal she was in a fight. Dr. P. J.

Palm, in Cody, Wyoming, wrote Mr. Holliday about a dog he had bought from him:

I claim the Airedale I bought from you is the most useful and intelligent dog in Wyoming, and if you could see him at work you would understand my claim. In addition to retrieving ducks and standing sagehens, he is the leader of my pack on bear, lion, etc., and has killed several coyotes and bobcats single-handed. On a fairly fresh track he leads way ahead of the Hounds, and has a record of four lions already this season, never having lost one started—some record for a youngster. Am enclosing clipping from the local paper describing our latest catch, an eight-foot lion.

Wherever "lion" is referred to in hunting in this country, the mountain lion (also called cougar, panther, and "painter") is meant.

W. D. Sanders of Irwin, Idaho, wrote about Lionheart Primary:

He is the constant companion of myself and wife and a royal pal he is. I just returned from a six day bear hunt on which we secured two bears, largely due to this dog. He took the lead of my two Walker Hounds on the track and it was his hard fighting that made the bears tree. Also he is a better chicken dog than most Setters and Pointers, and will retrieve ducks nicely.

Doctor Deacon gives this report of one of his hunts:

Every man has a hobby. Mine is hunting varmints with dogs. For over thirty years I have followed this sport, my first pack was composed solely of Hounds. Later on I tried a mixed one. The last fifteen years I have used nothing but Airedales. In my opinion the Airedale is the dog of dogs. His courage and intelligence are unequalled and he can be taught anything that a canine can. He can be as gentle as a lamb or as courageous as a lion, more so in fact, for a real Airedale never knows when to quit. Every year I spend all the time I can in the mountains, and in the fall, with a few friends and twenty to thirty Airedales, at least a month.

The Airedale has been used in Africa on the "real" lion, to stop him and bring him to bay. Of course the more courageous dogs, if not also prudent, quickly get killed in this work, but those that only get close enough to harass the lion until the hunters come up for a shot, live to fight again. In this they are like experienced bear and boar dogs, for a big, full-grown bear or a husky sabre-toothed wild boar cannot be killed by a dog any more than an African lion can.

One hunter in Northern Rhodesia used Airedales in hunting baboons, which are about the most formidable and ferocious animal a dog ever might have to face. They have much stronger biting power than any Bull Terrier ever bred, and their ape-like ability to use their hands in fighting does not help matters at all, except for the baboon.

In France Airedales find their big game limited to wild boar—no small adversary, either in tonnage or ability to kill. Boar hunting is not common in America, since there are no wild boars similar to European and Indian varieties, but there are the wild peccaries, or *javelina,* and in the mountain districts of the South, the feral "razorbacks." These have been hunted with Airedales by W. D. Scarborough, a Tennessee Airedale breeder.

Mrs. S. H. Stroud, from Texas, tells of an example of the "show type" Airedale's disproval of the myth that it is only a bench-warmer:

In attempting to breed and sell *good* Airedales in West Texas, believe me we constantly fight the battle of "sissified ribbon" winners vs. "hunting strains." Major Cargill, about 30 miles from us, made the initial dent in this area with his Cactus and Cactus Blossom, which he took with him to England after their coyote hunting adventures, and we are carrying on. Although it was only a sanction match, we took the Terrier Group at Plainview last Sunday with a bitch that less than a week before had made a darn good job of trailing and made a kill on an all-night 'coon hunt. And for the pure "helluvit" we took one of her pups, now 4½ months old, which was already sold as a working stock dog, and showed her through her puppy class and second to her mama in open, over grown bitches! She was picked up, together with her ribbons, by her owners the following morning and a phone call from them this morning assured me how pleased they were with their show type Airedale, that she charges the Herefords if they mill around the yard or too close to *her* children, yet goes down to the corral where the cattle belong, 15 minutes later and licks the same cattle on their noses. Our dogs, essentially of Dalehaven breeding, are over the 23-inch standard, but our area market is for "big ones"—hunting, working stock, or a woman's guard dog for the woman whose husband works all night in the oil fields.

Airedales are, of course, used in fighting bobcat, and pictures of such fights have often been printed in magazines and books. Among the most spectacular were the full-color photographs in a four-paged spread of *Sports Illustrated,* showing Bonny, the Airedale owned by Sam Shaver of Bend, Oregon, in a free-for-all with one of the feline hellions. The pictures show her work graphically, her head and the 'cat's often a blur, but the 'cat's huge, wide-spread, knife-clawed feet were very much in evidence although Bonny's planned attack managed to avoid most of the very considerable damage those claws could have done.

In the *Jungle* series on TV, an Airedale was shown in a bobcat sequence also. Here, again, the Hounds tracked the 'cat to a small cave, then, faced with a spitting, slashing invitation to suicide, decided they had done their part and retired to watch. The Airedale was unleashed and without further ado rushed to the cave, paying no heed to the inevitable damage, and pulled the infuriated varmint into the open, where the Hounds decided to help out.

Few champions of any breed ever make the headlines by killing a full-grown bobcat, but Ch. Comrade Speed King, owned by Ben Bishop of Bethany, Oklahoma, did just that, and when he was officially just a pup, too, under a year of age. He was no slouch in the show ring either, winning the Terrier Group, among other honors.

A very entertaining article on Airedales, entitled *My Friend Buck,* by J. P. Williams, was featured in a 1955 issue of *The Alaska Sportsman.* Buck was used for about everything that could be expected of a trapper's dog. His breeding was unknown, but he was supposed to be of a famous strain on Vancouver Island, B.C.

Obedience Airedales

Previously we mentioned the Comet family from which many Airedale bird dogs descended, as well as May Pridham's line of obedience dogs which come down from Ch. Sierradale Chica, U.D.T. This outstanding kennel of bench and obedience winners of Glendora, California, produced the following *champions* with obedience degrees: Rusty Dusty, U.D.T.; Sierradale Chica, U.D.T.; Sierradale War Drum, U.D.T.; Sierradale Cherokee, C.D.; Sierradale Osalita, C.D.; Sierradale Firefly, C.D.; Sierradale Sioux, C.D.

The Riveraire Kennel of Mr. and Mrs. John Schohner of Sacramento, California, is another fine example of what can be done with Airedales if the owner is obedience minded. Starting with Big Dipper Dare, U.D.; and his daughter Goldipper Sierra Spice, U.D., the Schohners later bred champions that attained high obedience degrees. The acquisition of Lionheart Irene, trained to her title by the Schohners, brought them into the bench-show angle. Irene's daughters Ch. Riveraire Rock-C, U.D.T.., and Ch. Riveraire Revel, U.D., by Ch. Eleanore's Royalty of Lionheart, obviously did well in both fields.

Other Utility Dog degrees won by Airedales were those of Farmer's Daughter, Kiowa's Bonnie Welcome, and Bellville's Skylark. The latter, owned by Eileen Larkin of Allentown, R. I., has made some spectular wins, and one of the most unusual was when she and her kennel mate, Belwings Supreme Riot, U.D., a Lakeland, tied for first in their class when trying for a Canadian degree at one show, and tied for second at a show the following day, both of the classes being well filled. Another Airedale to place high in his classes was Ch. Elroy's Top Kick, C.D., winner of several Groups in bench competition. Topper was first in his class of 43 dogs with a score of 199 plus, and was runner-up for high score of the day, later in his career taking the high score honor also.

The vocations of the Airedale have ranged from the frivolous to the serious, the predisposition toward any particular line of work depending on the combination of environment and the type of training or sport favored by the owner, with heredity possibly having less to do with it than with some breeds. Each dog is an individual, with litter mates sometimes showing completely opposite tendencies. Not only can a bold pup and a bashful pup be litter brothers, but a free-ranging hunter that especially likes retrieving from water can have a brother that hates to go out in a heavy dew, and heels so close in the field that he is useless as a gun dog. It is for reasons like this that we do not place all emphasis on inheritance as contrasted with individuality, experience, environment, and training.

Down the trail.

Under the rocks.

Out again.

Finis!

11

Obediently Yours

OBEDIENCE degrees won by Airedales, especially champions, were mentioned in Chapter 10 which covered the time period up to approximately 1960. Along with the great increase in numbers of Airedales being shown in conformation classes there has also been a surge of interest in obedience training, including the more difficult advanced degrees.

According to the list compiled by Marjorie Schohner, there were four champions which became Companion Dogs from 1961 through 1964, one of which Ch. River-Aire Bonnirogue, was C.D.X.; in 1965 there were two C.D.s; in 1966 only one, and there were three in 1967. The following year saw a goldrush of degrees, with six C.D.s and one C.D.X. One of the C.D.s was Ch. Cyndale's Shawney Sabu, who took time out between litters for such training, and from those litters she produced twelve champions. The year 1969 saw three C.D. Airedale champions and one C.D.X. with 1970 almost the same, except for an additional C.D. In 1971 we find another great producer of champions on the list of three C.D.s and one C.D.X. This is Ch. Triumph's Benaire Daffodil, C.D., dam of thirteen champions. One of her champions is Eden Jokyl Sunpiper U.D., of which more later.

There were six champions which qualified for the C.D. degree in 1972, one of which was the Airedale Bowl winner Birchrun Bartender, but the next year there was a slump, with only two making the grade. This number doubled in, and 1975 brought out three C.D.s and two C.D.X.s. It was in 1976 however that the breed proudly carded eight

233

degree-winners, of which two earned the C.D.X. title and one of the C.D.s won the same degree in Canada. During 1977 four champions annexed the C.D. degree. One is Cyrano Apollo, winner of the SCAA specialty.

Mrs. Schohner lists approximately 61 champion Airedales with Companion Dog degrees ("approximately" since some others had two legs on the degree and may have finished) Of these twelve were earned prior to 1961, and 49 since. Those with the C.D.X. degree number thirteen, The elite group of "higher learning" (or "training"), namely Utility Dogs, Utility Dog Trackers, or Tracking Dogs alone, number 47. As before, these are also champions. Of this group, four were U.D.T.s, and divide as to sex with 29 bitches and 18 dogs. The four U.D.T.s are "half and half" of each. So the grand total of champion Airedales with obedience degrees is 121—"approximately."

It was noted that several champions had two legs on the title (degree) but their owners decided to concentrate on the conformation ring instead. One of these prospective title-holders was Ch. Jerilee's Jumping Jericho, who had scored very high in his tests. But his concentration on the show ring was amply repaid, as seen earlier. While some individuals try for an obedience degree before going in for championship points, it is usually the other way around. A few even go in for both at the same time.

All Tracking Dog, or Utility Dog, Tracking, (champion or not) title holders seemed to have been Southern Californians up to and including 1953. Then Belle of Honeysuckle Acres U.D.T. joined the group in 1965 to represent the Midwest, and Seca, C.D. added the T.D. to her titles to bring Northern California into the game in 1968, along with Beachnau's Rosey, U.D.T., another Midwesterner. But 1976 saw real variety in the homelands of such experts, with Hollye of Honeysuckle Acres, U.D.T. scoring for the Midwest, Burdock of Briarpatch, C.D. added the T.D. for the Northwest and Dingo's Daphne of Erika, T.D., whose name starts out with an Australian flavor, is instead from the far north, in Alsaka. The totals give 11 T.D.s and 6 U.D.T.s. Four of these U.D.T.s were champions.

Geraldine Hagaman is the owner-trainer of Belle and Holly of Honeysuckle Acres and the only owner of two U.D.T.s, other than May Pridham (of earlier years) with three. But what makes Ms. Hagaman unique is that she is deaf, and consequently any training she does has to also be unique in itself, and that it is successful is amply proven. Marjorie Schohner's River-Aire Rock-C and May Pridham's Sierradale War Drum are the only champion U.D.T.s in the last twenty-five years. In fact they are the only champions to get any Tracking degree in that period. Lack of sufficient space (or the right sort) in which to practice tracking is given as a major reason for failure to complete

234

Ch. Cyrano Apollo, C.D., a winner in conformation and obedience with his handler, Wood Wornall.   *Yuhl*

Ch. Rusty Dusty, U.D.T. (1937), an early obedience standout.

Ch. River Aire Revel, C.D.X., Ch. River Aire Rock-C, U.D.T. and Lionheart Irene, U.D. (left to right) taking a high jump together.

236

Ch. River Aire Rock-C, U.D.T., shown in tracking harness, at work.

Triumph Toni of Pancho Villa, U.D.

237

Willow Aire Proud Piper, U.D.

these degrees. Lack of time to continue training can be another factor, for these are the most difficult of all degrees.

The foregoing C.D. and C.D.X. dogs are all champions, so of course there are many more non-champions who also hold such degrees. Other successful obedience Airedales have already been mentioned in connection with their achievements in breed competition and/or as producers.

Ch. Triumph's Benaire Daffodil C.D., referred to in one of the previous lists, is the dam of Ch. Eden Jokyl Sunpiper, U.D. She is the twelfth champion U.D. Airedale, and the first in the last ten years, and has started Tracking training. Triumph Toni of Pancho Villa, U.D. is the "aunt" of Sunpiper since she is a litter sister of Daffodil. She was the first U.D. Airedale in the Southwest; the first Airedale to place in Group IV top ten, and was the top working Airedale in the United States for three years. These two most "utilitarian" bitches are owned and trained by Estelle D. Francisco.

Another "Piper" to gain Utility fame is Willow Aire Proud Piper, U.D. She has been the highest-scoring Airedale in the United States for four years in a row (1973-76) based on the Shuman system as reported in *Front and Finish*, the obedience work newspaper. This is based on points accumulated from trial scores. She is also highest ranked Airedale for the second year in a row based on the Kent Delaney system (which is based on points accumulated by wins or class placings in obedience). She has two High-in-Trial wins and at least ten class firsts, with numerous seconds, thirds and fourths. At the Gaines U.S. Obedience Classic Trials held in New Jersey and St. Louis in 1977, she was tenth-place "Super Dog" *both years*, competing against all breeds.

Piper is proudly owned by Nancy and Frank Foster who say that "She is a 'typical' Airedale—very smart, independent, great with kids, death on intruders. She may be small in size but she is great in spirit and sets a wonderful example for her breed. She is a sweet, loving, devoted pet and a marvelous worker."

Now what better tribute could you find that that? She does indeed sound "typically Airedale."

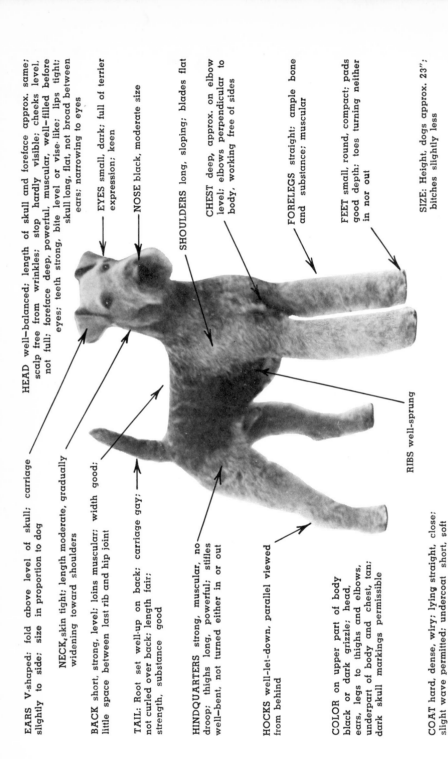

EARS V-shaped; fold above level of skull; carriage slightly to side; size in proportion to dog

HEAD well-balanced; length of skull and foreface approx. same; scalp free from wrinkles; stop hardly visible; cheeks level, not full; foreface deep, powerful, muscular, well-filled before eyes; teeth strong, bite level or vise-like; lips tight; skull long, flat, not broad between ears; narrowing to eyes

EYES small, dark; full of terrier expression; keen

NOSE black, moderate size

SHOULDERS long, sloping; blades flat

CHEST deep, approx. on elbow level; elbows perpendicular to body, working free of sides

FORELEGS straight; ample bone and substance; muscular

FEET small, round, compact; pads good depth; toes turning neither in nor out

SIZE: Height, dogs approx. 23"; bitches slightly less

NECK, skin tight; length moderate, gradually widening toward shoulders

BACK short, strong, level; loins muscular; width good; little space between last rib and hip joint

TAIL: Root set well-up on back; carriage gay; not curled over back; length fair; strength, substance good

HINDQUARTERS strong, muscular, no droop; thighs long, powerful; stifles well-bent, not turned either in or out

HOCKS well-let-down, parallel viewed from behind

COLOR on upper part of body black or dark grizzle; head, ears, legs to thighs and elbows, underpart of body and chest, tan; dark skull markings permissible

COAT hard, dense, wiry; lying straight, close; slight wave permitted; undercoat short, soft

RIBS well-sprung

Visualization of the Airedale Terrier Standard, reprinted with permission from Dog Standards Illustrated, © 1975, Howell Book House.

240

12

Official Standard
and Blueprint
of the Airedale

"O wad some Power the giftie gie us
To see our dogs as ithers see them!
It wad frae mony a blunder free us
  And foolish notion.

What errors of make and gait would
  lea'e them
  But not devotion."

(With apologies to Robert Burns)

OH WOULD indeed we had the power to see our dogs
as others—judges, for instance—see them! The nearest approach to
such a faculty is that rare gift, "an eye for a dog"—the ability to
appraise the qualities of a dog at a glance, so far as such can be ascer-
tained by outward appearance. Most of us were born without that
power, and consequently we have to learn through experience and
constant study how to evaluate the points of a dog.

241

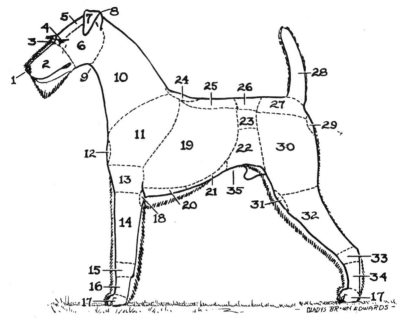

Points of the Dog
as shown on the Airedale Terrier

1—Nose
2—Muzzle; foreface
3—Stop
4—Eye
5—Skull; forehead
6—Cheek
7—Ear
8—Occiput (hidden by ear in this view)
9—Throat
10—Neck
11—Shoulder
12—Point of shoulder
13—Upper arm; arm
14—Forearm
15—Knee
16—Front pastern
17—foot; paw

18—Elbow
19—Ribs
20—Brisket
21—Abdomen; belly
22—Flank
23—Coupling
24—Withers
25—Back
26—Loin
27—Croup; rump
28—Tail; stern
29—Point of buttock
30—Thigh
31—Stifle
32—Gaskin; second thigh
33—Hock
34—Back pastern

35—Tuck-up

Length is measured from point of shoulder to point of buttock (12 to 29)
Height is measured from withers (24) to ground. Length should approximate height on the Airedale.
The QUARTERS are the thighs; the HINDQUARTERS include the croup and hind legs.
The FOREHAND is that point in front of the center of gravity.
The BACKLINE includes the withers, back, loin and croup.

Points to Consider

There are two pitfalls that trap the newcomer to the dog game, slowing his progress, one being that self-satisfied rosy glow known as "kennel blindness," the other a superficial and usually short-lived egotism that brings on a pernicious affliction known as "fault-judging." The misted vision of kennel blindness glorifies one's own dogs and at the same time makes the dogs owned by others, like Gil Blas' mule, "all faults." Fault-judging affects the owner's dogs as well as his competitors, and in his own dogs he can become so conscious of a fault he is striving to eradicate that he cannot see good points even though they may completely outweigh the fault in question. This attitude, applied to others' dogs, can make them seem worthless because of one obvious fault, such "pet hate" possibly being the only fault the fault-judger knows on sight.

The Airedale is a dog of normal conformation, square in proportion of length to height, and in basic points the Airedale Standard is similar to that of other normally conformed dogs. That is, there are no gross exaggerations of any points.

The current, official Standard of the breed follows. The balance of this chapter is a point-by-point analysis of the word picture of Airedale perfection. Careful study of the Standard and the analysis, or blueprint, herein will give the reader an excellent basis for understanding what makes an Airedale an Airedale. If the reader will also objectively observe as many specimens in the flesh as possible, he will be well on the way toward really developing an in-depth knowledge of the "King of Terriers."

Official Standard of the Airedale Terrier

Head—Should be well balanced with little apparent difference between the length of skull and foreface. *Skull* should be long and flat, not too broad between the ears and narrowing very slightly to the eyes. Scalp should be free from wrinkles, stop hardly visible and cheeks level and free from fullness. *Ears* should be V-shaped with carriage rather to the side of the head, not pointing to the eyes, small but not out of proportion to the size of the dog. The topline of the folded ear should be above the level of the skull. *Foreface* should be deep, powerful, strong and muscular. Should be well filled up before the eyes. *Eyes* should be dark, small, not prominent, full of terrier expression, keenness and intelligence. *Lips* should be tight. *Nose* should be black and not too small. *Teeth* should be strong and white, free from discoloration or defect. Bite either level or vise-like. A slightly overlapping or scissors bite is permissible without preference.

Neck—Should be of moderate length and thickness gradually widening towards the shoulders. Skin tight, not loose.

Shoulders and Chest—Shoulders long and sloping well into the back. Shoulder blades flat. From the front, chest deep but not broad. The depth of the chest should be approximately on a level with the elbows.

Body—Back should be short, strong and level. Ribs well sprung. Loins muscular and of good width. There should be but little space between the last rib and the hip joint.

Hindquarters—Should be strong and muscular with no droop.

Tail—The root of the tail should be set well up on the back. It should be carried gaily but not curled over the back. It should be of good strength and substance and of fair length.

Legs—*Forelegs* should be perfectly straight, with plenty of muscle and bone. *Elbows* should be perpendicular to the body, working free of sides. *Thighs* should be long and powerful with muscular second thigh, stifles well bent, not turned either in or out, hocks well let down parallel with each other when viewed from behind. *Feet* should be small, round and compact with a good depth of pad, well cushioned; the toes moderately arched, not turned either in or out.

Coat—Should be hard, dense and wiry, lying straight and close, covering the dog well over the body and legs. Some of the hardest are crinkling or just slightly waved. At the base of the hard very stiff hair should be a shorter growth of softer hair termed the undercoat.

Color—The head and ears should be tan, the ears being of a darker shade than the rest. Dark markings on either side of the skull are permissible. The legs up to the thighs and elbows and the under-part of the body and chest are also tan and the tan frequently runs into the shoulder. The sides and upper parts of the body should be black or dark grizzle. A red mixture is often found in the black and is not to be considered objectionable. A small white blaze on the chest is a characteristic of certain strains of the breed.

Size—Dogs should measure approximately 23 inches in height at the shoulder; bitches, slightly less. Both sexes should be sturdy, well muscled and boned.

Movement—Movement or action is the crucial test of conformation. Movement should be free. As seen from the front the forelegs should swing perpendicular from the body free from the sides, the feet the same distance apart as the elbows. As seen from the rear the hind legs should be parallel with each other, neither too close nor too far apart, but so placed as to give a strong well-balanced stance and movement. The toes should not be turned either in or out.

Faults

Yellow eyes, hound ears, white feet, soft coat, being much over or under the size limit, being undershot or overshot, having poor movement, are faults which should be severely penalized.

Scale of Points

Head	10	Color	5
Neck, shoulders and chest	10	Size	10
Body	10	Movement	10
Hindquarters and tail	10	General characteristics and	
Legs and feet	10	expression	15
Coat	10	TOTAL	100

Approved July 14, 1959

Size

The Standard states that the ideal Airedale should be "approximately" 23 inches in height, but actually a dog measuring exactly this height looks rather small today, the average ranging from 23½ to slightly over 24 inches, with an occasional "big 'un" going 24½. Any height over 24 inches is called "big," but when an Airedale gets close to the 25 inch mark he really is a whopper, if in correct balance and with good substance. Most of the truly tall ones, however, are inclined to be

245

Main Points of the Skeleton

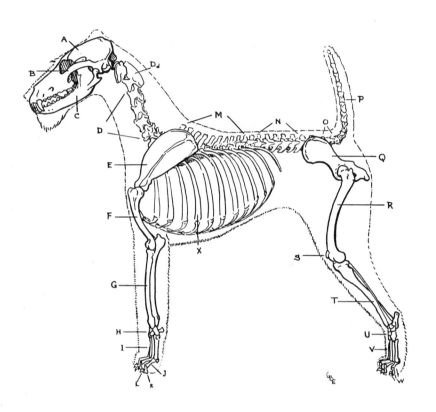

A—Cranium
B—Malar bone (Zygomatic process of,)
C—Mandible
Dd—Atlas (1st cervical vertebra)
D—Cervical vertebrae
E—Scapula
F—Humerus
G—Radius and Ulna
H—Carpus
I—Metacarpus
J—1st phalanges
K—2nd phalanges

L—Distal phalanges
M—Thoracic vertebrae
N—Lumbar vertebrae
O—Sacrum
P—Caudal vertebrae
Q—Pelvis
R—Femur
S—Patella
T—Tibia and Fibula
U—Tarsus
V—Metatarsus
W—Phalanges

X—Ribs

Superficial Muscles of the Dog

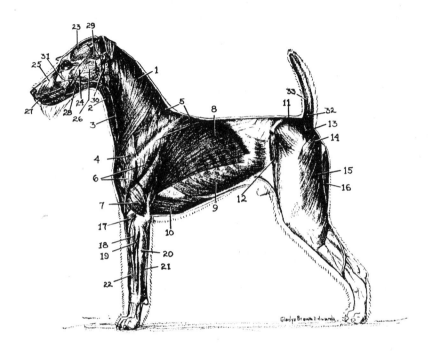

1—Sterno-cleid-mastoid
2—Sterno hyoideus
3—Jugular Vein
4—Inferior levator anguli scapula
5—Trapezius
6—Deltoid
7—Triceps brachi
8—Latissimus dorsi
9—Obliquus abdominis externus
10—Pectoralis
11—Gluteus medius
12—Anterior part of sartorius
13—Gluteus maxiumus
14—Trochanter major
15—Biceps femoris
16—Semitendinosus

17—Extensor carpi radialis
18—Extensor digitorum communis
19—Extensor digiti minimi
20—Extensor carpi ulnaris
21—Flexor carpi ulnaris
22—Abductor pollicis longus
23—Temporalis
24—Zygomaticus
25—Levator nasolabialis
26—Masseter
27—Buccalis
28—Molaris
29—Exterior adductor of ear
30—Depressor auris
31—Facial vein
32—Adductor of tail

33—Levator of tail

rangey and light in substance, usually lacking Terrier type as well. Height is measured from the highest point of the withers to the ground, while length of body is measured from the forward point of the shoulder to the point of the buttock—the length of the whole body, and only the body. The average "square" Airedale of about 23 inches weighs at least a good 55 to 60 pounds, variation in substance and bone making the few-pound difference.

In certain breeds, such as the working Terriers that must go to ground after their quarry, size is very important, but in the Airedale there is no real reason for an absolute decree as to height and weight, and slight variance in either is not too serious. However, when the Airedale is so small he resembles a Welsh Terrier or is so large and rangey that he looks like a black and tan Irish Wolfhound, then size becomes a problem.

Secondary Sexual Characteristics

The Airedale Standard does not mention sex characteristics, although it does state that the bitch should measure "slightly less" than the dog. Actually, the bitch is more refined throughout, and must be just as feminine as the dog is masculine. A "doggy" bitch is coarse of head and unfeminine, while a "bitchy" dog lacks strength of skull and foreface for his size and substance, often having a less aggressive attitude also, but not necessarily. The male Airedale should have that fierce, keen-eyed gaze known as "the look of eagles," hard as nails when he sizes up another dog. A bitch can be as large as a dog without being doggy if she has true feminine character. Most Standards concede that bitches may be a little longer in the coupling than dogs, and the neck of a bitch should be lighter and more elegant, though the dog's neck should not be coarse by any means.

General Appearance

The Airedale is a stylish dog when on parade but a very workmanlike dog when in the field. The sleekly trimmed Airedale, ready to prance into the show ring, looks long of head and lean of skull, his neck is elegant and arched, his body coat may have a slight wave but lies flat, and his furnishings of muzzle and running gear are brushed out to a bristly fluffiness. This same dog in his "working clothes" has a protective layer of hair on his head and neck, but his coat rarely has the well-tailored flatness it shows when well groomed. The hair on his skull, even though lying fairly flat, adds thickness to the appearance of the skull, and the muzzle looks shorter and even snipey through contrast with the broad-appearing skull.

Head

The Standard describes the head as being well balanced, with little apparent difference between length of skull and foreface. In spite of

248

Deeper Muscles of the Dog

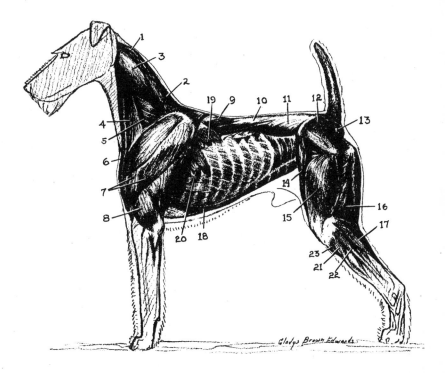

1—Head part of rhomboideus
2—Rhomboideus
3—Splenius
4—Inferior levator anguli scapulae
5—Cervical portion of serratus anterior
6—Suspraspinatus
7—Deltoideus
8—Triceps brachi
9—Spinalis dorsi
10—Longissimus dorsi
11—Iliocostalis

12—Gluteus medius
13—Gluteus maximus
14—Anterior portion of sartorius
15—Quadriceps femoris
16—Semimembranosus
17—Gastrocnemii
18—Rectus abdominus
19—Anterior portion of serratus posterior
20—Thoracic portion of serratus anterior
21—Extensor dig. pedis longus
22—Flexor hallucis longus

23—Tibialis anterior

The Skull

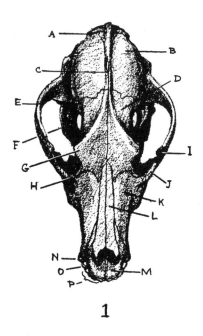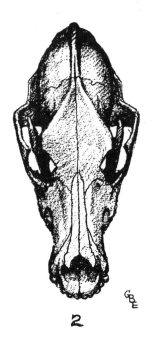

1   2

"1" Skull of a dog of Samoyed type. "2" Skull of an Airedale. Note that the much wider appearance of the former is due to the wide spacing of the malar bones and that the size of the cranium—the "brainroom"—is the same in both.

A—Interparietal bone
B—Parietal bone of the cranium
C—Parietal crest
D—Frontal bone
E—Zygomatic process of the temporal bone
F—Coronoid process of mandible
G—Supraorbital process
H—Lacrimal bone

I—Zygomatic process of the malar bone
J—Malar bone
K—Maxilla
L—Nasal bone
M—Body of premaxilla
N—Canine tooth
O—Canine tooth (lower)
P—Incisors

this, some breeders are very proud of producing dogs with very long muzzles—which are certainly not in balance. The skull is fairly well described in the Standard as long and flat, not too broad between the ears, and narrowing slightly to the eyes. The flatness should be apparent both from side view of the skull and also from front view, for the skull should be more inclined toward the rectangular than the cylindrical. Some very narrow-skulled Airedales have a prominent bump just above the stop, but this is undesirable.

The stop should not be "browy" even if the facial furnishings are sopping wet; and the expression "well filled up before the eyes" means *very* well filled, so that the upper jaw, when viewed or felt from the front, should resemble the top of a quonset hut rather than the roof of a Swiss chalet. In other words, the top of the muzzle should be rounded, giving a good feeling of solidity when grasped in the hand. A narrow muzzle, dropping quickly away from the bridge, is not the muzzle for an Airedale. Some muzzles are dished below the eyes, also a weak formation and not worthy of a Terrier.

In critiques of Airedales, "long, lean head" or "head of terrific length" is often mentioned. Certainly the head should be long and lean, provided it is in proportion to the size and conformation of the dog, but it should not be so exaggerated that all one can see is head. Nor should it be so narrow that the impression of brainlessness is automatically given.

Cleanness of cheek has been interpreted at times to mean entirely cleaned of muscle, so that the dog lacks jaw power. The cheek muscle need not bulge to be powerful, but certainly it must be present. And the temporal muscle, forming the "corner" or "edge" of the skull, should be well developed.

Ears

The description of the ears is not too clear in the Standard, unless the reader already has a good idea of how the ears should look. Nothing is said about the Airedale's ears being of the drop type—the Standard merely states that the top line of the folded ear should be above the level of the skull. It does not specify whether the ear is normally folded, or if you do the folding yourself to see where the fold will be, just as you might pull a Cocker's ears toward his nose to see how long they are. Assuming that knowledge of the side-carried drop ear is understood, it should be noted that the inner edge of the ear should lie close to the cheek, and should not point to the eye—as with the Fox Terrier—but rather should point to the ground.

Expression

Expression is a combination of several factors: size, shape, color,

The Skull and Dentition

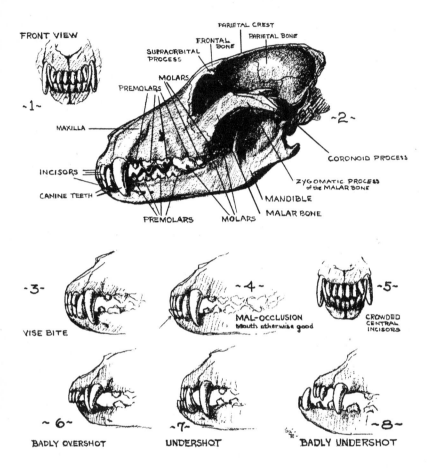

Nos. "1" and "2" show the perfect scissors bite, with No. 3, a vise or pincer bite, considered equally good. On the live dog the teeth of course are partially covered by the gums, and in the front view the lower lip fits in between the canine tooth (fang) and the jaw. The smaller premolars are almost buried in the gums in some cases, but ideally are of fair size. Occasionally a premolar is missing, but is usually compensated by larger size of the others. The mal-occlusion of the incisors, shown in No. "4" is due to the centrals growing forward in too flat an angle. The mouth shown is otherwise excellent. No. "5" is a common fault, with central incisors too small and crowded by unusually large corners and intermediates. Aside from "looks" this is not a serious fault, except that it might be inherited, while a mal-occlusion may be due to late shedding of milk teeth; "6" is a "pig jaw," badly overshot, and an abomination in a Terrier, accompanying a weak lower jaw. "7" Undershot jaw. Note the obvious difference between this and the mal-occlusion, especially the position of the fangs, and the face-to-face position of the premolars, rather than interlocking. "8" should never be seen on a Terrier, and is the deliberately-bred undershot jaw of a Boxer.

252

Heads and Expression

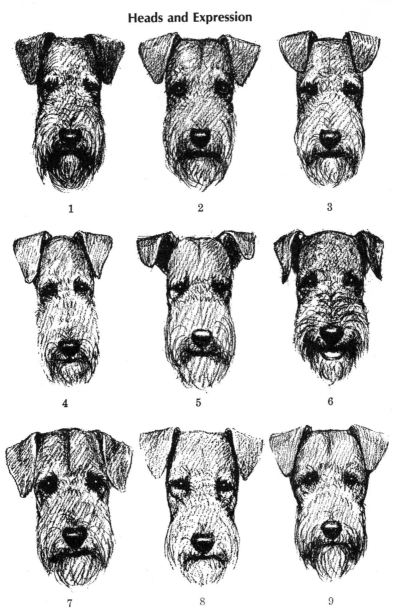

1   2   3

4   5   6

7   8   9

"1" Typical expression. "2" Staring expression due to large, round, light eyes. "3" High, Fox Terrier ears, pointing to the eye. "4" Very narrow head, with little space between eyes or ears. "5" Flying ears. "6" Same head as No. 1, but in a less stern mood, and ears relaxed. "7" Broad head, large eyes, Houndy ears. "8" Same type head as No. 1, but trimmed too close in front of eyes and at corners of mouth, making the head appear cheeky. "9" Broad, coarse skull.

and placement of the eyes; size and carriage of the ears, together with the general shape of the head; and it is sparked by the glow from within. The correct expression is keen and hard-bitten, and the dog seems to look right through you.

Eyes

Eyes are well described in the Standard, and the subject needs little clarification other than to mention that they should not be round. Rather, they are oval, sometimes even giving a somewhat triangular appearance, but not so exaggerated as in the Bull Terrier. The color of the eyes is described as "dark," but the nearer to black the color is, the better. The eventual color of the eyes cannot be determined until puppies are three or four months old. Some eyes that are dark when first clearing from the bluish haze of very young puppyhood become light as the puppy gets older, so it is well not to be too smug about eye color until the puppies are at least three or four months old. In contrast, there have been cases noted where eyes have become noticeably darker as the puppy got older, the change occurring when the dogs were about two years of age.

Nose

The Standard has little to say about the Airedale's nose, except that it should be black and not too small. Since the Standard calls for a black nose, breeders are occasionally worried by the appearance of pink-nosed newborn puppies in a litter. The pink is usually limited to a streak down the center of the nose, and sometimes inside the nostrils. Ordinarily the nose turns black by the time the puppy starts to teethe, and usually well before, but a very rare one will retain a faint light-colored streak. Although called a Dudley nose, it is not truly one, in that the color is just washed-out, not a light pink and black combination with a distinct edge, and in any event is extremely unusual in mature dogs.

Teeth and Bite

The upper jaw furnishes the foundation for the set of formidable teeth, and the more solid the foundation, the firmer the teeth. The lower jaw should complement the upper in strength, and should be relatively deep, furnishing a solid base for the lower teeth and acting as a powerful level in the use of those teeth.

The Airedale Standard is similar to most others in regard to teeth, actually referring only to bite, except for a short reference to "strong and white and free from defect." There is more to a dog's mouth than the incisor teeth, but a novice would never know it by referring to most Standards. The average person takes a quick look at the incisors, and if they meet in a pincer bite, or overlap closely in a scissors bite, he

254

considers the dog to have a good mouth. The dog could have tiny or missing premolars, yet such superficial glancers would not know it, or even know if inadequacy of these teeth made any difference, since the Standard ignores their presence. Overshot and undershot jaws are mentioned as faults, but the distinction between these conditions and a malocclusion of the incisors is not given. When either jaw is out of alignment—i.e., overshot or undershot, the condition is quickly proven by the canine teeth, better known as fangs. When these teeth do not fit closely along their length, the mouth is less than good. But when there is a distinct space between them, and the lower fang is well ahead of the upper, then the jaw is undershot.

In a malocclusion, the jaws can be normally placed with the fangs fitting closely, but the lower incisors may grow out at a greater angle than necessary to meet or fit behind the upper teeth. Occasionally the two center incisors will be too small, the others too large and crowding the small ones into irregularity. Whether this is inherited is anyone's guess, but irregularity or malocclusion of these teeth is often attributed to the milk teeth staying in too long, forcing the permanent teeth to grow in crooked.

An overshot jaw, especially one that is obvious, is an abomination in a Terrier. Since the overlapping of the upper teeth in the scissors bite can hide this fault to a degree, many dogs with an overshot jaw go scot-free as far as condemnation for the condition is concerned, while the unfortunate dog with a strong jaw and a perfect set of teeth except for a couple of crooked incisors is blasted as undershot by the novice.

Neck

The Standard describes the neck as of moderate length and "gradually widening into the shoulders," but some confusion has arisen as to whether this last is in reference to top or side view. In profile the neck is neat at the throat, descending in a graceful arch to the shoulders and blending into the withers without an abrupt angle. The "widening" refers to the profile view. From above, the neck is of about the same width throughout until it reaches the shoulders. The reference in the Standard as to the skin being "tight" is in regard to the skin of the throat, and any dewlap (also called "throatiness") as seen in certain Hound breeds is most objectionable. The desired clean throat line, free from folds of loose skin, is called "dry," with a "wet throat" being the Houndy sort.

Front, Chest and Ribbing

The front is described under the heading of "shoulders and chest" and is indicated to be of moderate width. Possibly "moderately narrow" would be more exact, for the Airedale front is typical of all the

255

Angulation of Shoulders

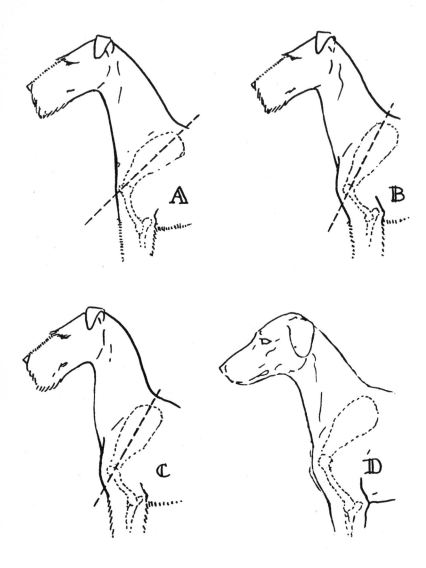

"A"—good Terrier front. "B" and "C" show straight shoulders and the undesirable "ewe" neck and "swan" neck, respectively. "D," the sort of front common to most breeds of dogs, different from the Terrier front in the length and angle of the upper arm (humerus). The greater length of the humerus places the leg farther under the dog.

Angulation of Hindquarters

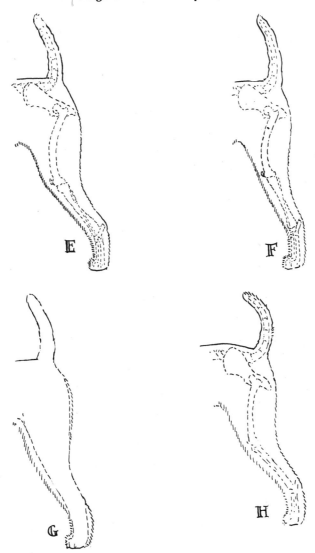

"E," correct angulation and tailset. "F," straight stifle and hock. Note that the bones of the thigh (femur) and the gaskin (tibia and fibula) are shorter than in the leg having good angulation. In this sort of leg the hind pastern is long, therefore NOT placing the hock "close to the ground." "G" shows how trimming can minimize the faults of this leg somewhat by leaving well-carved long hair in front of the leg and in back of the pastern, and leaving a padding of hair on the buttocks. "H"—hindquarters having a steep croup and low tailset, due to sharper slope of pelvis. This sort of croup often accompanies a curved tail.

257

high-stationed Terriers. The shoulders, according to the Standard, are "long and sloping well into the back." Naturally this wording means well "toward" the back rather than into it, for no shoulder could possibly reach the back proper. The common theory is that if the shoulder blades are too close together at the top the dog will travel basewide—that is, will paddle—while if the shoulder blades are too far apart the dog will be out at the elbows and toe in.

The Airedale's front is narrower than the Hound's and is flatter, the muscling being long and lean. Lean musculature has proven necessary in the long-legged Terrier types in the freedom of movement it permits—not just back and forth, but to the side as well. The value of the Terrier front on a dog the size of an Airedale is dubious. But it certainly enhances his appearance as a Terrier even though it may, in its extreme form, cut down his length of stride and liberty of action. Faulty conformation of the shoulder can also cut down efficiency of front movement, and the shoulder of a straighter than forty-five degree angle, even with the ideal right-angle upper arm, will have no longer stride than a Terrier with a typical, nearly straight front.

As in all dogs in which speed and stamina are important, the chest is deep rather than wide, and in the mature Airedale reaches the elbow in depth. The ribs under the shoulder are long and elliptical in shape, allowing free play of the shoulder fore and aft. This also gives the proper background for a clean, flat shoulder assembly. Round ribs naturally would make wide, rounded shoulders, which add to such faults as out-at-the-elbows, bowed legs, and rolling or paddling movement. The back ribs are more "sprung," with the last ribs extending up toward the coupling rather than straight down. This creates the "well-ribbed-up" conformation, as it not only makes the last ribs longer, automatically giving more lung room together with greater expansion, but it also shortens the coupling, since the last rib is much closer to the point of the hip than in the case of the short, round, or down-pointing rib. The withers are just prominent enough to help blend the neck cleanly into the back, and fair height of the withers also helps the illusion of great depth of chest.

Back

Most of us confuse the "back line" with the back proper. The former can include the withers and certainly includes the loin and croup, while the back itself is that fairly short area between the withers and the loin. The ideal back line for the show dog is dead-straight, and as short as possible without sacrificing length of croup. Those who use field dogs do not like a too-short back as such conformation inhibits free action.

A roached back is very unsightly, but should not be confused with the faint rise of a strong loin. Just how it is possible to obtain a back line with a slight rise but without a dip behind the withers and before the tail is not quite clear, for where something goes up, something must at least appear to go down. Other types of back lines not pleasing to the eye are the "soft" or sway back in which the back line dips from withers to croup; the slack loin or slack coupling in which the top line falls off abruptly in front of the croup but does not sag the entire distance to the withers; and the "roller-coaster" back line which dips in back of the withers, rises over the loin and drops in front of the tail, which is usually curved as if it were a continuation of the curvaceous back line. Often a back will appear perfectly straight when the dog is standing in show stance, but will prove to be slack when the dog trots; hence, the dog should be trotted so he can be viewed from the side.

The croup is the area from the point of the hip back to the point of the buttock, including the section above as well as between these two points. It is, in other words, the sector above the pelvis, and its slant depends in part on the slope of the pelvis itself. The levelness of the croup decides to some extent the position of the tail-set. In the mad desire for shorter and shorter backs, it sometimes happens that there is "nothing in back of the saddle"—i.e., the croup is so short it is almost non-existent and the dog appears to lack balance. From the leverage point of view, this naturally lessens the power of the hindquarters.

The sacrum is that part of the vertebrae directly in front of the tail, and in the Airedale does not slope in the same approximate degree as the pelvis—in fact, it is usually quite level. The sacrum is not immobile, and rises slightly if the tail is pushed forward, or when the dog pulls itself together.

Tail

The tail is described in the Standard as being "set well up on the back," a phrase that could conjure strange pictures if taken literally. Naturally, it means that the croup (also called rump) should be level, as designated by the position of the sacrum especially, but also the pelvis, with the tail's root about halfway forward along the croup. The tail is further described as "carried gaily but not curled over the back," but there is nearly always a slight forward curve to the tail. One that is absolutely straight is of doubtful authenticity. A tail that bends forward abruptly is called a "squirrel tail," and although not exactly pleasing to the eye in that it lessens the balance of tail and neck, it is infinitely more pleasing than a tail that curls between the dog's legs. A dog that normally carries his tail in the ideal position will squirrel it to some extent when on his toes and tightened up—this tightening actually involving the whole back line, drawing up the tail and bringing it forward. Ordinarily, a puppy with a tail that is fairly thick at the base will be more

Faults of Conformation and Type

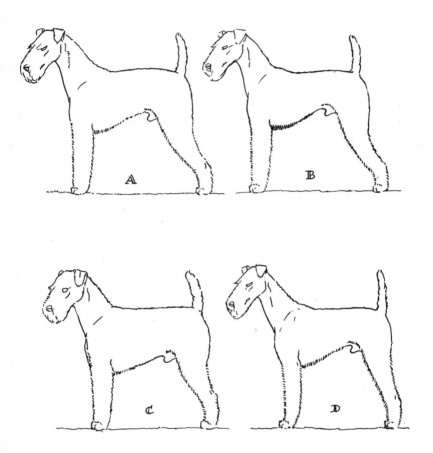

A—A roached back. Otherwise the dog is of good conformation.

B—A weed of somewhat racy lines.

C—A thick-set, cloddy dog, with broad skull, low ears and round eyes. He also has a short gaskin and long back pastern. Though he has a straight backline it looks longer than it is, due to a complete lack of withers.

D—An angular dog, with "nothing in back of his ears." Neck is upside down, shoulders are straight and upper arm too slanted, and the front pastern "soft." Tailset is low and hindleg is very straight of stifle.

Conformation

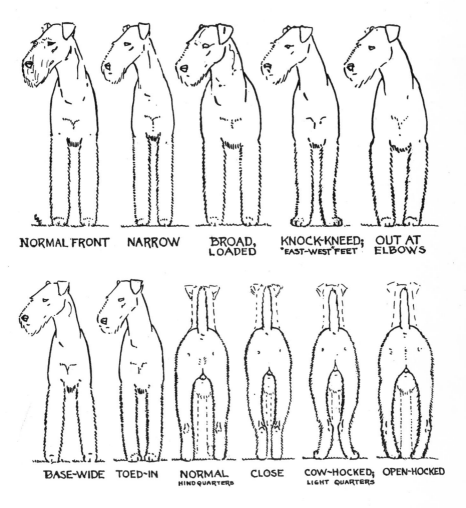

NORMAL FRONT   NARROW   BROAD, LOADED   KNOCK-KNEED; EAST-WEST FEET   OUT AT ELBOWS

BASE-WIDE   TOED-IN   NORMAL HINDQUARTERS   CLOSE   COW-HOCKED; LIGHT QUARTERS   OPEN-HOCKED

The normal front is "moderately narrow," and straight. Good hindquarters are broad, well-muscled, and straight, in rear view. The very narrow front is typical of the "pipe-cleaner" type of Airedale, and is undesirable, as are also the "broad," "knock-kneed," "out at elbows," "base-wide" and "toed-in" fronts. The "close" stance of the hindquarters is not necessarily the counterpart of the "narrow" front; it often occurs on otherwise good hindquarters. It is generally conceded that the "open-hocked" conformation is much less serious a fault than "cow-hocks."

inclined to squirrel his tail, due to the strong muscling, than will a puppy with a tail that is nearly the same thickness throughout its length.

The Standard assumes that everyone knows an Airedale's tail should be docked, but it does not specify to what approximate length, other than stating that the tail should be of "fair length," which is exactly the same wording as used in the Standards of certain undocked breeds. The tail is docked to a length that will balance the length of neck, and this usually means that no more than one-third should be removed. However, since puppies do not all have the same length tail (the cobby ones usually have a naturally shorter tail), reliance will have to be placed on general balance rather than mathematics.

Quarters

There is a tendency to confuse "hindquarters" with the more restricted term "quarters," which latter term means the thigh muscles only, and never includes the legs. Thus a dog can have excellent quarters—i.e., heavy muscling—but be poor as to angulation of the hindquarters.

The quarters of the Airedale should be powerfully muscled, though the muscle may only be seen on the inner part of the leg, the outside being rather hidden by furnishings. Although heavy muscling is more important in a galloping dog, it is also desirable in a dog-of-all-gaits, and a Terrier needs strong hindquarters to hold himself up while digging. The well-angulated, but not *over-angulated* hind leg is desirable because it increases length of stride and improves action. Viewed from behind, the ideal hind legs are straight in that an imaginary line drawn through point of buttock, hock, pastern, and foot would center all four. However, the average Airedale in show stance is placed with hind legs farther apart than this in order to make the back look straighter and the quarters wider.

A cowhocked dog is often also a light-quartered dog, even so deficient in muscling that he is "split up," and in fact malnutrition or lack of condition can in itself cause a cowhocked appearance. But extreme cases are born that way and stay that way—some inherit the malformation. Airedales are no more prone to cowhocks than any other breed, but that does not mean the condition is rare. However, the most common fault in Airedale understructure is the straight stifle. Very heavy-quartered dogs are often openhocked, this being conformation in which the stifles turn in, the hocks turn out, and the back pasterns turn in so that the feet are close together and toe in. While this is not an especially beautiful rear, at least it is strong. Another variation from the ideal is the close stance, in which the stifles may or may not turn out as in the cowhocked dog, but the hocks turn neither in nor out

262

and the pasterns are parallel down to the feet but so close together that they brush throughout their length when the dog moves.

Legs and Feet

The forelegs are tersely summed up in the Standard as "perfectly straight, with plenty of muscle and bone." It is assumed that the reader knows this means when viewed from any angle and that the pastern should be upright, not sloping. For some reason, dog books always mention that the dewclaws of the hind legs on most breeds should be removed, but rarely mention that in most Terriers no hind dewclaws are present but that the front dewclaws—always present—should be removed. These are useless appendages, often getting caught and making the dog lame. In addition they detract from the clean, straight lines of the front leg. And when the furnishings are groomed, the dewclaws often snag the comb, hurting the dog and making him foot-shy.

The stifle, which corresponds to the human knee, should be well bent and the gaskin (often called the "second thigh") should be long. The long gaskin makes the hock (the joint between the gaskin and back pastern) close to the ground, or "well let down." If the stifle is well angulated, the hock, too, is well bent, for these angles come in pairs. On the other hand, a very open angle results in a stilty hind leg.

The feet should be round, fairly small, high-knuckled and compact, like a cat's. The toes should be close together, although a worse fault than an open foot is a flat one—weak in every part and thin of pad. It is generally thought that too long nails will cause a young dog's foot to be more open than normal, and that puppies allowed to become too fat will be rather flat-footed. Kennel runs laid with pea-gravel are believed to improve the arch of a dog's feet, and adequate road-work will also help. However, the best way to get good feet is to breed for them.

Coat and Color

The coat, according to the Standard, is "hard, dense and wiry, lying straight and close, covering the dog well over body and legs. Some of the hardest are crinkly or just slightly waved. At the base of the hard, very stiff hair should be a shorter growth of softer hair termed the undercoat." No mention is made that the Airedale has facial and leg furnishings, and some have this hairy adornment in Afghan-like profusion. Furnishings originally had a distinct purpose in protecting a Terrier working in heavy or thorny cover, and the ruff of hair on the neck (now trimmed off to give an impression of length to the neck) protected the dog in fighting. In the early days of the breed, furnishings lay rather flat in comparison to those on modern dogs, and many of the old-timers could sport only a rudimentary goatee. This is the sort of furnishings favored for the utility Airedale, for it does not accumulate a leg-load of

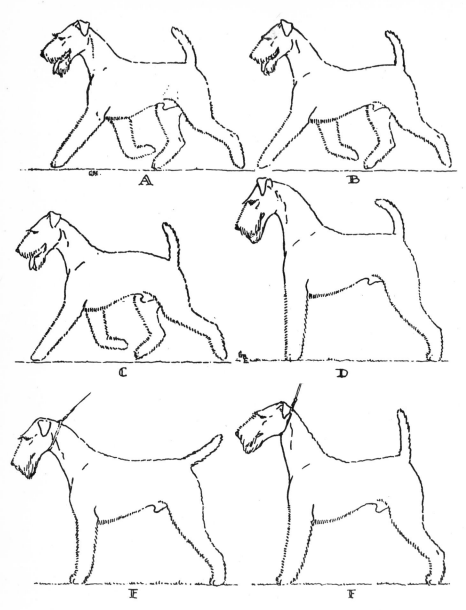

"A" is a dog with a good backline which stays straight when the dog trots. "B" is the usual result, a slight sag of the back, not evident when the dog is standing. "C" is an unpleasant roach, not noticed until the dog moves. This backline usually goes with very poor hind movement of the "rubber-legged" sort. "D"—A dog "on his toes" and showing off, on his own. "E"—Same dog, half asleep, making the backline seem much longer and the front less straight, especially notable in the slant of upper arm and pastern. "F"—Same dog, over-handled. Strangled by the lead, he "props" in self-defense, his hind feet come forward, and his back goes down. The neckline is far from the graceful arch the dog shows when allowed to spar against another dog.

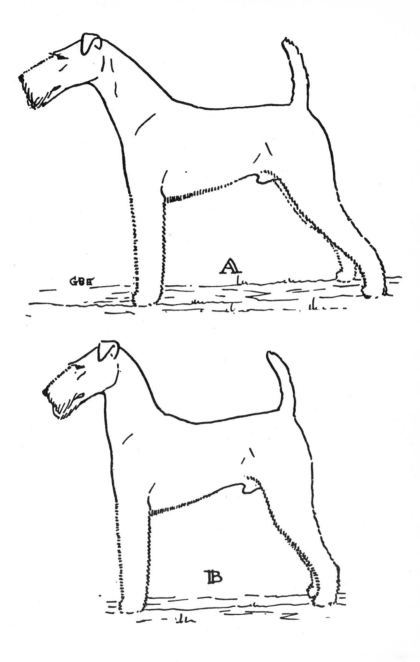

"A" shows a dog with rather plain neck and slightly high croup, posed to offset these faults. The neck is pulled forward by "baiting," and the hind feet are placed far apart to lower the croup, levelling the backline. "B," the same dog, improperly posed, with neck too upright, showing a bulge underneath; hind feet too far forward and close together, making croup appear even higher, and back consequently showing a dip.

265

foxtails, burrs, and balls of mud, nor does it ever snarl into a myriad of knots between combings. Very hard-coated Airedales as well as many having coats of average texture often have scant, equally hard furnishings, creating a headache for their owners if the dogs are show prospects. Except for those with the pin-wire, often single coat, the texture of the furnishings usually changes by the time the dog is about eighteen months of age, whether because actual fining of the texture lessens the breakage, or just because "two hairs grew where only one grew before." If the owner has been faithfully applying the recommended remedy for this condition—oil or some lanolin preparation—he will be convinced that it turned the trick, even though furnishings can become more profuse with no such industry whatsoever. The oil application is helpful in saving the whiskers of dig-happy Airedales, however, for it reduces breakage, and there is also a believable theory that applying oil, especially when it is rubbed in with a stiff brush, steps up the circulation and makes the hair grow faster.

From the utility point of view there would be no reason for trying to encourage growth of heavier, thicker furnishings, but from the show point of view ample furnishings are a necessity. A dog with few whiskers looks short in head, snipey and short in muzzle, and broad of skull as compared with a dog having normal furnishings. Even a heavy "barrel" muzzle will look lighter than will a light foreface well padded with hair and carved to the desired shape. The good length of beard accompanying normal furnishings gives the illusion of a longer head and heavier jaw than may actually be the case, while the "wide" muzzle, the whiskers trimmed skull-width, makes the head seem rectangular its full length, rather than pulling in at the muzzle, as is the case of a dog with few whiskers. Usually, a scantily furnished dog will look leggy, light-boned, and shallow-chested, and even though he may have a good bend of stifle, his hind legs will look straighter than those of a heavily furnished dog in which the curve of leg has been accentuated by artful trimming. A dog that is somewhat less than perfect in conformation can be helped materially in appearance by trimming to counteract faults. Of course, the faults do show up when the dog moves.

The wiry texture of the coat has been well described in the Standard, but there are certain aspects confusing to the novice. One is the character of the hair itself. The shaft of a wiry hair varies in gauge from root to tip. The older or longer the hair, the longer is the fine section toward the root. The thick, wire-textured portion tapers toward the tip, which is sharp pointed. Clipping will leave only the soft, fine section unless a new coat is already coming in, in which case the cut hair will still be hard. Individuals vary as to the distance from the root at which the hair thickens, so some can be clipped without "Kerry-izing" the coat. However, it is preferable that the dead hair on a hard-haired

Terrier be pulled rather than cut, and the construction of the root is such that it pulls much easier than fine, constantly growing hair. Ordinarily, the hair on a hard-coated (but not extremely hard) Airedale will never grow more than three inches in length, and even then does not appear this long, since it does not stand straight out.

Coloring varies throughout the shaft of the hair in most cases, the root being light and the tip black. Often this change of color is abrupt, not blended. While this characteristic is most common on the black saddle, it can occur on the tan also, especially the head and the furnishings over the thighs, the tip being slightly richer tan, not black. The two-tone coloring of the hair is called "badger grizzle."

Novices are usually surprised when the jet black saddle of their young Airedale turns grizzle, as often happens, some becoming almost gray of saddle by the time they are four or five years old. The hardest coated Airedales often have a red grizzle area over the croup, called the "red diamond" though it is more like a triangle; these dogs usually have quite a few red hairs throughout the coat, although they are not prominent. Some Airedales turn red grizzle over the complete saddle, showing very little black. The richly colored dog with his gleaming jet saddle and burnt-sienna tan is a thing of beauty as a show specimen, but in hot weather the less glamorous grizzle dog has much the best of it because the black saddle tends to absorb heat.

Airedale puppies are black with tan points when first whelped, their coloring being similar to that of Manchester Terriers or black and tan Dobermans and Dachshunds. Many a litter of new-born Airedale puppies has been destroyed because the owner did not know this elementary fact and thought his bitch had become involved with a Dobe or Coonhound. The short hair of the Airedale whelp confuses the novice as much as the typical coloring, the average person believing that the newborn Airedale puppy should have whiskers. As the Airedale matures, the black gradually recedes from the head; the tan first outlines the dark on the ears, then the black retreats to the center of the ear, in most cases finally conceding completely to the tan; the tan goes up the legs, up the shoulder and up to and over the thigh; and the black recedes on the neck, sometimes going clear down to the saddle, but usually staying along the crest and often ringing the neck in a blend of black and tan hairs on the under part. This transition from black with tan points to tan with black saddle is usually complete at a year, and from that point on the only change is a possible lightening of tan and the grizzling already mentioned.

The sheep-coated Airedale is ordinarily very light of tan, almost wheaten, and often slate blue or slate black of saddle, with dark ears and quite a bit of dark on the muzzle, usually around the underjaw. As a rule, the sheep-coat can be detected by color alone, but a quick glance also shows the soft texture of the coat, and feeling of the coat will dispel any doubts as to whether the dog is sheep-coated. Such hair can rarely be plucked as easily as wiry hair, and dogs sporting this type of coat are usually clipped for it makes no difference to the texture whether it is pulled or cut. Furnishings of such dogs are even thicker and longer than their coat and have to be thinned and trimmed down often if the dog is shown. Soft-coated and hard-coated (even single-coated) puppies may be found in the same litter, and wooly bitches often have hard-coated pups, as do wooly sires. Since soft-coated dogs are usually bred to hard-coated ones to counteract this fault, ancestry doubtless accounts for sheep-coats in litters from hard-coated parents, and vice versa

To be useful, the undercoat must be piley and oily. It insulates, and acts like the down of a duck in waterproofing the dog. During a rain the outer hair will divide and form points, running the water off without its penetrating the hair, but when the dog gets in really "wet" water, as when swimming, then the undercoat lives up to its purpose, and the water rarely gets through to the skin. Naturally, when a dog is shampooed and soap is rubbed into the hair, the water penetrates the undercoat easily. As a rule, sheep-coats do not have a true undercoat and lack the protection of the hard outer hair.

Movement

The Airedale Standard states: "Movement should be free. As seen from the front the forelegs should swing perpendicular from the body free from the sides, the feet the same distance apart as the elbows. As seen from the rear the hind legs should be parallel with each other, neither too close nor too far apart, but so placed as to give a strong, well-balanced stance and movement. The toes should be turned neither in nor out." Actually, the legs remain absolutely perpendicular only at the walk and slow trot—the faster the gait the more the leg will incline inward under the body to maintain balance. On a two-beat gait such as the trot, the weight is divided on each side and the leg does not have to go as far under as in the gallop, in which one leg can bear all the weight so must be well under the center of gravity. According to our own observation, tracks of a dog at full gallop are never in a direct line—i.e., with the tracks of the right legs on the same line as those of the left legs; rather, they are on each side of an imaginary center line. If the dog places one foot directly in front of another, he is "single-tracking" or "rope-walking," wasting motion in bringing one leg around the other instead of placing it in its own line of travel. This faulty form of travel is also called "weaving" and "plaiting" and the dog does look as if he could braid a rope in transit. These latter terms are usually used when

Movement

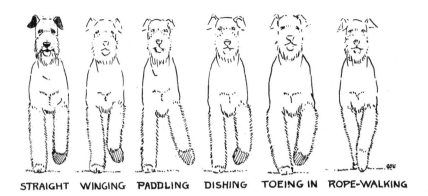

STRAIGHT   WINGING   PADDLING   DISHING   TOEING IN   ROPE-WALKING

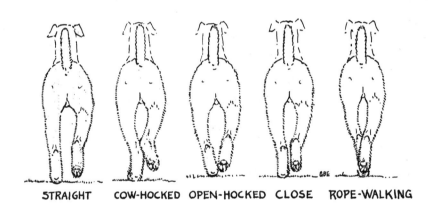

STRAIGHT   COW-HOCKED OPEN-HOCKED CLOSE   ROPE-WALKING

Correct and faulty movement, front and rear view. The faster the gait the more the leg inclines under the center of gravity.

the dogs throw their feet more than in the ordinary rope-walking movement, and in exaggerated cases actually seem to cross their legs.

Confusion between "single-tracking" as a virtue and as a fault can arise from mention of the fault called "two-tracking," also known as "side-wheeling" or "side-winding." In this the dog actually leaves two *sets* of tracks—those of his front feet and those of his hind feet, the latter well to one side of the former due to his crabbing along his course, his body diagonal to the direction traveled. This defect used to be much more common than it seems to be today, and we have so far not observed it in show quality Airedales.

At the trot the action should be as long and free as is possible in a dog with a straight, Terrier front, and should not be short, trappy, or stilty. Some Airedales, when strutting and showing off, will prance and throw their legs a little, or even paddle a bit, but when getting down to business at a smart trot they will step out straight and true. Hackney action is characteristic of some individuals but is out of place on a sporting Terrier. Both the high, Hackney action and the assorted ills of paddling, rope-walking, etc. cause wasted motion and tire a dog in the course of a day's work. Out-at-the-elbow conformation will make a dog toe in and "dish" when moving, this latter fault being an inward arc described by the foot when brought forward. "Winging" is similar to paddling, in that the foot describes an outward arc, but the movement in winging starts from the knee, not the elbow or shoulder as in the paddle.

Balance is important, not merely of the over-all dog, but of the two "ends." In other words, a dog that has a beautiful, long, sloping shoulder and great reach is out of balance if his hindquarters are light and straight. Conversely, straight, short conformation of the shoulder is out of place on a dog with a strong, well-angulated hindquarter. It is better that a dog be moderately good fore and aft rather than extremely good in one place and extremely bad in the other.

One often hears the expression that if dogs "are built right they will move right." Well, they should, but they do not always do so. However, the opposite is certainly true—when a dog is built wrong he moves wrong. There are many reasons why a beautifully built dog does not live up to his promise when he trots out. Often you will see a dog with a faultless shoulder, yet the dog will paddle, with a peculiar action from its elbow only, as if the elbow were pinned to the body, the shoulder moving but little—although this is not the sort of paddle that includes the shoulder in its movement and is caused by too-close placement of the shoulder blades at the top. There is also the dog with a broad stern end, with legs that are perfectly straight and true when viewed from behind—but when he moves he nearly tramps on his own toes or brushes his pasterns throughout their length. Another sort that would be expected to move with plenty of drive is the dog with the beautifully bent stifle and otherwise ideal conformation of hindquarters, including heavy muscling; yet dogs of this sort often have appallingly bad movement in which the leg shows as much solidity as overcooked spaghetti, the stifle turns out, the hocks turn first in then out as the dog moves—an indescribable and impossible movement. Yet it is there, and has even been seen on some of the few Airedales having very well-bent stifles.

Physical Faults

The Standard severely penalizes "yellow eyes, Hound ears, white feet, soft coat, being much oversize or undersize, being overshot or undershot, or having poor movement." Light eyes are still to be found, but the yellow, staring sort are comparatively rare. White feet are occasionally found in even the best of litters, to the horror of the novice breeder and to the displeasure of the old-timer if the white extends past the toes. If the white is on the tip of the toes only, it invariably goes away, replaced by tan, and the first indication that this is happening is the change of the pink toe-nail and pad to black. On a newborn puppy the white often seems more extensive than it really is, a white foot looking like a whole pastern, but when the pup gets up on its legs the white shows to be only on the foot, and this may disappear. If it is any higher, the chance is that it is permanent. Many Airedales have a white blaze on the chest as young puppies, the small blazes disappearing, the larger ones remaining, but the Standard states that a blaze is "common in certain strains" so there is no need to worry about it.

Arguments on size have been going on for over half a century and will be going on from here to eternity. The trend in size seems to go in cycles—for a while a crop of whoppers, then a few years later the worry is about undersize. At any rate, when a dog gets entirely too tall he is usually rangey, so is off-type and not likely to do much winning, while the undersized dog seems always to be at a disadvantage.

The old Standard made reference to the now-banned practice of "touching up" the color of Airedales. Fortunately, the AKC cracked down on the employment of coloring arts, and now the rich coloring of most Airedales is their own, not factory-made. The other "agent" mentioned formerly as "unsporting" is "stiffening the coat." Various cleaning agents, such as chalk and resin, used to be left in the coats of show dogs, but this also is now banned. The ban has, like that on coloring, brought about an improvement in the dogs themselves, and coats are either harder or the soft ones are not shown. The American Kennel Club's August 1977 ban on the use of hair spray should encourage even further breeding for good coats.

Temperament

Temperament is completely ignored in the Airedale Standard. Consequently, only a judge's conscience stops him from putting up a beautiful but shy dog over a bold but less glamorous individual. Although Airedale temperament is less volatile than that of the smaller Terriers, a dog should show plenty of Terrier fire in the show ring, even though it is tempered somewhat by the dignity natural to a big dog. The Airedale should show with animation, but without rowdyism or savagery. He should not be meek, but, above all, he must not be shy. With due allowance for youth, inexperience, strange surroundings, and possibly a dislike of being handled, due to previous experience the dog should be able to put up a good show, especially when faced off against another dog.

Symmetry

Since many people are confused by an often heard phrase—"the Terrier should stand like a cleverly made hunter, covering a lot of ground, yet with a short back"—it is not out of place to clarify this statement. A hunter is a horse ridden to Hounds over varied terrain and many jumps, and must carry a rider safely and comfortably. Such a horse must have a long, well-sloped shoulder, short back and long croup, the latter giving the propulsive power, the shoulder acting as a shock absorber through the good slope therof, which also increases length of stride. The long, well-laid-back shoulder places the forelegs forward and the *back* (not the *back line*) is made shorter. The long croup takes inches off the back from the other direction and places the hind legs farther back; so, with the back short, and the forefeet a good distance from the hind feet, the wording becomes self explanatory —the horse "stands over a lot of ground." This wording first appeared in the Fox Terrier Standard, obviously drawn up by horesemen who, at that time, had no inkling that several generations later the general public would know vastly more about internal combustion engines than the points of the horse.

A Final Point

The average dog owner may or may not be impressed with the beauty of a dog; more important for his purpose, the family dog must have devotion, brains, reliability, stability, trainability, and a sense of humor, plus the extra talents he may need for the multitudinous things the breed does well.

272

13

Selecting an Airedale Puppy

ASIDE FROM the critical prospective buyer of a future show dog, most people select a puppy that appeals to them in temperament, cussedness, brashness, or lovability, and are willing to put up with faults in conformation, coat, and gait, provided the pup gallumphs up to them, ears bobbing and tail whizzing, just asking to be chosen. Some, however, wanting a watch dog, will be more impressed by a pup slower to make friends, one which calmly appraises the newcomers and perhaps scorns them, but which certainly is not afraid of them. Others want the pup that can lick the stuffing out of every other pup in the litter, even if he might be a bit man-shy. On the other hand, there are buyers who want a dog that will not fight until openly invited to do so.

What to Look for

Whether the pup is selected as a show prospect, for breeding purposes, or to serve as a pet and companion, breed character and conformation should be important considerations in making the choice. This is more than a matter of evaluating visible assets—potentials must also be taken into account, along with the realization that a puppy can as easily retrogress as improve.

The head of a high-class Airedale puppy at one day of age will be almost flat from nose to occiput; very clean and flat of cheek; blunt and heavy of muzzle, yet long—the head shaped like a small brick. A coarse-headed puppy, on the other hand, will be apple-domed, snipey of muzzle and rounded of cheek, or just too wide of skull. As the puppy grows he loses some of the long, clean-cut quality of head, then after a few months, starts to regain it if he lives up to his early promise.

Coat type is fairly easy to foretell, as a hard coat will at an early age be of harsh texture, though appearing smooth, very much like that of the Smooth Fox Terrier. Some coats become passably hard after the puppy grows his second coat, and these are neither hard nor soft at first, yet not at all like the chinchilla sort of "fur" sported by the sheep-coated pup. The "off" coat can be of good color, but the sheep-coat is usually slate black, with wheaten or grayish furnishings, and retains black on the ears, muzzle, and thighs long after the hard-coated pups clear. In fact, the sheep-coat sometimes does not clear of black at all. The hard-coated puppies will not have the whiskery appeal of the well-furnished, softer coated ones, and a few will have heads about as beardless as a Dobe's and will be turned down by some customers because they are not "cute." Other characteristics of the coat, including the change of color of the puppies (which are whelped black with tan points) are discussed in Chapter 12.

A fair and possibly optimistic estimate of the puppy's future balance and conformation can be made at about six weeks of age, when the pup usually shows the back line he will have at maturity, something of the balance, and usually the tail carriage. As he goes through the long-bodied, short-legged stage, he loses his well-balanced and cobby effect; then he will, as a rule, go through a gawky, all-legs-and-feet stage, very nonchalant, with tail carried as an afterthought.

The average pup will grow at different rates in different parts—sometimes higher in front, then higher behind; he will be long-bodied, then long-legged. Only the rare ones, the Best in Show prospects, retain balance throughout growth, keeping the short, level topline all of the time and having few discouraging anatomical changes.

Good movers can be picked out at a fairly early age; the bad ones, especially the cowhocked ones, will show up from the time the pups can first hold a true course without floundering. Some pups will have a good bend of stifle up to about four months of age, then will straighten somewhat. Some which as young pups are perfectly straight and true in movement will become open-hocked and toe in slightly as they pass the gawky stage. The *badly* open-hocked or bow-legged ones will show the fault from the beginning, as will those that are out at the elbows, or which have "east-west" feet due to splayed pasterns or knock-knees. Many a litter that is poorly cared for will have every fault in the book, so far as running gear is concerned, mainly due to rickets. Bone is rarely good on ill-fed pups, but is of the light "chicken-bone" variety, and such individuals, with all their faults of conformation, are terrible movers.

A really good dog will usually have a deep chest even as a youngster, and his back line will be level and short. But some late developers are slack of back line as youngsters and do not drop in brisket until at least a year of age. It may seem hard to believe that the chest could deepen, but it does, possibly due to the upper arm and shoulder blade stopping their growth before the ribs do. Some puppies will look rather goose-rumped during the gawky stage but on maturity will be level of croup with high tail-set.

Although the Standard calls for small feet in the adult stage, the average Airedale pup will have large feet. But even young puppies should have feet that are high-arched, round, and cat-like. If the puppies are grossly fat due to limited exercise and unlimited feed, the feet may be rather flat, and might be improved by reduction of weight and plenty of exercise. For the half-grown youngster with rather open or flat feet, road-work is recommended, and lots of it. Long toenails are a prevalent cause of poor feet, so many breeders prefer cement runs. which act as a natural abrasive in shortening toenails.

At about four months, the head may seem narrow in contrast to grown dogs of average conformation, and may also be a bit peaked of occiput and wrinkled of forehead. This last is in specific defiance of the Standard, but is evident only when the pup has his ears at attention, the tendency toward wrinkles gradually disappearing as the dog's head widens slightly with maturity. The widening is a general strengthening all over—of muzzle, skull, and especially of the muscle along the temples. Cheek muscles should be strong but should not bulge.

Teeth and bite are a doubtful quality until the permanent teeth have attained their growth. Many a puppy with a perfect bite has done less well with his second set of teeth, either developing a malocclusion, or crooked, small, or otherwise defective incisors. An undershot or overshot jaw can, of course, be detected in a young pup, for such conditions are due to malformation of the jaws, not the teeth, although causing the teeth to be mis-aligned. It is thought that the late shedding of the milk teeth may cause the second set to grow in crooked or at a greater angle than normal. Some judges are rather harsh in condemnation of distemper-pocked or discolored teeth, which would seem unjustified, although there is a contention that teeth that damage easily may be of poor quality. At any rate, even if one buys a puppy with a perfect set of teeth, he may find that the second teeth are not quite as good—but certainly he cannot blame the breeder, since this comes under the heading of "imponderables."

275

Ears and Ear Pasting

Ear carriage, on American Airedales at least, is often given a lift by aid of a liquid surgical adhesive. Whether some Airedales would have the proper ear carriage without its aid is unknown, for in most kennels the ears of the pups are "glued" to their heads any time from two months on—and kept up at intervals until the desired ear carriage seems permanent. In some cases little more than a week is required, but in others it may take several months; and if the ears are large, creased, heavy, or low-set, the cause is nearly hopeless. Attempting to improve ear carriage is not necessarily done to fool the judge, but just because the dogs look better with good ear carriage than with droopy, Hound-type ears. If ears were improved by an artist with a knife, the anger and penalties of the AKC would descend upon the owner, whereas setting the ear with glue seems to have full approval—a rather "white lie" type of improvement, although the actual strengthening of the ear muscles is done by the dog himself with every flick of the ear.

There are several methods of setting ears, the oldest of which is to bring the ear directly forward, flat along the skull, and to fasten the tip to the skull approximately over the depression of the temple. The most approved method is to draw the ear up about the width of a finger, then align the edges, glue them together at the fold, hold the ear long enough for the glue to set, then bring the ears forward toward the center line of the head as far as they will go, or else straight down from the break of the ears to the point just above the eyes. Some prefer that the tips of the ears nearly touch, thus giving the most pull and making the muscles work more each time the ear is moved. Ears that are fastened up in this manner will sometimes develop a crease, so as a preventive measure a thin dowel or lollipop stick may be fastened along the inside of the ear at the fold. The stick should first be wrapped with adhesive tape, then the loose ends of the tape should be brought up over the flap of the ear before "gluing" the ear to the head. If the ear stays up well and not much air can get inside, it is usually taken down for a day or so, then reset.

Advice on selection of Airedale puppies usually advocated choosing the puppy with the smallest ears, despite the fact that too-small ears usually fly. A small ear with an aerial tendency is much harder to correct than a slightly large ear that can be glued. A number of methods for bringing down "flying" ears have been recommended; among the suggestions is gluing dimes or nickels to the inside tip of the ear. This certainly works as long as the dog carries the change around with him, but the minute he loses it, up goes the ear and down goes the owner's hopes. Instead of coins, pieces of leather, or folded pieces of adhesive tape have also been mentioned for this purpose but with no better luck. It has even been advised that the ears be glued to the desired position, but this merely adds to the flippant tendency in most cases.

276

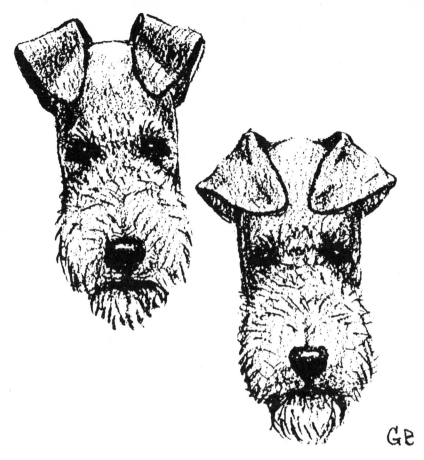

GE

Two Types of Ear "Glueing"

On the head at the left the ears have first been lifted about a finger-width above the head, then the inner edges glued together with liquid surgical adhesive; after this has set, the ears are pulled straight forward to a point above the eyes. On the head at the right, the ears are pulled forward and affixed to the head closer together than in the former method. A light dowel may be wrapped with adhesive tape and fixed at the "break" of the ear to prevent creasing, in the first method.

The Standard as a Guide

Again referring to the usual advice given on selection of an Airedale puppy, the list goes on with the hardest coat, the smallest eyes, the narrowest head, the heaviest bone, etc. Superlatives all. The natural reaction to the Standard is to believe that if "long" is good, then "as long as possible" is much better. It is rather like the assumption that if some salt is good, a lot is better, though the error of such reasoning is soon discovered. And so it is with superlatives, which can so easily become exaggerations. The *hardest* coat can be so hard that it is single-coated with no protective undercoat; the *smallest* eyes can be beady, expressionless, like those of a snake; the *narrowest* head can be so splinter-thin that it is squeezed to a minimum; and the *heaviest* bone can be on a pup that will on maturity be a shapeless clod, sausage-bodied, and utterly devoid of quality. So all of the "ests" should be taken with a grain of salt and a full measure of sound sense.

The eyes of a classy Airedale pup are dark, glinting with humor and impish deviltry, and fairly deep set. The "not prominent" dictum in the Standard is included for a good reason, for a prominent and large eye on a Terrier is liable to all sorts of damage—from dirt and seeds, or from cuts and serious injury in fights. Consequently, the typey Airedale puppy has small eyes, but not exaggeratedly small to the extent of being dull and devoid of humor and expression. The eyes are more triangular than round, or may be oval, but they certainly are not so distinctly triangular as those of the Bull Terrier, nor nearly so small in proportion to size of head.

In most Terriers "the darker the better" is the motto with regard to eyes. Although a light eye cannot affect working ability, it is undeniably true that a very light eye—hazel or lighter—ruins the expression completely, changing the bright, alert expression to a blank, stupid stare. Unless a puppy's eyes are really yellow, they will, after the original blue stage, appear dark until eight to ten weeks of age. Eyes that will be light later will show lightning-like streaks in them when the puppy looks directly into the sun. The streaks will develop into a nearly solid bluish shade, then eventually a too-light brown.

When intent on another dog or any game, the expression of an Airedale puppy is as hard and "varminty" as any tough adult of the breed. When emitting such sparks of canine fire, the eye is actually smaller than at other times, just as a human's eye looks smaller when squinting, and the piercing stare of a hard-boiled Terrier is a form of squint so far as the muscles are concerned. When the dog rolls his eyes upward, they look rounder and larger than normally, so the eyes should be judged when the dog is looking intently at you.

Most breeders wait until their choice of the litter has its permanent teeth before deciding whether or not it will make the grade as a show

278

dog. By this time, although still immature and a rather rough sketch of the picture it will present as an adult, the youngster will have outlived some puppy faults and its gait and conformation can be evaluated more truly. The puppy may need "tightening up" and filling out, but if the essentials are there, embellished by the ornamental triviata, and the temperament is happy and brash, then this one is undoubtedly a flyer. Buyers of show prospects also wait until this age, as a rule, before selecting a new jewel for their string, but the buyer of a pet ordinarily wants it as young as possible so he can have the fun of raising it and watching it develop.

It is asking rather a lot of any buyer to expect him to decide on one puppy in a few minutes time, for the breeder himself will moon hours away trying to decide whether he likes this one best, or that one—at least while the puppies are young. Once the choice is narrowed down to one or two puppies, they can be taken from the pen and stacked and gaited for the benefit of the buyer's close appraisal.

Conditioning

Most breeders will take each puppy out for walks, into the house, and for rides in the car in order to get him gradually accustomed to the sights and sounds of the noisy world. Then a puppy of normal temperament will not be submitted to "shipping shock" and its resultant shyness. It has been found that young puppies—from weaning time to three or four months of age—rarely are bothered by shipping, for the younger they are the less chance there is that they will "think." When a pup starts to think about noises and strange sights, and shows that they bother him, then he is at the age when he might react badly to shipping.

Tail Docking and Dewclaw Removal

Airedlae puppies' tails are docked at about the fourth day after whelping, and although the average amount removed is approximately one-third, this is not true of puppies which may have unusually long or unusually short tails. There are various methods of gauging the ideal length of tail. One is to hold the puppy by the head and the tip of the tail and then note the place on the tail that appears to balance the length of neck of the puppy. However, newborn puppies seem to be all body, with large head and no neck, so much of the "neck length" will have to be imagined by visualizing the balance of the puppy when adult. Many experts advise that the tail be docked so that when it is held up it is approximately the same height as the head, but imagination has to be used here, too, by visualizing future balance of the pup. A simpler method (though not always reliable) is to feel down the tail, noting where the bone abruptly begins to taper toward the tip, and dock at that place. The drawback is that some tails are slim throughout their length, having little taper.

At one time tails were sometimes docked by the excess being bitten off, but this does not appeal to finicky people nowadays. Scissors are often used, knives have been used, but bone shears are recommended if available—although they usually are not in the average home. Their nearest counterpart is a pair of side-cutting (diagonal) pliers, which should be new, undamaged of edge, and showing no space when held to the light, for if there is any visible space between the edges, the skin will not cut cleanly, although the bone will cut easily enough. The pliers must be sterilized, of course.

Most instructions advocate pulling the skin down toward the root before cutting, but this is almost impossible when the puppy is wriggling and squirming. The cutting is done with one clean crunch, and the puppy rarely yelps and as rarely bleeds more than a drop or two. In using either the bone shears or side-cutting pliers, the straight side should be toward the root of the tail (the cutting edge being on that side), making it easier to see where the cut is made. If the owner is unnerved by the prospect of docking, he should have a veterinarian do the job.

While sewing the end of the tail is unnecessary, most veterinarians will take a couple of stitches to make a finished job of it. Some people put the puppies back with the dam right away, while others dip the stub of the tail into healing powder first. It is well to watch the puppies carefully after putting them back with the bitch to see that she does not lick the tails so industriously as to cause them to bleed.

Dewclaws are removed from the forelegs at the time the tail is docked, and care must be taken that they are removed cleanly, for otherwise they may grow back, often deformed and crooked. Large manicure scissors, curved scissors, or bone shears can be used for this, but we recommend instead that a veterinarian should remove dewclaws. The small rudimentary toes are at the soft-bone stage at four days, but because of the care that must be exercised to cut close to the leg, the removal of dewclaws is a little harder on the nerves of the shaky-handed novice than is docking.

Some breeders now believe that it is best to wait until the puppies are two weeks old before docking, as by that time a better idea can be had of the proportionate length of the tail. There is no doubt that during this period the body seems to grow much faster than does the tail, consequently a tail that is docked early may prove later to be too short, whereas waiting a few days longer might have eliminated this chance. However, by the time the pup is two weeks of age the bone has hardened and the operation must be performed by a veterinarian. If, after docking, the tail seems obviously too long, the owner usually waits until the dog is almost full grown before re-docking, since often a dog will grow into a longish tail, possibly because he and the tail are both of a gawky, long nature, and maturity brings all into proportion. When there is nothing to do but re-dock the tail, it is, of course, the veterinarian's work, not to be tackled by a novice, and must be done with the use of an anesthetic.

A badly squirrelled tail can be corrected by cutting certain tendons, but this is expressly against the "faking" clause of the AKC and known offenders are given the quick heave-ho from the dog game. The same applies to anyone known to have "fixed" ears by illicit methods. The major number of artful dodges that have been perpetrated were strictly for the purpose of fooling the judges and possibly other breeders, but occasionally a tail that lies almost flat on the back will be fixed just because it is an eyesore and the dog looks so much better with the correct tail carriage even though he may be far from show quality. Airedales rarely have tails that emulate the Pekingese and Basenji, but quite a few do carry their tails at an abrupt forward angle. However, a squirrel tail is infinitely superior carriage to the tail clamped between the hind legs. No cure for the latter tail carriage has yet been devised, except through work on the other end of the dog—his mind.

A New Puppy in the Home

Most breeders will give a menu for the pups they sell, and often a few days' supply of meal so that a change of diet will not throw a puppy off his feed and make him more upset than he might already be. They will also advise of the last date of worming and give a certificate showing the dates of distemper and hepatitis shots, as well as the rabies shot if the puppy is old enough for the latter.

Anyone with a young dog, whether it is an Airedale of some other breed, can look forward to occasional arguments with him on the matter of dug-up petunias, or his digging under the fence with an eye to a quick getaway. I do not know the value of "dog manure" as a fertilizer, but as a discourager of gophers and gopher-chasing dogs, it has few equals. It is a most unusual dog that will dig where this has been buried.

For a determined pup that is going to dig out, come what may, the best thing is to nail a length of twelve or eighteen inch chicken wire along the bottom of the fence, burying the netting its width underground. Any time the dog starts to dig along the fence he will catch his toenails in the chicken wire, which is more discouraging to him than if he hits hard ground or cement. If he is a jumper, this same type wire in the narrow width can be placed along the top of the fence facing inward, so the dog bops his head with every leap, and cannot possibly get a toehold so he can climb out.

281

Trimming Chart

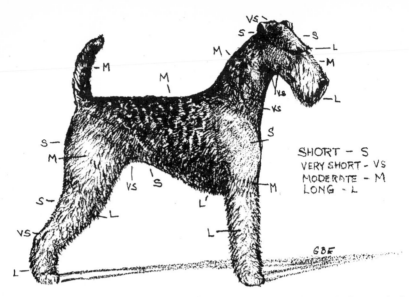

SHORT — S
VERY SHORT - VS
MODERATE - M
LONG - L

For the final trim the Airedale should appear as shown here. Body coat is about an inch long, that on the shoulders is from one-quarter to one-half inch in length, lying very flat. The "very short" areas are taken down as close as possible, hardly measurable as to length. "Long" is never of such a length as to give a lank or flowing effect.

Trim of the Head

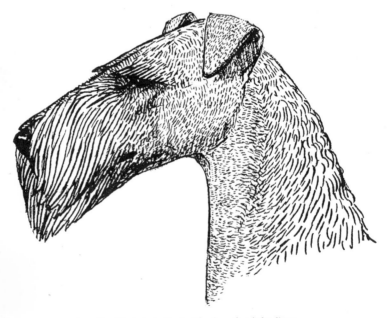

Length of hair is indicated by length of the lines

14

Grooming the Airedale

THE WIRE hair of the Airedale coat is not constant-growing like human hair, but grows to a certain length, then dies. It does not necessarily shed as soon as it dies, but will cling half-heartedly until it is pulled out by the dog, by brambles, or in the grooming process. Unlike other types of hair, it will pull out quite easily at almost any stage of growth. It is easiest, however, to strip the hard-coated dog when the coat is well "on the blow," long and open. Then a quick jerk on a tuft of hair will pull it out with gratifying ease, showing that it is "ripe" for stripping.

Wire hair is not ordinarily the same "caliber" throughout its length. It is fine near the root, coarse and stiff toward the end, with a tapered, pointed tip. There is variation in individual dogs as to the length of the wiry part before the hair fines down, which is one cue to the difference in even the best of coats, and in the time elapsed before certain coats need "topping," with the type having a short amount of hard portion not being adapted to proper topping at all. The fine portion of the hair, as a rule, is lighter color than the tip, although some coats are dark nearly to the skin. It is because of this change in both color and texture of each individual wire hair, plus the increasing presence of undercoat, that a clipped coat is ordinarily softer and quite unlike the normal, "garden fresh" new hair of the stripped coat. The thick, soft undercoat is completely different in makeup, never coarse at any time. On a clipped dog, cut portions of the outer coat can hardly be distinguished from undercoat. If a coat has been clipped repeatedly, it can take as long as a year (or even longer) to return to correct texture and color, hence the disrepute in which clipping is held.

When the coat has been properly stripped and is the correct length for show, there is little of the fine part of the wire hair yet grown out, so, except for the undercoat, only hard, wiry hair constitutes the coat. If a dog is clipped often, there are times when the coat will be reasonably hard, since, by the law of averages, there is bound to be a time when the dead hair was cut near the root and if, through brushing, it has been removed, the new wire hair will come in. But, even so, there will be plenty of the cut hairs in view.

Condition of the dog will also affect the condition of the hair—a dull, lusterless, staring coat being one of the signs of ill health. But such things as washing too often, no care at all, and the dog's swimming in salt water also affect the condition of the hair even though the dog is in good health.

Because dogs vary in the length of time it takes to grow a new coat, if it is at all possible, a dry run or two should have been made before the dog is to be prepared for show. Even this is not too accurate a guide, though, for condition, climate, age, and many other unpredictable factors affect growth of a coat. The average time is eight weeks for a hard coat, but somewhat less for the sheep type, which is quick growing. Practice trims are beneficial in other ways, too, for a butched practice job will not be disastrous, though temporarily spoiling the dog's looks. And the beginner in the art will usually have learned a lesson from mistakes made in practice and will not repeat them when every hair counts.

What to Emphasize

In grooming the Airedale coat, we want to emphasize the following: length of head, flatness of skull, cleanness of cheek and barrel-like muzzle; length and arch of neck; flatness of shoulders and moderate narrowness of front; levelness of topline; absolute straightness of front legs, with feet small and hardly visible beneath moderate furnishings; and the well-bent stifles of the hind legs, viewed from the side, and their well-muscled straightness, viewed from the rear. If the dog is good in the foregoing points, that is fine. But if he is not, then, even though we do not intend actually to fool anyone, we at least do not wish to emphasize a bad point through mis-trimming.

Grooming for Show

In grooming the Airedale for show, either of two methods of stripping may be used. One requires no tools, the thumb and forefinger doing the work, while the other is done with a dull stripping comb, preferably one made especially for the outer coat, and coarse-toothed.

Trimming to Minimize Faults

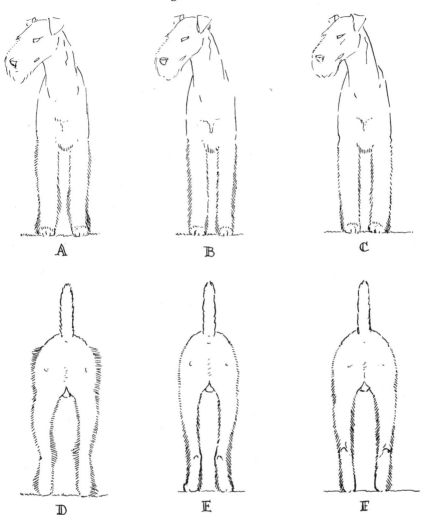

A   B   C

D   E   F

"A" Straight front which appears splayed because of long hair in the wrong places—inside of knee, outside of forearm, and outside of pastern. "B" Knock-kneed front made to appear more straight through trimming. "C" Bowed legs, which though not made to appear straight, look more straight than they would if hair had been left on the same length clear down to the feet. "D" Good hindquarters, improperly trimmed. Hair left on too high outside the legs, and too long. Cow-hocked appearance is given by the long hair inside the hocks and outside the feet. Short hair outside the hocks adds to the illusion. "E" Cow-hocked hindquarters, trimmed to minimize this bad fault though trimming cannot hide it. Hocks are taken down close on the inside, and the feet are trimmed close on the outside, the hair left long inside. "F" Bowed hindquarters. Long hair outside the feet and very short inside, helps disguise this fault slightly. If the hair had been shortened inside the gaskins the legs would have looked more bowed.

285

Since the object is to *pull* out the hair, the first is the preferred method. Both the finger-and-thumb method and the tool-assisted stripping are loosely termed "hand stripped" to avoid confusion with clipping. In the restricted sense, however, hand stripped should mean the finger and thumb method. In either method, the right way to remove the hair is with a quick jerk, not an actual pull at all, and only a small tuft is taken at once.

As an aid to hand stripping, the latex finger stalls obtainable at stationery stores work wonders. They not only ward off soreness, but also seem to have a magnetic effect in pulling out hair in that they "find" more fine hair than can the fingers alone. Scissors with blunted points will be needed, and clippers and thinning shears are necessary for Airedales with very heavy coats. A razor-type stripping knife may also be used, but only for topping. In topping, the sharp stripping tool is used in a manner similar to that employed in using a stripping comb, but more hair is taken at a time, and only the ends are removed.

For a dog that has never been in show trim, or for one whose coat has not been kept in show trim, at least six months should be allowed from the beginning of the grooming process until the time the dog is to be shown. And the grooming should be done in four distinct stages.

First Stage: As the first step, the furnishings should be thinned drastically, preferably by plucking out the old hair by the finger-and-thumb method. This can immediately change the color of the furnishings to a surprising degree, as the light hair lightens the whole effect. The facial and leg hair takes much longer to grow than does the body coat, so any time this is stripped down to the skin, at least six months should be allowed for re-growth. Again, the sheep coats may be the exception to prove the rule, due to their more rapid rate of growth.

Second Stage: Approximately four months after the furnishings were plucked, the coat must be taken off the entire body, clear down to the skin. In removing the coat at this time, it is recommended that a dull stripping comb be used for the top coat and a fine one for the fuzz.

It is the custom, also, to strip at this time the head, neck, shoulders, and other parts on which the hair should be shorter at show time, although the coat on these parts will have to be taken down again a few weeks before the show. If the dog is to be more or less out of sight, so that his appearance is not of importance, these areas can be left until the later stripping—and there is no doubt that it is easier to pluck the long hair than the new crop.

If the dog is a bit low in back and tailset, it is recommended that these two areas be plucked a couple of weeks before the rest of the body coat is done, giving a head start thereon, and making a thicker, longer fill when the time comes to straighten the topline in the final work-over.

286

UNTRIMMED

BODY STRIPPED DOWN CLOSE,
FURNISHINGS "TIDIED"

BODY STRIPPED, but
FURNISHINGS ROUGH

"Untrimmed" shows a dog with an unusually long coat, so is either inclined to be somewhat soft-coated, or has not been trimmed for at least a year. The second view shows
the dog when freshly stripped down to the skin but the furnishings as yet untouched.
Some "clip jobs" are left like this, and the clipper actually expects to be paid for this
half-done work. But whether the dog is clipped, or is waiting for a stripped coat to
grow, he can look like the third drawing merely by blending in the furnishings, raking
out dead, long hair, and straightening the outline where needed.

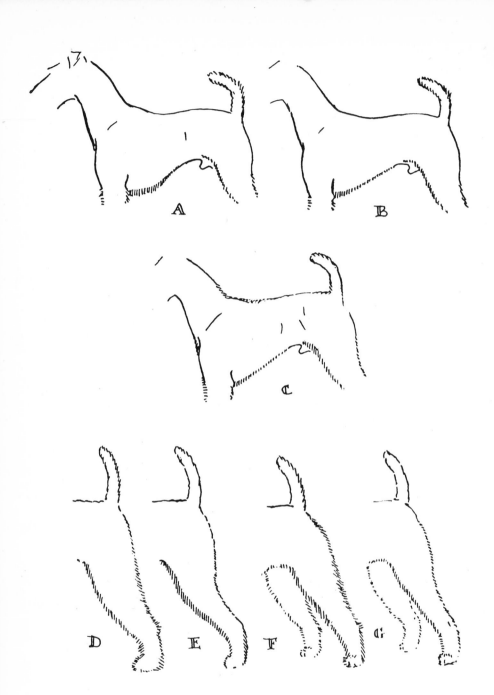

288

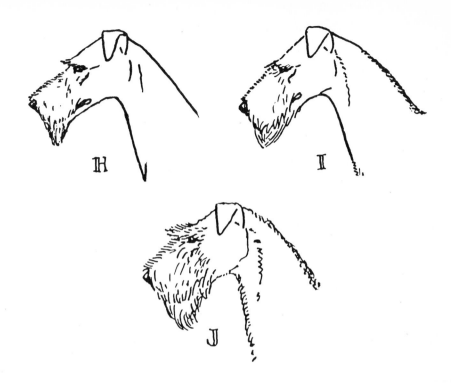

H   I

J

Trimming Tips

"A" shows a dog with a dip in back and low tailset, these faults accentuated by too much hair on the chest and curved underline. "B"—Same faults, but minimized slightly by giving a diagonal trim to underline. Tail is slightly squirrelled and made to appear more so by too much hair in the wrong places—under tip and at the outside bend of tail. "C"—Same dog trimmed to minimize all faults—topline levelled as much as possible by leaving hair long in the hollows and short over withers and loin. Neck blends into withers better due to longer hair at juncture of neck and withers. Neck also improved by leaving more hair as it nears the chest, while too-angulated upper arm has longer hair in front to disguise this fault. Hair is left longer at flank and leading down to stifle. "D" and "E" show the illusion of a straight hindleg due to long hair along back of leg; also the disappearance of this effect by a closer trim along the back. "F" and "G"—Same thing, three-quarter view. "H," "I" and "J" are the same head and neck over-trimmed; correctly trimmed; and not trimmed enough. Neck is angular, so hair along crest as on "I" gives effect of arch; while too much hair on neck makes it look thick in "J."

Care During Intermediate Stage: After "Old Baldy" has been stripped, he can be bathed (unless he was bathed before the stripping was done). Stripping after bathing is preferable, unless the dog is very dirty, with oily hair.

After the bath, the skin should be rubbed with oil or a good lotion, and, of course, the dog kept indoors until he is thoroughly dry. Ordinarily, in cool or cold weather he should wear a blanket at night (and also during the day, if outside in very cold weather) until he becomes adjusted to the "skinless frankfurter" condition. If the furnishings are scanty, as on a young dog, and so hard they are inclined to break, any good lotion, cream or oil can be rubbed into the beard and legs by hand, or with a brush—a stiff one to increase the circulation. Consideration must be given to the fact that a dog whose coat is saturated with oil will be an unwelcome guest in the house. There are hair preparations that soften and improve the hair but which are not greasy, and it may be well to use one of this type. They may be a bit more expensive, but hardly so costly as a rug-cleaning bill, or new upholstery. The softening effect of any hair preparation lasts only while the oil is on the hair. The hair will not remain soft or silky after the preparation has been washed out.

As part of the routine of the dog's care, the coat should be brushed regularly, and, if necessary, superfluous undercoat kept raked out with either an undercoat comb or wire hound glove, and the coat should be checked for ragged hair and too rapid growth in certain areas.

Third Stage: As the hair grows, it will be approximately the same length all over the body and neck, though possibly not so long on the head. The hair on the shoulders and chest must be shortened, because it is desired that these areas look flat and not too broad. The hair must also be shortened on the forechest and buttocks, for if the hair is long on these areas, the dog would look long of body. Since it is desirable that the chest look deep, the hair is left long on the brisket unless the dog is very deep of chest without this artificial aid.

The stripping for this third stage of the grooming should be done at least two weeks before the show. The hair on the skull, neck, and shoulders should be stripped down close. When hair is the ideal length for these parts, it looks like natural, rather short and wiry hair, averaging nearly a half inch in length on the shoulders. Cut or clipped hair can never simulate new growth in color or texture, but some handlers do use a sharp stripping comb on these parts.

The ears are preferably stripped but may be clipped with a No. 15 blade, bringing the clippers over the edge of the ear to taper the edge, and cutting ragged hairs with the scissors. The skull is trimmed quite close from the eyebrows back, and the cheeks trimmed from the corner of the mouth back to the jawline.

Since the hair under the throat should be very short, it is often clipped and the cheek hair is also clipped on coarse-headed dogs if the hair cannot be stripped close enough. The neck, to emphasize the arched effect, is trimmed very close underneath, less short on the sides, and only moderately short on top, tapering into the shoulders and withers. It is also trimmed shorter immediately in back of the head than at the crest.

The shoulder hair may be tapered into the leg hair at this time, or it may be done in the final stage, as preferred, but a more natural look is obtained if the tapering is done now.

If the backline shows need of remodelling, the work can be started at this time in order to have it perfect by show time. The high spots may either be topped, by cutting off the tips of the hair, or they may be levelled by use of thinning shears. The latter is the better method, if done correctly, since only the underneath hair is cut, allowing the hair to lie flat, while topped hair will often stand up like stumps on logged-off land. Also, topped hair looks obviously cut and may cause the judge to be aware that the hair is shortened in that particular area to disguise a fault.

Since the buttocks should not be too short-haired, the sector below the tail should be taken down only moderately on the higher part, but close on the area inside the quarters. The furnishings along the back of the hind leg should also be fairly short, so that they outline the leg properly and do not look ragged, yet are not so freshly done that the leg looks half skinned.

Final Trim: This is done two or three days before the show and is no place for the amateur to practice, because the final work (especially the trimming of the head) can make or mar the dog's appearance. Since the head should look oblong, both from above and from the side, the trimming should emphasize that effect. A straight line from occiput to nose is desired, with only the eyebrows breaking the line. The beard is brushed forward (adding to the rectangular effect), all too-long hairs evened up, and any part of the furnishings on the muzzle that interfere with the straight profile are leveled to the right height. If the cheeks need further flattening they should be again worked over, but clipping at this late date is not recommended.

One point where novices usually fail is on the trim along the edge of the mouth. On most Airedales the hair should be trimmed close at the corner of the mouth, unless the muzzle pulls inward, as it would on the snipey type. The average person does not realize that the head will look different, even from the front, when the dog pants. But if any scraggly hair is left along the lower lip, at the corner of the mouth, the dog, when panting, will look like a grinning Cheshire cat or a fringe-whiskered sea captain. The straight outline (viewed from above) is, of course, destroyed by this billowing of untrimmed hair, so care must be taken to remove just enough to achieve a look of neatness when the dog's mouth is open, yet not so much that there will be an indentation of outline. Too much hair above the corner of the mouth also increases the "sea captain" effect, so the facial furnishings must be gradually tapered into the shorter hair of the head, and the hair below the eyes must never, under any circumstances, be scooped out, such over-industry being sure ruin to expression. It should always be remembered that the idea is to make the muzzle look as heavy as possible and well-filled below the eyes. Viewed from the front (at a level with the eyes), the muzzle should appear cylindrical, not peaked, and especially not concave. Only enough hair should be removed from in front of the eyes to create this powerful-muzzle effect by rounding it off, assuming of course that a mass of fluff has not been left on the muzzle, *a la* Kerry, in which case the eyes could hardly be seen and some carving would be necessary.

Since long hair tends to lie flat, any hair beneath the eyes which has shown an inclination to become over-long and limp may be hand-plucked in the earlier stages of trimming so that by show time the hair will be new and of the stand-off type. However, even at a preliminary stage, the hair of the muzzle directly in front of the eyes should never be scooped out, for this makes the foreface look weak and dished. Only the long, flat-lying hairs should be taken out, and by the finger-and-thumb method, not with a stripping comb. Facial furnishings take a long time to grow—much longer than the body coat—and this fact must always be borne in mind with every tuft of hair removed. Hair on the top of and between the eyes may be trimmed with the scissors, but only enough to make the topline of the head appear level.

The eyebrows are a tricky problem, and the art of trimming them must be studied first-hand to really learn it. Even then the first attempt or two may be bungled. The eyebrows are trimmed very close on the outside corner, longer on the inside corner, with the length varying according to the shape of the dog's head, the size (and color) of the eyes, etc. Longer brows are usually left on to help disguise light or large eyes, and the shape of the trim on the eyebrow also has some effect on the latter. The top of the eyebrow should blend into the hair of the head, the stripping comb doing most of this work, but scissors can be used, provided care is taken. The hair over the cheek bone and on the ridge below the eye should be shortened sufficiently for it to start the taper into the facial furnishings. If this hair is too short (as well as the hair on the muzzle just in front of it), the muzzle looks too light, so care must be taken here also.

The ears should again be checked for ragged hairs along their edges and underneath. Small ears that tend to fly can be aided a little by not clipping or stripping the hair at the tip too close, and leaving enough hair underneath to weigh the tip down. It isn't necessary to leave much and it must not be obvious. Ears that do not lie close enough to the cheek need not be trimmed so close along the inner edge, although very close on the outer edge, which will help slightly in fooling the eye. Naturally, while the edge need not be cut close on small ears, it must be trimmed to the skin on large ears.

The neck is given the once over again at this time, and if the neck is heavy underneath, it is again trimmed as close as possible at the bulging part—the center. If the dog is a bit "wet-throated," the hair at the throat also should be especially short. The neck should blend gradually into the withers, not coming in at an acute angle like a stovepipe.

The backline should be straight—in back of the withers—so a good deal of attention should be given this area if it needs any artful carving. The dog should be viewed on the ground as well as on the trimming table, and preferably sparring with another dog, for this will change the outline. The higher viewpoint will show up any uneven spots that may have been missed, and since the withers will rise somewhat when the dog tightens, it should be especially noted whether additional hair need be taken off, even though the withers are not too high when the dog is relaxed. Any further retouching on the "straightening" process already started a couple of weeks earlier will have to be done, and all stray hairs that will not lie flat when brushed should be topped or pulled.

The tuck-up should be clipped at this time, and the lower line should be evened up. Shallow-chested dogs need a fair amount of hair on the brisket, but too much will call attention to their deficiency. Dogs that are unusually good in this department are usually taken down quite close on the chest to show the world that the depth is all theirs, not merely a hirsute adornment.

The shoulders, by this time, should have a close, new crop of hair, as will also the upper arms. The problem now is to blend in the leg furnishings with the coat of the upper arm, with no sudden billowing out of cowboy chaps. This means that the hair on the elbow, both on the outside and on the point of the elbow, will have to be trimmed close, and the forearm will also need attention, especially if well-muscled; otherwise, the dog may look a bit out at the elbow when moving, for a surplus of hair on this section will fluff out when the dog trots and spoil the clean outline. Consequently, the dog should not be trimmed from the table's-eye-view only, but should also be checked for incorrect trim (or conformation) as he trots toward you. A knock-kneed dog will have to have a bit more hair taken off the inside of the knees than would a straight-legged dog.

The forelegs should be, if possible, absolutely straight from any angle. The Cocker-type feathering around the foot should be taken off completely, and the foot stripped close around the lower edge and nails, although the back of the pastern may curve gradually up to the rest of the furnishings rather than straight, if desired. Any long hair between the pads should be cut out, and the nails filed as close to the quick as possible. Although the furnishings should be moderately heavy, they should by no means be in Afghan-like profusion, nor should they be ragged. Again, remember the straight lines. The hair on the forechest should also blend gradually into the hair of both the chest and the upper arm, with no noticeable tufts, and should be very short.

The coat should come down over the hips, mingling with the leg furnishings at the top of the thigh muscle. The furnishings should never be allowed to extend above this point, as is done on Dutch-cut Poodles, although that is of course exaggerated. Neither should the furnishings be taken down so close on the hindquarters that they seem to be nonexistent. The hair inside the quarters is trimmed short to show the strong muscling.

A first-class conditioner of hard-coated Terriers can keep a dog in show coat for months at a time by going over the dog nearly every day, using the finger-and-thumb method, pulling out any dead hairs. This keeps replacements growing in—a sort of "rotation of crops" idea— and it works. The hair is then always bright and new, very different from the hacked-off, blunt-ended appearance of topped hair, even though topped hair may have been tapered by singeing. This last is an art which is strictly for those who know how, with speed and dexterity the first requisites.

Grooming the Pet Dog

Although clipping is considered unethical, it is nevertheless being done, even by Airedale exhibitors, who, no longer showing a dog, do not have time to keep it in trim otherwise. Clipping also eases the problem for pet owners who want their Airedale well-groomed in appearance but who have not been able to find the time (or the person) to strip the dog.

The general effect of the clipping job is similar to that obtained in grooming for show, but is much easier. There is no worry about a gouge in the wrong place, and the job is done all at once, too—no waiting for the hair to grow at different times in various places, although, as was pointed out before, the coat will not appear so crisp and wiry as when stripped.

Keeping in mind the general effect achieved through stripping, the dog is clipped on that part of the head normally stripped, on the neck, and on the body. The furnishings are tapered down to the clipped hair with a sharp stripping comb, freed of dead hair, and thinned and shortened enough so they can be readily combed without snagging or snarling.

The clipped area should extend down the ribs and under the flank, but not under the chest, for there the hair should be blended into the coat with the sharp stripping knife. Thinning shears or the clippers themselves can be used for this tapering process, easing the latter into and then out of the longer hair. The No. 10 blade is commonly used, but a higher-cutting blade, called the stripping blade, may be used if it is desired that the coat be longer from the beginning. The ears are better clipped with a finer blade, such as No. 15.

Since clipping can cause a sore known as clipper burn, oil or lotion should be applied to the skin afterward, especially under throat, jaw, and tuck-up. If the dog is bathed after clipping, the oil should, of course, be applied after his coat has been thoroughly dried.

Bathing

Some Airedales can be bathed the day before a show and not have the coat curl in places, but some cannot, so it is well to know the characteristics of the dog's coat. A dog that has been well brushed during the pre-show period will need no washing at show time unless he has become dirtied to an unbrushable degree. The furnishings, however, are normally washed just before the day of the show, for the more they stand out and fluff up—in a crisp way, of course—the better.

If the dog's entire coat must be washed just before he is shown, the coat should always be dried by rubbing a towel with the lay of the hair, never against it. If the dog is toweled in a back, forth, and whirlwind fashion, his coat will look as if he had been combed with an eggbeater. The furnishings, however, should be rubbed every which way—to make them stand out as much as possible.

15

Showing the Airedale

by June Dutcher

THE CONFORMATION, or breed classes at a dog show are essentially beauty contests. The dog which most nearly fits the official AKC-approved Standard as the judge interprets it is the winner. The Standard is the word-picture of the perfect dog, and the same words can mean different things to different people. This is why different judges will select different winners from among the same group of dogs competing on the same weekend or circuit of shows.

Lead Breaking

How do you go about showing a dog? First, the dog must be lead broken. This means he must walk briskly and under control on a lead, neither pulling or lagging behind. He must literally put his best foot forward. The easiest way to accomplish this is to put a string lead on a young puppy and encourage him to move along with you. Great patience is the most essential asset in lead breaking a puppy—make it play and not work. Children are often more successful than adults when it comes to introducing a young hopeful to the lead. A child probably makes it more fun for the puppy and has more patience than most adults.

Many times the initial attempt at lead breaking results in a puppy that refuses to move and a frustrated owner. You want the puppy to walk, but you should not resort to dragging him. It is often helpful to entice the puppy with a bit of boiled liver, chicken or some other tasty morsel to get his cooperation. Any lesson, successful or not should never last longer than five or ten minutes. Young puppies have a very short attention span, so prolonging lessons is a bad mistake. The best showman is the dog that enjoys the spotlight and this association should be imprinted early in the dog's life.

When the puppy will walk nicely on the lead on the handler's left, it is ready for the second step—stacking.

Stacking

Some people call it "stacking," others say "posing," "setting up" or "standing for examination." However you refer to the exercise, stacking means getting the dog to stand in such a way as to approximate the breed Standard as closely as possible. An Airedale that is properly stacked will be standing with its front legs straight down from the shoulder and its front feet pointing forward. The rear legs are set back until the vertical line from the hock joint to foot is perpendicular to the ground. Ideally, this pose should also show a straight topline. However, if you find your puppy roaching his back a trifle, as most will, move the rear legs slightly farther back or spread them slightly farther apart to improve the picture.

As with lead breaking, lessons in stacking should start early. Many breeders will start posing their puppies when they are able to stand. It helps to begin stacking lessons on a table as puppies will be more manageable off the ground. Early lessons in stacking are always worthwhile, especially with a male puppy. A full-grown male Airedale who has never been taught to stack will not appreciate having his testicles handled and will actively resist the attempt to do so. In the show ring a judge will physically handle every part of your dog from head to toe. The dog that resists the judge will have almost no chance of winning despite any merits it has, while the dog who stands well can be properly evaluated. It is not unusual for a better dog to lose to a lesser rival because the latter made the most of itself while the former did not.

Many people find it beneficial to stack the dog in front of a mirror; it shows how the puppy will look to the judge and tells you if any adjustments are needed. Stack the dog holding the lead above his head in your right hand with your left hand holding up the tail if necessary.

Your puppy should be taught to stand quietly once properly stacked. As mentioned earlier, the judge will examine the dog all over and he (the dog) must not move or come unglued during the examination. Most good handlers, professional and amateur, will carry some boiled liver into the ring with them to tempt or "bait" the dog while the judge is performing his inspection ritual. A dog thus baited often forgets all about the stranger going over him. He will raise his ears and tail, pull himself together and be the picture of Airedale alertness. Your dog may even quiver a bit when baited, but so long as he presents the desired picture, keep the liver in play. A dog that baits well can always be in the proper position when the judge looks at him, whether close-up or from a distance.

Show Ring Procedure

To be eligible to enter a dog show held under AKC rules, your Airedale must be at least six months old on the day of the show and must be either registered with the AKC or be from a registered litter. To enter your dog in a show, obtain an official entry form from the show secretary or the superintendent. Fill it out and return it with the proper entry fee to the secretary or superintendent prior to the published closing date. Shortly before the show you will receive the *Schedule of Judging* and your exhibitor's pass in the mail. The schedule will show the approximate time of judging and the number of dogs entered in each breed.

As an exhibitor it is your responsibility to get to the show on time and to have your dog groomed and ready at ringside when your class is called. Dogs shows go on whether you get there or not, so allow enough time for travel, grooming and normal snafus.

Once at ringside, check in with the steward who will give you an arm band printed with your dog's catalogue number on it. When your class is called you enter the ring with the dog on your left and line up as the judge directs. Usually the judge will have all the dogs gaited around the ring together in a large circle; you gait your dog at a trot counterclockwise around the ring, always keeping the dog between you and the judge. When the judge signals the class to stop, you do so, stack you dog and wait for your turn to be examined. The judge will conduct a detailed examination of each dog. He will check general conformation, coat, teeth, bite, testicles (male dogs must be entire), eye color and anything else that interests him. Following this examination he may ask your dog to be moved or he may go on and check the next dog, saving movement testing for later.

Regardless of his procedure, he will want to see your dog gait in a pattern of his own choosing. Many judges will use the "triangle" in which the dog is to move straight away down the ring, across to the opposite corner and back to the judge on a diagonal. Another popular pattern is the "L." Here the dog is moved straight down the ring, across to a corner, back to the center and back to the judge. In the "T" the dog moves straight away down the ring, across to one side of the ring, back across to the other side of the ring, back to the center and then returns to the judge. "Up and back" is just what is says—straight away down the ring and straight back to the judge.

When you are completing your individual gaiting pattern and are just a few feet away from the judge, have your liver or a small squeaky toy ready to alert the dog, thereby presenting him in the best possible manner. At this point most judges will thank you and send you to the end of the line, going on to the next dog to repeat the same procedure. The sharp handler will be watching the competition to see if he can out-show them. Learn to keep one eye on the competition, one eye on your own dog and an "extra" eye on the judge. The name of this game is Dog *Show* so teach your dog to *show* on command. You won't be sorry.

After all the dogs in the class have been examined and gaited, the judge may have the class move again in a circle around him. Perhaps he may want to compare a few dogs he liked best. After making up his mind he will send his first four placings to the designated markers, mark his book and distribute the awards. When all the dogs have left the ring the next class enters and the whole procedure will start afresh. You are expected to take your wins or losses graciously. Good sportsmanship is very important in dog shows as in any other competitive activity.

If your Airedale has won first in his class, he must return for the judging of Winners. This class is comprised of all the first-prize winners in the regular classes for one sex and is judged immediately following the judging of all the classes for that sex. It is this class that carries the championship points, thus if your male is designated Winners Dog, he receives points. The number of these coveted points will depend on the number of other dogs in the regular classes present and competing. A second best in the sex or Reserve Winners is also chosen in the event that the Winners Dog is disqualified for any infraction of the rules. In that event the Reserve would then move up and be credited with Winners.

After judging for Reserve Winners Dog, all bitch classes are judged in the same way. When judging has been completed for Winners Bitch and Reserve Winners Bitch, all champions entered will compete for Best of Breed. This class is comprised of champions of record, dogs who have completed their championships but who have not yet been officially confirmed by AKC, the Winners Dog and the Winners Bitch. The judge will examine this class as he did all others and will select from it his Best of Breed, Best of Winners and Best of Opposite Sex. The Best of Breed Airedale will then be eligible to compete in the Terrier Group against the the Best of Breed winners from all the other Terrier breeds for a Group placement. The dog chosen first in the Terrier Group competes against the other five Group winners (Sporting, Hound, Working, Toy and Non-Sporting) in the last competition of the day for the coveted Best in Show.

How a Dog Becomes a Champion

Championship points are awarded in each breed to the Winners Dog and the Winners Bitch. The number of points won, from none to five, depends on the number of dogs of the same sex actually present and competing in the classes. The required number of dogs for a given point rating will vary from on part of the country to another depending on the number of dogs usually shown in a given location. The AKC revises the point schedule in May of each year and this is printed in every dog show catalogue.

To become a champion a dog or bitch must acquire fifteen points under at least three different judges, and two of these wins must be *majors*. A major is a win that carries three points or better and a dog's majors must be won under different judges. A technical point sometimes difficult for the beginner to understand is the computing of points for Best of Winners. The Best of Winners is awarded points equal to the higher rating in either sex for the breed. For example, if the Winners Dog earned four points by beating a large entry of males and the Winners Bitch earned two points by beating a smaller entry of females, and the Winners Bitch goes Best of Winners, she wins four points instead of only two. Similarly, if the Group winner comes from the regular classes, it wins points equal to the highest rating awarded any breed in that Group. In this case if an Airedale bitch were to win the Terrier Group from the classes, she would be entitled to the highest point rating in the Group if it were higher than what she won by going Best of Winners in the breed. So, if the Airedale bitch gained four points for Best of Winners enroute to Best of Breed and then went Group first, she could earn five points (forfeiting the four) if another breed had an entry present with a five-point rating.

Match Shows

Most experienced breeders routinely take their puppies to match shows for ring education long before they are old enough or mature enough for serious competition. Matches are held in many areas nearly every weekend, and many are open to all breeds. They are run along the lines of championship shows, but no points are offered and the atmosphere is pleasant and relaxed. The match show is intended as a training ground and is a good place for you and your puppy to learn show procedure.

Most entry fees at match shows are very reasonable and entries can be made on the day of the match when you arrive on the grounds. Many of the exhibitors will be helpful to newcomers, explaining the procedure and giving encouragement as needed. Match shows are also training grounds for aspiring judges, so don't let yourself be too elated or too deflated by their placements. You will find a great deal of additional helpful information in *The Forsyth Guide to Successful Dog Showing* by Robert and Jane Forsyth (published by Howell Book House, New York, N.Y.) on the subject of showing dogs.

An Important Reminder

Puppies change from week to week, and some very promising ones end up "also rans." On the other hand, some "ugly ducklings" turn into real "swans." So keep your sense of humor and remember that showing dogs is a "Gentleman's Sport." If you lose today, tomorrow will bring another show with a different judge and it may be your day. Most of all, never blame your dog if you don't win. He is only as good as you have presented him. Your confidence or lack of it goes down the lead; your dog reflects your state of mind. Borrow a motto from the Boy Scouts and *Be Prepared.*

Obedience Trials

Obedience trials are an entity unto themselves. This is where your dog shows off his brains. Obedience trials are held with most all-breed shows and sometimes as separate events by dog training clubs. In obedience the dog and handler work as a team and the trials have grown to be popular, well-supported events.

Many Terrier fanciers claim that obedience and Terrier temperament do not mix, but as you have seen earlier in this book many Airedales have acheived good success in obedience competition. Also, more than a few of them were and are also bench champions.

In obedience work it is only the dog's work that scores, not his looks. He can be trimmed or untrimmed, fat or thin, young or old. However, most exhibitors take pride in their dogs and try to have them looking like typical breed representatives while working for a top score. It is pleasing when your Airedale is both bright and beautiful.

The Bibliography on the last page of this book lists many excellent books on all levels of obedience training. Consult any or all of them for their excellent, detailed instruction regarding training programs and participation in AKC obedience competition.

A Final Word

The foregoing, as noted, was furnished by June Dutcher, whose Coppercrest Airedales are so successful. The dogs are sometimes shown by either June or her husband, or both, although they do engage professional handlers from time to time. Touching on handlers, it is a good idea to use professionals if you feel your own bumbling efforts at first might hurt your dog's chances. After you are as expert as your dog, you can do your own handling, right up to Best in Show, if you both have what it takes. Also in favor of using a professional handler,

Ch. Sierradale Squaw (1947).

Ch. Lionheart Ajax.

Ch. Lionheart Sandstorm (1953).

302

at least occasionally, is the opportunity afforded to see your dog compared to the competition much better than if you are actually in the ring with him. It can be quite a lesson to see this contrast. It can also be either encouraging or discouraging, depending on the quality of the competition and how they are showing.

If you decide to have a professional handler to show your dog, write or phone the Professional Handlers Association for recommendations. When this book went to press, the President of the PHA was Ted Young, Jr., Rocky Hill, CT 06067, phone 203-529-8641. If no longer President, Mr. Young will refer you to the current PHA Officer to contact.

The best of all worlds is having a dog that does not need to be "handled" at all—except to be led around the ring and moved as the judge directs. This ideal is the stylish Airedale who does all his own showing, striking a proper stance, with neck arched, ears alert and tail held up under its own power. In this respect it should be emphasized that nearly all long-legged Terriers of the Airedale stamp are assisted by the handler as to tail carriage, because usually when the dog comes to a stop he relaxes a little and the tail goes down—or back— somewhat. The tail doesn't relax much, but just enough to make the back appear longer. When a dog will show himself, especially when "sparred" against another dog, he tightens up all along the backline, and this automatically pulls the tailhead farther forward also. In the line-up most dogs will get a little bored, so the handler pushes the tail forward to improve the picture. The same is true when taking photographs, although at that point several people are trying to make the dog alert, so he may not be actually bored. This last still is not the same as when challenging another dog, so the tail may be held at 45 degrees instead of straight up. Consequently when you see all those pictures of dogs beautifully posed but with the handler pushing the tail forward, t'aint necessarily so that they *need* that assistance at any other time. In other words, they are not shy. As a rule.

BIBLIOGRAPHY

ALL OWNERS of pure-bred dogs will benefit themselves and their dogs by enriching their knowledge of breeds and of canine care, training, breeding, psychology and other important aspects of dog management. The following list of books covers further reading recommended by judges, veterinarians, breeders, trainers and other authorities. Books may be obtained at the finer book stores and pet shops, or through Howell Book House Inc., publishers, New York.

Breed Books

AFGHAN HOUND, Complete	Miller & Gilbert
AIREDALE, New Complete	Edwards
ALASKAN MALAMUTE, Complete	Riddle & Seeley
BASSET HOUND, Complete	Braun
BEAGLE, Complete	Noted Authorities
BLOODHOUND, Complete	Brey & Reed
BOXER, Complete	Denlinger
BRITTANY SPANIEL, Complete	Riddle
BULLDOG, New Complete	Hanes
BULL TERRIER, New Complete	Eberhard
CAIRN TERRIER, Complete	Marvin
CHIHUAHUA, Complete	Noted Authorities
COCKER SPANIEL, New	Kraeuchi
COLLIE, Complete	Official Publication of the
Collie Club of America	
DACHSHUND, The New	Meistrell
DOBERMAN PINSCHER, New	Walker
ENGLISH SETTER, New Complete	Tuck & Howell
ENGLISH SPRINGER SPANIEL, New	
Goodall & Gasow	
FOX TERRIER, New Complete	Silvernail
GERMAN SHEPHERD DOG, Complete	Bennett
GERMAN SHORTHAIRED POINTER, New	Maxwell
GOLDEN RETRIEVER, Complete	Fischer
GREAT DANE, New Complete	Noted Authorities
GREAT PYRENEES, Complete	Strang & Giffin
IRISH SETTER, New	Thompson
IRISH WOLFHOUND, Complete	Starbuck
KEESHOND, Complete	Peterson
LABRADOR RETRIEVER, Complete	Warwick
LHASA APSO, Complete	Herbel
MINIATURE SCHNAUZER, Complete	Eskrigge
NEWFOUNDLAND, New Complete	Chern
NORWEGIAN ELKHOUND, New Complete	Wallo
OLD ENGLISH SHEEPDOG, Complete	Mandeville
PEKINGESE, Quigley Book of	Quigley
POMERANIAN, New Complete	Ricketts
POODLE, New Complete	Hopkins & Irick
POODLE CLIPPING AND GROOMING BOOK,	
Complete	Kalstone
PUG, Complete	Trullinger
PULI, Complete	Owen
ST. BERNARD, New Complete	
Noted Authorities, rev. Raulston	
SAMOYED, Complete	Ward
SCHIPPERKE, Official Book of	Root, Martin, Kent
SCOTTISH TERRIER, Complete	Marvin
SHETLAND SHEEPDOG, New	Riddle
SHIH TZU, The (English)	Dadds
SIBERIAN HUSKY, Complete	Demidoff
TERRIERS, The Book of All	Marvin
TOY DOGS, Kalstone Guide to Grooming All	
Kalstone	
TOY DOGS, All About	Ricketts
WEST HIGHLAND WHITE TERRIER,	
Complete	Marvin
WHIPPET, Complete	Pegram
YORKSHIRE TERRIER, Complete	
Gordon & Bennett	

Care and Training

DOG OBEDIENCE, Complete Book of	Saunders
NOVICE, OPEN AND UTILITY COURSES	
Saunders	
DOG CARE AND TRAINING, Howell	
Book of	Howell, Denlinger, Merrick
DOG CARE AND TRAINING FOR BOYS	
AND GIRLS	Saunders
DOG TRAINING FOR KIDS	Benjamin
DOG TRAINING, Koehler Method of	Koehler
GO FIND! Training Your Dog to Track	Davis
GUARD DOG TRAINING, Koehler Method of	
Koehler	
OPEN OBEDIENCE FOR RING, HOME	
AND FIELD, Koehler Method of	Koehler
SPANIELS FOR SPORT (English)	Radcliffe
SUCCESSFUL DOG TRAINING, The	
Pearsall Guide to	Pearsall
TRAIN YOUR OWN GUN DOG,	
How to	Goodall
TRAINING THE RETRIEVER	Kersley
TRAINING YOUR DOG TO WIN	
OBEDIENCE TITLES	Morsell
UTILITY DOG TRAINING, Koehler Method of	
Koehler	

Breeding

ART OF BREEDING BETTER DOGS, New	Onstott
HOW TO BREED DOGS	Whitney
HOW PUPPIES ARE BORN	Prine
INHERITANCE OF COAT COLOR	
IN DOGS	Little

General

COMPLETE DOG BOOK, The	
Official Pub. of American Kennel Club	
DISNEY ANIMALS, World of	Koehler
DOG IN ACTION, The	Lyon
DOG BEHAVIOR, New Knowledge of	
Pfaffenberger	
DOG JUDGING, Nicholas Guide to	Nicholas
DOG NUTRITION, Collins Guide to	Collins
DOG PEOPLE ARE CRAZY	Riddle
DOG PSYCHOLOGY	Whitney
DOG STANDARDS ILLUSTRATED	
DOGSTEPS, Illustrated Gait at a Glance	Elliott
ENCYCLOPEDIA OF DOGS, International	
Dangerfield, Howell & Riddle	
JUNIOR SHOWMANSHIP HANDBOOK	
Brown & Mason	
RICHES TO BITCHES	Shattuck
SUCCESSFUL DOG SHOWING, Forsyth Guide to	
Forsyth	
TRIM, GROOM AND SHOW YOUR DOG,	
How to	Saunders
WHY DOES YOUR DOG DO THAT?	Bergman
WORLD OF SLED DOGS, From Siberia to	
Sport Racing	Coppinger
OUR PUPPY'S BABY BOOK (blue or pink)